JOURNEY IN
FAITH AND
FIDELITY

JOURNEY IN

FAITH AND

FIDELITY

Women Shaping Religious Life for a Renewed Church

Nadine Foley, OP, Editor

CONTINUUM · NEW YORK

1999

The Continuum Publishing Company
370 Lexington Avenue
New York, NY 10017

Printed in the United States of America

Library of Congress Cataloging-in-Publication Data

Journey in faith and fidelity : women shaping religious life for a renewed church / Nadine Foley, editor.
    p. cm.
   Includes bibliographical references.
   ISBN 0-8264-1192-4 (alk. paper)
   1. Adrian Dominican Sisters.   2. Dominican sisters—United States—Religious life. 3. Monastic and religious orders for women—United States. 4. Vatican Council (2nd : 1962–1965) I. Foley, Nadine, 1924–   .
BX4337.38.J68 1999
255'.972—dc21   99-27653
                                                      CIP

To all women religious
and
women of faith
who act in fidelity
to the spirit of God moving in and among them

Contents

Acknowledgments

The compilation of this work has been the work of a community. I am grateful for the encouragement and support of two General Councils— Pat Walter, Pat Siemen, Anne Guinan, Christine Matthews, Molly Nicholson, Janet Capone, Molly Giller, Maureen Comer, Kathleen McGrail, and Barbara Rund. The manuscript could not have been prepared without the exceptional computer competence and attention to detail provided by Lorraine Reaume, Jean Tobin, Carol Bollin, as well as the support and research services rendered by Heather Stiverson, Joan Schroeder, and Melissa Sissen. A very special gift of sisterhood came through Thomas Josephine Lawler who put me in contact with our editor, Justus George Lawler of The Continuum Publishing Company, who mentored the preparation of this volume. I am grateful further to Evander Lomke who saw it through to its completion. Finally, to all of the sisters of my congregation who continually offer prayerful support, I will always be grateful.

NADINE FOLEY, OP

Introduction

Religious life has an organic quality that has sustained it from its beginnings through a variety of transitions in the course of history. Its dynamism stems from an enduring responsiveness to the signs of the times that has animated faithful members along the way. Particularly in the case of women religious in the active congregations, their vowed life has given them a freedom to observe the needs of people at various times and in various places and to reach out in creative ways to address them. Over time their efforts have given rise in American society to unparalleled developments in education, health care, and varieties of social services. Their zeal has led them also beyond national borders to peoples and cultures all over the world. The result has been an accumulation of experience among the members that has provided knowledge and insight into their reality as women religious within the church, as well as into global situations far removed, geographically, politically, and socially, from their origins.

Yet prior to Vatican Council II, within the religious congregations themselves, there was little or no communal reflection upon the implications of what was rising in the consciousness of so many of their members. Structures were in place, patterns of behavior and accountability were established in tradition, expectations and responsibilities were understood. The communal life of the congregations proceeded as it had for generations. In the years just prior to Vatican Council II, however, underneath the surface of the apparently serene life of women religious, there were unsettling currents. The questions and gradual discontent that were rising had little or no place within a highly controlled and efficient organization that had stood the test of time. But times were changing. No one understood that better than Pope John XXIII as he called for *aggiornamento*, for updating the entire church in light of challenging times.

Called to renew themselves in light of this agenda, women religious responded with a remarkable fidelity. The mandate was issued directly from the highest authority in the church and invoked the obedience that was and is a hallmark of religious life. At the same time, it opened an unprecedented opportunity for the most intense examination of religious life in light of the broad experience of the members, something whose time had come, for one of the prescriptions for the process of renewal was to "consult all of the members," in preparation for what came to be called the " general chapters of renewal."

The general chapters, or legislative assemblies, that are scheduled every four or six years in most religious congregations, like so many other aspects of women's religious life, had been fairly routine, focused primarily upon the election of the congregation's leaders. But this general chapter was to be different. In some congregations the deliberations lasted in successive sessions over two or three years.

Probably no one could have predicted the result. The members were scarcely interested in cosmetic changes for their congregations. The ferment that had been growing was now able to express itself in radical questions about the very nature of religious life, its place within the institutional church, the congregation's responsibility for the mission of the gospel, the manner of internal governance, the individual member's role in decision making and ministerial placement. The consultations raised these kinds of issues and many more. The ensuing general chapter deliberations were long and labored as members learned to listen to one another and to respect varying points of view.

For the process, however, the women were uniquely prepared. For many it was a time of awakening, discovery and conversion. Their formal academic studies in preparation for teaching, administration, counseling, and forms of social service provided a base of advanced knowledge that enabled them to analyze data and set directions. In areas where their preparation was limited, they brought in consultants and experts of various kinds to assist them. In many cases they authorized in-depth studies carried out with professional assistance. Studies provided demographic data as well as factual information on the members' understanding of, and commitment to, religious life.

These were exhilarating times when, for the first time in the experience of most, all the members had the opportunity to express themselves and to voice their concerns. Far from being superficial, those concerns probed deeply into the corporate psyche of the congregations themselves. Dissatisfaction was expressed in many areas and touched into facets of religious life that could not have been anticipated when women religious were told to "consult all of the members."

The renewal chapters of the late 1960s set in motion changes in religious life that exemplified in unique ways a church always in need of reformation. While such a statement might seem startling initially, it seems appropriate to an entity that has often been called a "microcosm of the church." What this description might mean is contingent upon an understanding of "church." Traditionally, religious life in its organization and governance had been patterned on that of the institutional church. Supreme authority was vested in the "major superior," who to one degree or another expressed the will of God for those under her governance. The pattern was replicated in other governmental units and in local houses. But now women religious found that distinctions of superior and subject were inappropriate for contemporary mature and self-actualizing women and seized the opportunity to remove the language from their proceedings and documents. They chose to authorize and empower leadership for their institutes, but leadership that acted in concert with the membership in setting directions for their lives in ministry. In that respect they, perhaps inadvertently, inaugurated a new meaning of being "microcosm of the church," but a church only in process of becoming.

The reflections that follow in this volume detail the kinds of influences that effected change. The study of Scripture and theology had not been a primary emphasis for most women religious in their formation and preparation for ministry. But the kinds of discernment required for the renewal of their institutes brought the need for such studies to the fore. The sisters themselves avidly sought opportunities for deepening their knowledge and competence in these areas. The congregations generally made a priority of providing financial and personnel resources to meet the need. The effects on the members and on the congregations were profound as they began to assess their identity and their experience in light of the gospel and as they adopted prayer forms that were biblically based in new ways.

These studies in particular led to reflection upon the nature of religious life in relation to the church. Vatican Council II had proposed several understandings of "church" and at the same time was ambiguous about the place of religious life within its categories of bishops, clergy and laity as these articles show. Theological reflection, however, revealed the identity of "church" with "mission," from which it follows that all Christians are baptized into mission. For apostolic religious congregations this realization gave new meaning to religious life as an intensification of baptismal commitment. In the 1995 post–Synodal document on religious life, Pope John Paul II expressed with emphasis what had at that point become axiomatic for most religious congregations. ". . . it can be said that *the sense of mission is at the very heart of every form of consecrated life"* (VC 25).

It is out of this sense of mission and commitment to mission that the religious congregations had begun the task of renewal. Pivotal questions were: How do we identify our priorities in mission in light of our founding charisms? How do we actualize the gifts and talents of our members to serve the mission? How do we best organize ourselves for mission? How do we relate to, and cooperate with, all others baptized into mission in order that the teachings of Jesus may be rendered effective for the people of our times and in our shrinking global society? How do we as ecclesial women respond to the social agenda found in the teachings of the church and to our own experience of the problem areas to which these teachings apply?

What women religious have done in response to such questions, which are ongoing in our congregational lives, is not always understood by those outside of our religious life. What the writers offer here is an effort to inform our readers of the influences that have brought about profound change. It may also assist those of us in religious life to reflect together upon our experience as we move forward to a future that is implicit in processes that have begun and are ongoing. It may help us, furthermore, to dream toward a renewed future church that may benefit from our experience and to prepare for the challenges to faith and fidelity in a new millennium.

NADINE FOLEY, OP

Abbreviations Used in This Book

Vatican and Synodal Documents

AA   *Apostolicam Actuositatem* (1965)
      Decree on the Apostolate of Lay People

AAS   *Acta Sanctae Sedis* (1931)

AGD   *Ad gentes divinitus* (1965)
      Decree on the Church's Missionary Activity

CD   *Christus Dominus* (1965)
      Decree on the Pastoral Office of Bishops in the Church

CU   *Convenientes et universo* (1971)
      Justice in the World

DAS   *Divino afflante spiritu* (1943)
      Inspired by the Spirit

DV   *Dei Verbum* (1965)
      Dogmatic Constitution on Divine Revelation

EN   *Evangelii nuntiandi* (1975)
      On Evangelization in the Modern World

ES   *Ecclesiae sanctae* (1966)
      Apostolic Letter (implementing several decrees of Vatican Council II, including CD and PC)

ET   *Evangelica testificatio* (1971)
      On the Renewal of Religious Life According to the Teaching of the Second Vatican Council

GS   *Gaudium et spes* (1965)
      Pastoral Constitution on the Church in the Modern World

NOTE: All quotations from the documents of Vatican Council II are taken from *The Basic Sixteen Documents. Vatican Council II. Constitutions, Decrees, Declarations: A Completely Revised Translation in Inclusive Language.* Ed. Austin Flannery. Northport, NY: Costello Publishing Company, 1996.

All biblical quotations are taken from *The New American Bible.*

II *Inter insignores* (1976)
    The Question of Admission of Women to the Ministerial Priesthood
LE *Laborem exercens* (1981)
    On Human Work
LG *Lumen gentium* (1964)
    Dogmatic Constitution on the Church
LHM This Land Is Home to Me (1975)
    Pastoral Letter. American Bishops of Appalachia
MM *Mater et magistra* (1961)
    On Christianity and Social Progress
MR *Mutuae relationes* (1978)
    Directives for the Mutual Relations between Bishops and Religious in the Church
OA *Octagesima adveniens* (1971)
    A Call to Action
PC *Perfectae caritatis* (1965)
    Decree on the Up-to-Date Renewal of Religious Life
PP *Populorum progressio* (1967)
    On the Development of Peoples
PT *Pacem in terris* (1963)
    Peace on Earth
QA *Quadragesima Anno* (1939)
    On Reconstructing the Social Order
RD *Redemptionis donum* (1984)
    To Men and Women Religious on Their Consecration in the Light of the Mystery of the Redemption
RN *Rerum novarum* (1891)
    On Conditions of the Working Class
RHP Religious and Human Promotion (1980)
    Sacred Congregation for Religious and for Secular Institutes
SR *Sollicitudo rei socialis* (1987)
    On Social Concerns
UR *Unitatis redintegratio* (1964)
    Decree on Ecumenism
VC *Vita consecrata* (1996)
    The Consecrated Life

Other Abbreviations

ADA   Adrian Dominican Archives
ADC   Adrian Dominican Constitutions
 CA   Call to Action
CCC   The Catechism of the Catholic Church
 EJA   *Economic Justice for All*
            Catholic Social Teaching and the U.S. Economy
  IB   *In Between*
            Adrian Dominican Quarterly Publication
RMRCI Report on the Moral Responsibility of Corporate Investments,
            March 11, 1973, May 8, 1973, ADA

1.

◆

The impetus toward biblical studies that began in the 1940s and received new emphasis in *Dei Verbum* from Vatican Council II inspired women religious to pursue modern methods of interpretation and to develop scriptural forms of prayer. A God who moves within human history and enters into the experience of people, especially the poor and the marginated, changed long prevailing notions of the church and religious life as static realities separated from the mainstream of human life. The incarnation in Jesus Christ took on new meaning as women religious realized the full import of a God who took on human form and shared the sorrows and joys of ordinary people. Religious life could no longer represent separation from the world but had to be a force within the world for imparting Gospel values.

◆

God in Search of Humanity

The Effect of Modern Scripture Studies on Religious Life

Miriam Mullins, OP

The tradition that comes from the apostles makes progress in the church, with the help of the Holy Spirit. There is a growth in insight into the realities and words that are being passed on. This comes about through the contemplation and study of believers who ponder these things in their hearts. (DV 8)

Lived experience and reflection on that experience provide the means of growth and maturity, the ongoing attainment of true wisdom. For women religious, the later part of the twentieth century has been a time of reflection on their lived experience and a time of renewing religious life in the spirit of their original charism as called for by the Second Vatican Council. From this shared reflection, a renewed understanding of religious life has evolved for the living out of mission and ministry in an ever-advancing technological society.

One of the major factors influencing the adaptation and changes of the lived reality of religious life in the twentieth century has been the progress and growth in the study of sacred Scripture. Through modern biblical studies women religious have come to an awakened and renewed realization that the God of our Jewish and Christian ancestors is a God of salvation history. This God of people, Yahweh, comes to us today through the history of our times, calling us to a deeper relationship and understanding of who we are as God's covenanted people and who we are to be for one another in our era. Given the reality of modern technology, the world's inhabitants in most places have instant access to information about events in the global community. Such knowledge impels women religious to mission and ministry in ways unknown to previous generations. Through our probing of the scriptures we have come to know that God has called us into a unique covenant relationship. The very nature of our religious life is a manifestation of covenant, something that we did not always realize.

The study of sacred Scripture has led us to a profound realization in these recent years. If we are to be faithful to our Covenant God, the God in search of humanity, who calls us to mission in the new millennium with all its challenges, we must turn to the prayerful study of the Scriptures as a constant feature of our lives. Especially to the Gospels, we find our source of inspiration, hope and fidelity in following Jesus, the Christ. Just as Jesus responded to the physical and spiritual needs and hungers of God's people during his earthly life, we are called to be salt and light for our people in our time.

Fresh Air

For women who entered or were members of a religious congregation in the first half of the twentieth century, the study of sacred Scripture was not part of their formation nor was it a significant part of their day-to-day religious life. For the majority of women religious, common prayer was an adaptation of the breviary that was prayed in common by the monks and nuns and said privately by the secular clergy. For those religious communities who prayed or chanted the hours of the breviary in some form, the prayer was usually chanted in Latin rather than the vernacular. The celebration of the Eucharist, referred to at this time as the Mass, was also prayed in Latin and the major responses within the liturgy were sung in Latin. Following the Gospel reading in Latin, the priest presider repeated it in the vernacular and then gave a sermon that sometimes was a reflection on the Gospel passage but many times was on a topic extraneous to the Scripture readings of the Mass. Other communal times of prayer were spent in praying the rosary in the vernacular, reciting various litanies such as the Litany of the Sacred Heart of Jesus and the Litany of the Blessed Virgin Mary, and following special devotions honored in the tradition of each congregation.

Formation in religious life during this early part of the twentieth century focused on the explanation of the particular rule of living followed by the community, such as the Rule of St. Benedict or the Rule of St. Augustine. Community customs for the day-to-day living of religious life were the content and source of the instructions that were presented to the prospective members by the directors of postulants and novices. The legacy of the community founder, the spiritual classics, and the lives of the saints were the focus of conferences and times of retreat. During the novitiate, the *Catechism of the Vows* (1873) was the main source used as the preparation for profession of vows in most religious congregations of many differing religious traditions. The aim of the spiritual life was striving for perfection, which was seen as fidelity to the observance of the rules and regulations of the particular congregation of which one was a member. The daily particular examen and the periodic chapter of faults or other similar practices were the means to assist one in attaining the perfect observance of religious life that was identified with holiness. In fact, being a woman/man religious was considered a "higher calling."

Communal periods of meditation usually occurred in the morning and evening gatherings of the community. At the beginning of the meditation period a short reflection was read aloud by a designated reader. Sometimes the passages were related to the Scriptures, but more frequently they were pious reflections on an aspect of religious life. For women religious living in the first two-thirds of the twentieth century, the sacred Scriptures did not have an intentional, significant role in their lives. In fact, at this time the majority of religious did not possess a personal copy of the Bible. This was true not only for women religious but also for Catholic Christians in general. Most Catholic homes had a copy of the Bible in the vernacular that had been translated from St. Jerome's Latin Vulgate Bible of the fourth century. The principal use of this home

Bible was to record the dates of the births, reception of the sacraments of first Holy Communion, confirmation, marriage and the deaths of family members. This lack of using the Bible as a source for prayer and reflection stems principally from the fact that the translation, usually a second or third translation from the original manuscripts, produced an unfamiliar, stilted style of the vernacular that lost the fullness and vibrancy of the original text, making it difficult to understand.

In the early 1940s, there was a great need among both English-speaking Catholics and Protestants for a new translation of the Bible that would speak to the twentieth century. In 1941, the United States Bishops' Committee for the Confraternity of Christian Doctrine authorized a revised translation of the Rheims-Challoner New Testament that had been published in the middle of the eighteenth century. The footnotes in this revision were very helpful since they incorporated the knowledge and perception of the original Greek text. The translation of the text, however, was made from the Sixto-Clementine Vulgate Bible and followed it even in the instances where it deviated from St. Jerome's original translation.

Providentially, a new era of study and knowledge of the sacred Scriptures began on September 30, 1943, when Pope Pius XII issued his encyclical letter, *Divino afflante spiritu*. In this encyclical, the pope enumerated a program for greater progress in the study and understanding of sacred Scripture in the light of recent discoveries in archaeology, ancient history and literature, and other sciences. He encouraged the study of the Bible through investigating the biblical texts in their original languages, emphasizing the importance of textual criticism and taking into account the literary forms of ancient writers. The publication of this encyclical gave scripture scholars the ability and blessing to publish the work they had been doing in these areas of scriptural study.

Responding to *Divino afflante spiritu*, the Bishops' Committee of the Confraternity of Christian Doctrine discontinued the revision of the Douay-Challoner Old Testament and commissioned a new modern English translation of the entire Bible from the original languages. By 1952, some of the books of the Old Testament were published in three volumes. With each succeeding publication the translations and scholarship of the books improved. These continued endeavors by the Bishops' Committee resulted in the publication of *The New American Bible*, with historical introductions for each book and explanatory footnotes. *Divino afflante spiritu* had produced a new renaissance that continued to bear fruit for years to come. Sisters from many different congregations, although perhaps not the majority, followed these developments and eagerly awaited each new edition of the Bible. The seeds of biblical influence on religious life were being sown.

In the late 1940s and 1950s another strong influence upon the new interest in the Scriptures for women religious came through the catechetical movement. Stemming from Belgium, and promulgated through the publication *Lumen Vitae*, the study of Scripture for those engaged in catechetical instruction was promoted. A perusal of this periodical for these years shows that articles on biblical themes predominate. At the same time the American journal *The Living Light* had a similar emphasis. American women religious engaged in catechesis, always diligent in their preparation for their ministries, attended the catechetical workshops sponsored at the time and read the supporting materials. As was true in many other cases, as they prepared to instruct children and young adults in the new biblical insights they gained, there was an impact on their religious lives as well.

On January 25, 1959, Pope John XXIII made the surprise announcement of his plan to convoke the Church's Twenty-first Ecumenical Council, Vatican II. He spoke of the need for *aggiornamento,* "updating," "renewal," the need for the Catholic Church to open the windows and let in some fresh air. After almost four years of preparation the Council opened on October 11, 1962. The sixteen documents promulgated by The Second Vatican Council touched and affected the lives of the entire people of God. Religious congregations and their members were intimately affected in many ways by the Council pronouncements and took seriously the *aggiornamento* of their lives as individuals and as vowed members of religious congregations. It is in the convergence of the message of the documents that a new panorama for religious life emerged that called for focusing on the person of Jesus the Christ as presented and proclaimed in the Scriptures by

- nourishing one's daily life through the liturgy and para-liturgical prayer that was centered in and flowing from the Scriptures,
- embracing the fullness of Christian life with all Christians through the covenant of the paschal mystery,
- going with others into the modern world to carry forward the work of Christ himself: to witness to the truth, to serve rather than be served, to live the message of the Gospel.

This renewed perception and understanding of religious life and its mission demanded a deeper understanding of the sacred Scriptures. Never before had the people of God heard or read:

> The church has always venerated the divine Scriptures as it has venerated the Body of the Lord, in that it never ceases, above all in the sacred liturgy, to partake of the bread of life and to offer it to the faithful from the one table of the word of God and the Body of Christ. It has always regarded and continues to regard the Scriptures, taken together with sacred tradition, as the supreme rule of its faith and for all time . . . all the preaching of the church, as indeed the entire Christian religion, should be nourished and ruled by sacred Scripture. In the sacred books, the Father who is in heaven comes lovingly to meet his children, and talks with them. And such is the force and power of the word of God that it is the church's support and strength, imparting robustness to the faith of its daughters and sons, and providing food for their souls. It is a pure and unfailing fount of spiritual life (DV 21).

This constitution goes on to say, "Access to sacred Scripture should be provided for all the Christian faithful" (DV 22). Not since the early centuries of the Catholic Church had any official promulgation urged that the Scriptures be readily available for all the members. This was a watershed event that would eventually bring new life and a renewed living and coming together of God's people. The "how" of the coming together needed to be explored in the Scriptures themselves. Women religious took seriously this call for which many were ready and prepared to respond.

Remeeting the God of the Scriptures

Probing the Scriptures for the "how" of our being God's people involves interpretation of the sacred writings. The task of interpreting the text leads to investigating what meaning the writers really intended and what God wanted to communicate by their words. This requires

- knowing the literary forms through which the human authors conveyed the message,
- understanding the patterns of thinking and perceiving that prevailed at the time of the writing,

- becoming familiar with the current customs and manner of human interaction common in the society of the authors,
- probing the writers' images of God and their beliefs about God.

One of the most influential themes from the Scriptures that was to have a strong impact on religious life was that of salvation history. A God who moved within human history, entering into and influencing the experiences of the people of God was a new and exciting insight into who God is and a refreshing alternative to a static God far removed from ordinary human life. The Bible took on new meaning as the ongoing history of a relationship. This relationship was created, offered, accepted, and formalized centuries ago in the form of a covenant between God and the Hebrew people. The various writings of the sacred Scriptures are a faith account of the formation, living out, and the development of the agreement. The common thread binding all the books together is *covenant,* another transformative theme for contemporary religious women in their self-understanding, personally and communally.

Historically, the writings relate the covenant that God initiated with Abraham, blessing him as the father of all nations. The next phase of the covenant between God and the descendants of Abraham was made with the Hebrew people as a nation through the person of Moses. Under his leadership God prepares them for a broader understanding of the covenanted relationship with the One who had chosen them.

> You have seen for yourselves . . . how I bore you up on eagle wings and brought you here to myself. Therefore, if you hearken to my voice and keep my covenant, you shall be my special possession, dearer to me than all other people, though all the earth is mine. (Exod. 19:4–5)

This image of the mother eagle teaching her young to fly, bearing them up on her wings as they learn how to mature and use their wings, is a powerful image of Yahweh, the God of the Covenant. Such feminine images have particular appeal to those long accustomed to envisioning God as demanding, punishing and condemning.

The stipulations of the covenant agreement are recorded as the Ten Words, commonly referred to as the Ten Commandments (Exod. 20:1–17). The uniqueness of this agreement is the fact that the people's relationship with Yahweh is part and parcel of their relationship with one another, all of which is rooted in and built on respect and the dignity of one another as covenant partners with God and each other. The liturgical ritual for the enactment of the Sinai Covenant (Exod. 24:4–8) is a ritual comprising (1) a liturgy of the covenant word, the oral proclamation of the covenant agreement, and (2) a liturgy of holocausts and the sacrifice of young bulls as peace offerings to Yahweh. Moses used the blood of the sacrificed animals to seal the covenant. He splashed half of the blood on the altar signifying God's agreement to the covenant, and after the people verbally agreed to the covenant terms, he sprinkled the other half of the blood on the people saying, "This is the blood of the covenant which the Lord has made with you in accordance with all these words of his" (Exod. 24:8).

The people were not always faithful to their part of the covenant agreement, neither in their relationship with God nor in their relationship with each other. Many times they were their own worst enemies, bringing troubles upon themselves and then blaming God for the situation or wondering why God was not rescuing them. At other times, however, their faithful living of the covenant did put them at odds with the other people and cultures that surrounded them, and they suffered as a result of their fidelity. Or, as in the case of many of the prophets whom God raised up from their midst to call them back to covenant living, they persecuted their very own flesh and blood who were trying to remind them to care for each other, especially the poor and those in need. In such instances, their response to covenant living was wanting. Justice, peace, mercy, truth, righteousness, and love, the building blocks of the covenant, were not operative in their behavior with one another. Even though the code of the covenant did not mention the Passover feast, the Hebrews and their descendants, down to our own times, have yearly celebrated this major national feast commemorating their establishment as the covenanted people of Yahweh.

Entering into the life of Jesus as recorded by the Evangelists in the New Testament, we experience the continuing development of the covenant theme. The Gospel according to Matthew presents Jesus to us as the new Moses, going up the mountainside, sitting down with his disciples gathered around him and teaching them the Beatitudes, the attitudes of mind and heart that characterize a true member of the covenant. These "attitudes of being" might be expressed as

- holding things lightly, not putting one's trust and confidence in the possession of material goods, but rather placing one's trust in God's promises of fulfillment,

- mourning over what should be and is not, what is and should not be,
- striving to be oneself rather than striving to be like someone else, being happy with who one is and what one has,
- allowing the God who loves us so much to find us watching and waiting for the divine embrace in the very ordinary events of life,
- extending kindness to everyone, even kindness beyond what is deserved,
- having one's priorities in order and acting accordingly, respecting the dignity of others,
- striving to see a situation as others see it and appreciating their viewpoint even if you do not agree or cannot agree with it, striving for right relationships,
- being constant in one's fidelity to God and true to self even when one does not "fit in" and others shun, ridicule, and make life unbearable.

It is the attitudes of our being that form and direct our actions. How pertinent this message was for Matthew's faith community comprised of Jewish Christians and Gentile Christians who, in embracing Christianity, were frequently cut off from their previous companions and sometimes even family members. In reaching back to describe the birth of Jesus, Matthew has two priorities: not only to show that Jesus is a descendant of King David and came as the fulfillment of God's promises, but also that the Gentiles are members of God's people, coheirs with the Jews. In Jesus, God's promise to Abraham and the covenant on Sinai find a further realization of the Covenant God who out of infinite love searches for all peoples. The peak expression of the development comes in the passion, death, and resurrection of Jesus.

According to the Synoptic Gospels, the meal that Jesus celebrated with his apostles the night before his crucifixion was the Passover supper. It was during this ritual of the covenant meal that Jesus added to the blessing of the bread the mandate, "Take and eat; this is my body." And with the thanksgiving cup of wine at the end of the meal he mandated, "Drink from it, all of you, for this is my blood of the covenant, which will be shed on behalf of many for the forgiveness of sins" (Matt. 26:26–28). Following this meal Jesus entered into and completed his passion, death, and resurrection—his exodus—the further development of the covenant between Yahweh and the Hebrew people, now reaching out and embracing all peoples and nations.

In early Christian centuries the followers of Jesus met in private homes and continued to celebrate the Eucharist, the ritual of the New Covenant in Jesus the Christ. At times of persecution the Christians worshipped and celebrated the Eucharist in secret for fear of arrest. Not until the fourth century A.D. did the churches have a particular style of architecture and acquire recognition as public houses of worship.

Since the acceptance of Christianity as a religion, we have tended at times to become complacent and take the celebration of the Eucharist for granted, a routine ritual that moved into a development of a personal pietistic devotion and a "Jesus and me" theology, losing the depth of the covenant meaning and the covenant mandate. There is the tendency to operate on "automatic pilot" as we enter the assembly and move toward the "Amen" at the time of entering into covenant that is the Eucharist, claiming our covenant membership in Jesus with one another. Refocusing on the main scriptural theme of covenant, probing its depths and implications for our living at this time in history, will lead us to a deliberate, conscious "Amen"—"Yes." Yes, this is the Body of Christ. Yes, I am the Body of Christ. Yes, I accept the covenant and intend to live it as a covenant member. Yes, my life for the salvation of our people. Yes, we in Christ are covenanted!

It is such consciousness and understanding of the implications of entering into the covenant of the Eucharist that need cultivation in our lives if we are to truly be Christ in the twenty-first century. It is not a matter of striving for perfection. The God of Jesus, the God of the covenant, is "God in search of humanity," longing to create a renewed people. God will stay with us when arrogance or pride lead us to stray from what we are intended to be. God will live closer to us than we are to ourselves, bone of our bone, flesh of our flesh, and will companion us with others who will walk the covenant journey with us. Together God calls us into relationship, into divine love, so that others may be fed, clothed, educated, nourished and nursed, and given their rights to dignity, respect, and life so that they, too, might "live"! The God of the covenant is the Divine Lover who watches, waits, looks for us to come home and allow ourselves to be found. It is in the ongoing study and reflective probing of the Bible that the lives of women religious have truly found a deeper realization and meaning for ministry and for the understanding of religious life itself as a living of the covenant.

The Implications of a Covenanted People in Religious Life

The Vatican II document, *Dogmatic Constitution on the Church* (Lumen gentium), spoke of the new covenant in Christ as a calling together of a new people of God. The heritage of this people is the dignity and freedom of the daughters and sons of God in whom the Spirit dwells as in a temple (LG 9). All of the people of God, no matter what their state or condition in life, are called by God to the fullness of the Christian life (LG 11, 40). The *Decree on the Appropriate Renewal of the Religious Life* (Perfectae caritatis) outlined a renewal of religious life based on two simultaneous processes: a constant return to the sources of Christian life in general and to the primitive inspiration of the institutes, and their adaptation to the changed conditions of our time (PC 2).

These processes were to occur according to various principles: (a) the fundamental norm of religious life being the following of Christ as presented in the gospels, which is the supreme rule of all communities; (b) recognition and preservation of the spirit of the founder, the heritage contained in the particular goals and wholesome traditions of the community; (c) participation in the life of the church according to the individual community's purpose and trait or characteristic; (d) promotion among the members of each community an awareness of the inner spirit of the members of each community, a closer living of life in Christ that is prior to the promotion of exterior works (PC 2).

The decree also called for the adaptation of the manner of living, praying, and working to the physical and psychological conditions of the community members and to the needs of the ministry, the requirements of a particular culture, social, and economic circumstances, especially in mission areas. Reexamination of the mode of governance in communities was to occur in light of the above principles, and constitutions, directories, books of prayer and ceremonies, as well as custom books, were to be revised and brought into accord with the Vatican II documents.

Congregations of women religious took seriously the renewal that the Second Vatican Council addressed to them. This renewal caused consternation among some members of religious communities, evidenced by those who for various reasons left their congregations. The laity also found it very hard to adjust to having women religious out and about, ministering among them in ways with which they were not familiar. Religious life was no longer something hidden and mysterious. Laity and religious are all the people of God and need to be one body in Christ, ministering together and addressing the needs of God's people on every level. It was the broadening of involvement at all levels of service that women religious began to address.

In the late 1960s and early 1970s the congregations of women religious began to hold general chapters to address the renewal of religious life that had been mandated by the Second Vatican Council. In preparing for these official community gatherings, women religious invoked the Scriptures to find the source and foundation of their renewal. The Gospels were the foundation and focal point of their deliberations as they reflected on the original charisms of their congregations and their current ways of ministering to carry out their charisms. The Gospel of Matthew, Chapter 25:31–46, commonly referred to as the "Last Judgment," brought a renewed and broadening vision of ministry. It became obvious that, in order to address in this era what the gospel proclaimed, additional ministries needed to become a reality, ministries that would address the root causes of the hunger, the thirst, the homelessness, the alienation, the oppression of people in our time, if the covenant of God's people was to be lived and to be a reality.

One example of such new ministering was the formation of NETWORK, a national Catholic social justice lobby founded in 1971 by forty-seven women religious from a variety of congregations. It was, and is, a nonprofit membership organization of religious and lay women and men whose goals are to obtain and secure just access to economic resources for all people.[1] Through such lobbying that influences public policy in the United States government, federal budget priorities can be reordered. By ministering in this way, with concern for the whole of humanity, women and men, religious and lay, are putting into action Gospel mandates that touch and transform unjust relationships at all levels of society. This is one way, but not the only way, of working toward the reality of a just society and putting the Gospel into action with a scripturally based, covenant spirituality.

The Challenge of the New Millennium to Women Religious

Change is never easy or simple. Through the Second Vatican Council, not only religious life, but also the entire covenanted people of God, are

---

[1] See Chapter 11, "Women Religious Engage the Political Process."

being called to become what they must become for and in the modern technological world. In many instances, the *aggiornamento* process has resulted in factions within every part of the Body of Christ and the results sometimes have not been experienced as a renewal of life in Christ. A shortage of clergy, leaders in the clergy at odds on major issues, lack of young people entering religious communities, family life frequently in ruins, countries and cultures competing with one another, consumerism, greed, violence, and individualism characterize our society. They raise critical questions for all followers of Jesus the Christ, but uniquely for women religious whose very identity lies in a covenanted bond with him.

Where is the covenant in all of this? How are we to be a covenanted people of God in the twenty-first century?

When Paul's favorite Christian community in Philippi was going through some difficult times, his admonition to them was, "Have among yourselves the same attitude that is also yours in Christ Jesus. . . . [H]e emptied himself, taking the form of a slave. . . . he humbled himself, becoming obedient to death, even death on a cross" (Phil. 2:5–8). His appeal to the community is that they relate to one another in all matters in the same way that they relate to each other as brothers and sisters in Christ, i.e., serve each other as you serve Christ.

In the Gospel of John, Chapter 12, the Last Supper portrays Jesus in the model of servant leadership. His washing the apostles' feet was embarrassing and awkward for them and Peter was not about to have Jesus wash his feet. One might say that a power struggle was occurring: Peter believing that Jesus' insistence on foot washing was not an appropriate thing for the Master to be doing, and Jesus insisting that servant leadership was the call of every person. Rich or poor, leader or disciple, each one needs to see and know oneself at the core with gifts and talents, weakness and sinfulness, but as one who is madly loved by God. The disciple must learn not only to minister to others, but also to accept ministry from others. Such mutuality in living breaks the power struggle and unites us in compassionate service and love. Having the same attitude as that of Jesus means letting go, not clinging to the "now" as the only way of being, living, doing, and ministering. It requires that one remembers the fidelity of God in past circumstances and places oneself in God's hands for the future. Living this way is truly to live!

Catherine of Siena concluded from her experience of God's love that God needs us just as much as we need God. Catherine believed this kind of love because she saw God as the "Mad Lover" who had fallen in love with humanity. We are called to this same belief in our lives and in these times. The shape and form of religious life in the twenty-first century must be the living of covenant justice, peace, mercy, truth, righteousness, and love. The details of the outer reality we do not yet know.

One thing we do know for certain is that women religious must have among themselves the same attitude that is also theirs in Christ. E. Glenn Hinson in his article, "Having the Mind of Christ," suggests that having this servant attitude should result in a common understanding, mutual love, and harmony of spirit that "should lead to mutual servanthood out of mutual love to fulfill a common task, the mission of Christ" (20). This does not mean that there will be total agreement on everything. Being the Body of Christ and living the mission of Christ in our age and time according to the charism of the particular congregation is the core that unites. When there is disagreement on the "how," the love of Christ will be the bond that continues to bring unity. That common task, the mission of Christ, will require the recognition and the calling forth of the gifts of leadership needed for the particular tasks of our time and the encouragement of those who have these particular gifts to exercise them for the common good and the building up of the Body of Christ. Finally, the common task, the mission of Christ, will require the continual focusing on the attitudes that are called forth by covenant bonding: justice, peace, mercy, truth, righteousness, and agape-love: loving God above all and loving our neighbors as ourselves. Forgetting personal petty concerns and directing energies for the common task of mission is the very nature of having the attitude of Christ.

The foundation of such covenant bonding and focusing is found in personal and communal prayer. It requires a living of personal prayer where one prays life experience, listening to God in both the experience and the wisdom of the Scriptures, asking for the strength, courage and insight to respond as Christ Jesus would respond, in covenant love and selflessness. It also requires communal prayer reflection, listening for the voice of the spirit present in the assembly and speaking through the members. This is no easy task and requires the attitude of Christ himself to let go of whatever binds and to embrace the servant leadership of Christ. Courage and absolute confidence that God will lead the way, as God led our forebears in religious life, is the key that will guide women religious into and through the new millennium.

Works Cited

Catherine of Siena. *The Dialogue.* trans. Suzanne Noffke, OP. New York: Paulist Press, 1980.

Cotel, Peter. *The Catechism of the Vows.* Baltimore: John Murray & Co., 1873.

Hinion, E. Glenn. "Having the Mind of Christ." *Weavings* (Mar.-Apr. 1977): 17–21.

2.

◆

Study of the Scriptures with insights into its relevance for contemporary experience led to sustained reflection upon women's experience of religious life and a reexamination of its theological foundations. The call of the council to update religious life led to profound exploration into the very nature of religious life. But the enterprise was not merely theoretical. It involved a turn from a "classical" model of theological reflection to a "dialogical" one. Reflection upon experience was the beginning but it led to a new wave of women pursuing advanced studies in theology that helped to put many issues into perspective but also opened up new questions not only for religious life but for all of the people of God.

◆

Shifting Paradigms: A New Reality

Anneliese Sinnott, OP

In every age, the church carries the responsibility of reading the signs of the times and of interpreting them in the light of the Gospel, if it is to carry out its task. In language intelligible to every generation, it should be able to answer the ever recurring questions which people ask about the meaning of this present life and of the life to come, and how one is related to the other. (GS 4)

Introduction

Paradigms are interpretative models that tell us what "reality" stands behind a symbol. Every bit of information we receive gets processed through paradigms. Paradigms are the way we make sense out of our experience. For the most part, we receive experience through "programmed" paradigms, models we've inherited. If all the experience we have doesn't "fit" the paradigm, we take in what we can, and just let the rest stand by way of exception. Paradigms remain in place until the amount of experience we take in that doesn't "fit" far outweighs that which continues to fit. At this point, we experience a "paradigm shift" (Schillebeeckx 579–82). For example, when most adults over the age of forty hear the word *family,* they interpret it to mean mother, father, children. We do this even though many of us know intellectually that well over 50 percent of the world no longer fits that model. When the family we encounter doesn't fit our paradigm, we acknowledge it as family, but usually attach a descriptive adjective: single-parent family, foster family, same-sex parent family, extended family, etc. (Perhaps those growing up in the twenty-first century will develop a new paradigm that won't require so many adjectives!) Jon Sobrino describes the task of shifting paradigms as endless. But, he says,

> it becomes inescapable, and urgent, in moments of crisis and "unhinging" when the old, worn-out hinges no longer support the weight of the whole door. The creation of new hinges, so that history may turn again, and turn well—so that it may become a history in which men and women will live as human beings once more. . . . (46)

—is an ongoing process within human history.

There are many ways to look at the experience of religious life since Vatican II. In this chapter I will explore a paradigm shift that has taken place in theological methodology, from what has been called the "classical model" to what I will call a "dialogical model," and the effects that shift has had on the lived reality of women religious in the United States. I do this out of my own experience as a woman religious, assuming that it is somewhat representative of the experience of others in similar circumstances.

It is not just theologians who "do" theology. Anyone who seeks truth, who grows in understanding, is actually "doing" theology. Long ago Anselm defined *theology* as "faith seeking understanding." Theology is both a product and a process. Engaging in the process of doing theology leads us not only toward the discovery of truth and understanding about faith, but also toward truth and meaning in the whole of life. The questions life poses to us are deeply theological (Young, 8), and for the believer, are given meaning out of the context of faith. If theology as a product is to be effective it must address the real questions which permeate our existence.

What we perceive as truth forms the basis for our unique heuristic vision, our "window on reality." My heuristic vision is the lens through which I see myself, others, all of life. Some of the influences that have shaped this lens are inherited from family and from the society and culture into which we are born. For some of us, our heuristic vision is fashioned out of a faith tradition that recognizes God as the ultimate source of truth, and as the One in whom we discover who we are and what life is about. As we grow and mature our heuristic vision or "truth" is continually challenged and expanded by new experiences. If life is to be meaningful, we must bring its probing questions to the theology that forms the foundation of our heuristic vision, our faith which is our "window on reality."

"Doing theology" is a process in which the believer engages in a conversation between the truth which is already possessed and a new truth encountered. The result of the dialogue, if it is truly dialogue, can be a new truth. What is articulated we call "theology."

Theology, then, is both process, the dialogue through which one arrives at truth, and product, the articulation of a new truth. One impacts the other, and the product is often determined by the process. The way people carry on the dialogue (the process) can be limited by their views of what is truth, and their perceptions are almost always shaped by the age in which they live and the context out of which they come.

The medieval church of the West perfected what has come to be known as the Scholastic method of doing theology. This process was largely deductive: one began with "the truth" and then deduced its application to real life. Although in its day this method was an effective way to do theology,[2] one of the limitations of using the Scholastic method in later centuries was its tendency to depend on patristic and medieval writers to the exclusion of Scripture, and not to take into account the changing world.

Scholastic methodology remained largely unchallenged until the Renaissance awakened a new interest in human experience, and the Reformation called Christians back to the Scriptures as a source of truth. The Enlightenment brought a new respect for the role of reason and

---

[2]Thomas Aquinas gives us an excellent example of the relevance of Scholastic methodology. Drawing on Scripture, philosophy and the experience of the world of the thirteenth century, he arrived at a new articulation of what people ought to believe about God and the things of God. The drawback to the Church's use of his theology into the twentieth century was their failure to adapt it to seven hundred years of change, and to engage in the same process as he had done.

emphasized the validity of human experience. With these new insights, theological methodology began to be transformed, at least among Protestants.

The Catholic Church however, bruised from its battles at the time of the Reformation, retreated into a neo-Scholastic position which was to continue until the time of the Second Vatican Council. In the years following the Council of Trent in the last half of the sixteenth century, there was a widespread belief that truth had already been articulated in its final form, and the task of the church was simply to pass it on. By this time, "doing theology" meant using the Scholastic method: starting with "the truth" and deducing from it how life was to be lived.[3]

Roman Catholics growing up in the first half of the twentieth century were taught to do theology out of the classical model. From the church one learned "the truth," largely based either on the *Summa Theologiae* of Thomas Aquinas or the writings of Augustine, and from it the Catholic arrived at the answers to the questions of life. This method was considered to be "objective"[4] and adequate. But in the second half of the twentieth century some theologians in the Roman Catholic Church began to make a shift in the way they did theology. This shift came, in part, from the realization that the classical method of doing theology is not as objective as once thought, but is, rather, conditioned by a medieval worldview, and because we no longer share that worldview, it is not adequate for doing theology today.

There were a variety of forces that caused a change in the theological methodology of the Roman Catholic Church, but perhaps the most critical were World War II and the experience of the Holocaust, and subsequently, Vatican II. The horrors of the war had touched the entire world; Catholics were not exempt from its effects. When the bishops seated themselves at the Second Vatican Council, ready to take a new look at the reality of the church and the world in which it found itself, they discovered theologians like Karl Rahner, Yves Congar, Henri de Lubac and Bernard Häring already in the wings. These men had seen first hand the evils of the war years perpetrated under the guise of Christianity, and they said, "No more!" They knew there was something wrong with an understanding of theology that could allow many Chris-

---

[3]The Scholastic method modified somewhat over seven hundred years is what is identified in this work as the classical method.

[4]If one is not aware that one's experience is influencing the way one sees reality and the conclusions one draws, then one may believe that the result is "objective" theology.

tians to look the other way when human beings were being exterminated. These theologians and others like them were realizing already that the classical method was no longer adequate to the search for truth. It was their thinking that helped to give direction to the bishops gathered at the council to examine the Roman Catholic Church and its theology.

The impetus generated by the council, and the emphasis on religious freedom shaped by the thought of John Courtney Murray, had tremendous effect on the American Catholic Church, due in large part to the climate in the United States at the time. The rise and development of the mass media, the challenge to create a new world, the change of status for American Catholics, turmoil over the war in Vietnam, the restlessness of young people on college campuses all over the United States, the rise of the civil rights movement, the tragic deaths of John and Robert Kennedy and Dr. Martin Luther King, Jr., and the riots that followed in many cities, the demographic changes that affected institutions operated by the Catholic Church, the rise of the women's movement, and the growing awareness of poverty both in the "land of equal opportunity," and in newly "seen" Third World countries all had great impact on the American Catholic Church. Sobrino summarizes the challenge we faced:

> Current history, with it crises, its doubts and questions, its opportunities and demands for the construction of a human future, challenges human beings, singly and collectively. We can ignore this challenge. We can manipulate it or pervert it. But if we have our ears open, it voices once more the question of what we are and what we ought to be, what we hope for and what we could hope for, what we are doing and what we ought to be doing. From within history itself we hear the call to respond to that history and its truth, to shape it, and not be subjugated by it, or dragged along passively (46).

Because of the climate in which it was received, the call issued by the Second Vatican Council to do theology in a different way had almost instantaneous effects. The shift to a new paradigm of theological methodology was to inevitably affect American religious life.

Paradigm Shift: A New Theological Methodology

Truth can exist in many places. It takes form as orthopathy, orthodoxy, and orthopraxy. Jamie Phelps defines these terms:

Orthopathy is rooted in the Spirit of Truth revealed through human experience. Orthodoxy is rooted in the Spirit of Truth revealed through Scripture and the Church's Tradition, and . . . [o]rthopraxy is rooted in the Spirit of Truth which manifests itself as action on behalf of existential peace and social justice (55).

One of these forms alone cannot be the whole of truth; each is needed. It is in the process of theological reflection that they are brought together.

Theological reflection can be defined as

the discipline of exploring individual and corporate experience in conversation with the wisdom of a religious heritage. The conversation is a genuine dialogue that seeks to hear from our own beliefs, actions, and perspectives, as well as those of the tradition. It respects the integrity of both (Killen and de Beer, viii).

Theological reflection is not a new thing. People always have engaged in a dialogue between their own experience and their religious tradition. But the paradigms which shape that dialogue have changed throughout history. There are five aspects or steps that characterize the new paradigm of doing theology. To engage in theological reflection, in other words, to "do" theology, we must (1) know and understand our own experience and its interpretation, (2) be willing to encounter truth in others, (3) listen and reflect on these varied sources of truth in a dialogical way in order to gain new insights, (4) be ready to articulate these new insights and, (5) be prepared to act upon them (cf. Lonergan). These components do not suggest a nice, neat linear progression, but rather varied aspects of a holistic way to do theological reflection.

In the new paradigm, the first step in doing theology is the recognition that human experience is an important factor in the development of any theology. One cannot do theology honestly without being aware of one's experience. We must take our experience seriously, whatever it might be (Cone, 23–24). The conviction that *orthopathy* is an authentic form of truth enables us to explore and own the validity of our own experience and that of others.

Validity, however, is not the only factor of importance here, because it is not pure experience that shapes us, but the interpretation of that experience. We need to know why we interpret our experience the way we do, and we must know how our interpretation conditions us to receive a "new truth" to which we are exposed. The unique paradigms each of us has are not as important as is the realization that we do have paradigms and that they condition the way we receive information. If we are unaware of our paradigms and how we have acquired them, they are likely not to change easily! Once we are able to understand our unique worldview, and can admit that it is limited, we are better able to open ourselves to truth from many other sources. Theology can only articulate a perception of faith based on the lived circumstances of an individual or a community.

Because all theological reflection is done by human beings who have unique heuristic visions, all theology is done out of a particular context or *locus theologicus*.[5] One aspect, then, of the dialogical method, is the belief that all theology is contextual. Because all theology is contextual, it becomes extremely important to open oneself to varied voices, since each of them holds a piece of the truth.

A second step of the dialogical method is the recognition that truth can be present in others. Here we encounter both orthopathy (experience of others) and orthodoxy (experience of the believing community throughout its entire history and articulated in "normative documents" [Scripture, the Fathers of the Church, etc.]). Assuming that *one truth* is the *only truth*, whether it resides in an individual or a group, is inadequate and gives rise to a fundamentalistic viewpoint. In a dialogical model, theological reflection requires partners in the dialogue. We must share wisdom with one another and be willing to receive the same. There is a move here from a top-down giving and receiving of the truth to a shared wisdom model. We hear each other's truth and enter into dialogue.

One's grasp of the truth will be narrowed or expanded depending on what partners or voices are allowed into the conversation. If a partner is always a homogenous voice, one that shares the same context, one may be closing off valuable sources of truth. In the classical model, the major sources of truth are to be found in one's already articulated religious tradition. In the case of Catholic Christianity, these are seen as Scripture, tradition and magisterial teaching. The new dialogical model doesn't rule these out, but suggests that, in addition to these, there are many other voices of truth that are needed. Truth is found in literature, science, history, art, music, and in other cultures. We need to hear especially those voices we have not encountered, voices that challenge our paradigms and worldview.

---

[5]The term *locus theologicus* is a technical term that refers to the context out of which we do our theology.

We need to encounter not only truth in individuals but the truth of entire communities, particularly those communities whose experience is not reflected in our own. We need to be open to "the collective life experience of pain, oppression, and dehumanization" (Thistlethwaite and Engel, 25) of vast areas of the world. The more multivoiced our dialogue is, the richer will be our theological reflection.

A third step is the dialogical conversation that occurs in the reflective process. Growing in truth is not just a matter of piling up truth. We need to test the new truth to which we are exposed against our own truth to discover whether it makes sense to us. We need to place the new voice alongside our religious tradition to see how it measures up. Our listening of the truth of the other must be a critical listening (Goizueta, 51–52).[6] It is important to approach a partner with critical hermeneutical tools, recognizing that each voice reflects the experience and interpretation of particular persons or communities. Dialogical reflection will assist us in uncovering the conditioning that affects the interpretations of the other voices.

One of the most difficult struggles of life lies in trying to solve the tension that arises between one's personal interpretation of life and God as truth, and the other interpretations we encounter. The easiest thing to do is to accept one as truth and reject the other. It is far more difficult to reflect in a posture of dialogue because dialogue forces us to be open to the possibility that perhaps our truth may not as clearly reflect God's vision as the one we encounter, or that the "truth" of another may not be truth for us. We must be open to change. This process is called *conversion.*

Bernard Lonergan uses the term "horizon" when he describes conversion. He points to the fact that, throughout life we move from one horizon to another. A move to a new horizon implies that we are now different through some new insight. Life no longer looks the same. Our worldview has been altered. We are impelled to make new decisions.

He points out that some horizons change according to maturity, some are conditioned by one's special experience, but for all of us

there are fundamental conflicts stemming from an explicit or implicit cognitional theory, an ethical stance, a religious outlook. They profoundly modify one's mentality. (235)

---

[6]This is what Goizueta calls a "critical appropriation." Others identify it as critical analysis, social analysis, or evaluation.

It is these horizons that offer the greatest challenge to us because they call us to give up or change deep convictions. Conversion happens when we allow the dialogical conversation that is the core of our theological reflection to permeate the depth of who we are and what we believe. Change or conversion is a fundamental component of this theological methodology.

The last two steps in the process of doing theology challenge us with the responsibility to speak and to act. The effects of honest theological reflection include an integrated response to life with all its problems (Thistlethwaite and Engel, 22). This response must be spoken and shared with others. The goal of theology is ultimately praxis (Thistlethwaite and Engel, 22), action that flows from reflection. The articulation of truth is not enough; it must be lived out in action and action must be based on the truth that has been spoken.

Doing theology out of this model effects a change in our worldview, both individually and corporately. Because we see differently, we speak differently, and we act differently. When the process begins again we are different; therefore the conversation in which we engage is a new one.

No single theological methodology is definitive in the discovery of God's revelation. No theological process can guarantee the arrival at absolute unconditioned truth. But the theological process should encourage human beings to be both authentic and free. A good theological process should help the participant to continually explore the heuristic vision that gives meaning to that individual's life. A dialogical method, if entered into with integrity, will assist us in this ongoing task.

Effect on American Religious Life

Few institutions have changed so dramatically in so little time as American women's religious congregations. I believe that life in women's religious congregations has been altered significantly in the last thirty years, due, in great measure, to a new paradigm of theological reflection. Prior to Vatican II, those living religious life developed a pattern of life by studying the church's theology of religious life (already set down, developed substantially in prior ages, articulated mostly by medieval men) and putting it into practice. Today most women religious do theology by engaging in the process described above, and the results affect the entirety of their lives.

It would be impossible to identify which of the changes that have taken place in North American religious life have resulted directly from this new paradigm of theological methodology. It will be easy, however, to see solid evidence of the five components described above: knowing and understanding one's own experience and its interpretation; being willing to encounter truth in others; listening to and reflecting on these varied sources of truth in a dialogical way in order to gain new insights; articulating these new insights; and, acting upon them in a transformative way.

The recognition that personal experience is a source for doing theology and needs to be considered in the development of religious life did not come easily to women religious who entered their congregations in the pre–Vatican II years. We had been taught to be prayerful and reflective, and we were, but we had also learned what the church taught about doctrine and discipline, and our own experiences of God or life did little to alter that understanding. Especially in the area of human freedom, we seemed to have harnessed our potential. We had made one important choice: to enter religious life. From that point on, options for life's directions were someone else's responsibility. But that was soon to change. We had to learn that to truly "do" theology, we, both individually and as congregations, had to enter into a much more demanding process.

In 1965, the final year of the Second Vatican Council, two documents were issued which forever changed American religious life: *Perfectae caritatis* (Decree on the Up-to-Date Renewal of Religious Life), issued on October 28, 1965, and *Gaudium et spes* (Pastoral Constitution on the Church in the Modern World), promulgated on December 7, 1965. The impact of each of the documents of Vatican II was enormous, but several passages in these two documents are crucial to the paradigmatic shift in theological methodology that women religious made so quickly and so completely.

The Decree on the Up-to-Date Renewal of Religious Life stated:

The up-to-date renewal of the religious life comprises both a constant return to the sources of christian life in general and to the primitive inspiration of the institutes, and their adaptation to the changed conditions of our time (2).

The decree set four principles to guide the process of renewal:

(1) the Gospels must be taken as the "supreme rule";

(2) "the spirit and aims of each founder should be faithfully acknowledged and maintained";

(3) all institutes should "share . . . the church's initiatives and undertakings in biblical, liturgical, dogmatic, pastoral, ecumenical, missionary and social matters";

(4) the members should "have a proper understanding of people, of the contemporary situation and of the needs of the church";

(5) religious life must engage, above all else, in "a spiritual renewal." (2)

The renewal called for was to allow that

> the manner of life, of prayer and of work should be suited to the physical and psychological conditions of today's religious. It should also, in so far as this is permitted by an institute's character, be in harmony with the demands of the apostolate, with the requirements of culture and with the social and economic climate, especially in mission territories. (3)

In another document issued during that year, Pastoral Constitution on the Church in the Modern World, the Council directed all Catholics to become aware that

> [t]he joys and hopes, the grief and anguish of the people of our time, especially of those who are poor or afflicted, are the joys and hopes, the grief and anguish of the followers of Christ as well. (1)

In addition, the document challenged Catholics further:

> In every age, the church carries the responsibility of reading the signs of the times and of interpreting them in the light of the Gospel, if it is to carry out its task. In language intelligible to every generation, it should be able to answer the ever recurring question which people ask about the meaning of this present and of the life to come, and how one is related to the other. We must be aware of and understand the aspirations, the yearnings, and the often dramatic features of the world in which we live. (4)

These statements of Vatican II called into question the classical methodology that was so much a part of Catholic life. Especially important were the challenges to integrate a "return to the sources of Christian life in general and to the primitive inspiration of the institutions," and the "up-to-date renewal of the religious life" and its "adaptation to the changed conditions of our time as well as the call to read the signs of the times," and interpret them "in the light of the Gospel." To these ends we had to study, but also to examine our life as it was currently lived. We had to bring into dialogical conversation our experience of life, the intent of our founders, the Scriptures and the signs of the times. The mandate required a radical reorientation of doing theology.

The rapid response of religious congregations to the council's directives can be attributed to obedience. Religious life was built on obedience to God, to the church, to one's religious superiors. These were voices we were accustomed to hearing. We knew how to listen to these sources of truth, and so, when the church asked us to modify the past, we did it out of obedience.

The first concrete changes issuing from the council occurred in liturgical reforms directed at local parishes, and in revised catechetical materials used to teach religion. Many women religious were closely connected to Catholic elementary schools and found themselves immediately involved in the "renewal" experience.[7] We were expected to follow new directives and so we did.

Because religious were obedient and listened carefully to church teaching, we took seriously the challenges of Vatican II. It was out of obedience to the mandates of the council that women religious began first to read, reflect on, and discuss the documents of the council. We were then led to Scripture and contemporary theology, especially as it affected religious life.[8] We discovered new sources of truth. Our contact with works written on the theology of religious life led us to other theological reading which challenged and expanded our former pre–Vatican II thinking.

As women religious responded to the Vatican II call for the reexamination of their founders' original purpose for the establishment of their religious institutes, and renewed themselves in the founding inspiration, they were able to hear the voices of their founders anew, and often discovered that their congregations or orders arose out of needs for radical change in the established church structure of a particular era to address the problems of the church and society at that time and in

---

[7]In some dioceses, women were required to attend presentations on implementation of the new liturgical guidelines, whereas priests were only encouraged to do so.

[8]Examples of these early sources are: Jean Galot, SJ, "Why Religious Life?" (1965) and J. M. R. Tillard, OP, "Religious Life, Sign of the Eschatological Church" (1964).

that place. This insight provided the necessary impetus to move from church renewal in a particular historical era to religious life renewal in the twentieth century. If our founders could be innovative, so could we! We began to pay attention to "the signs of the times." These, too, were rather new voices for us. This was the mid-1960s, and the "signs of the times" were many! These were new voices to which we had paid little attention from behind our convent walls. But listen we did!

The process of renewal which began in most American religious congregations somewhere between 1965 and 1975 was tremendously influenced by the national events and issues that formed the context of American society's daily life at that time. The election of the Roman Catholic John F. Kennedy to the presidency marked a new era in the lives of American Catholics in the United States. Catholics took a fresh interest in politics and in the role of government. It was only natural that a reawakened concern among Catholics to make use of their political voice in participative-decision making in the political arena should flow over into the institutional lives of the members of religious congregations.

Other new voices that were raised in the late 1960s and 1970s were those of women, which led to the rapid rise of the women's movement. As women religious heard women's voices, for perhaps the first time as women, their own experience as ecclesial women led them to reflect on the role of women in the church. This process sparked a growing awareness that the structures of religious living, which, for the most part, had been designed and were kept in place by male clerics, were oppressive and presented difficulties that stood in the way of their maximizing their potential. Women religious knew that they had a contribution to make *as women* to both church and society, but first they had to work at removing the obvious obstacles.

In the 1960s, many Catholic Americans were engaged in the social action of the civil rights movement and the antiwar movement, but the involvement of women religious in issues of social justice was greatly restricted because of the minutely structured life of the convent. Their lives, for the most part, centered on the schools and hospitals in which they worked. Society was changing, however, and they soon found themselves inadequately prepared to deal with the social issues of the day, particularly with the sexual revolution that was finding its way into the culture and into Catholic education. The theology they had received in their Catholic school training and in the novitiate simply did not address these needs.

There was tension between what had been known as a traditional religious lifestyle and one that would allow members to respond to the call to mission in the spirit of Vatican II. Solving the tension through dialogical reflection led to a radical reassessment of the shape religious life would take and its relationship to apostolic activity. As a result of reading, reflection, and speaking newly discovered truth to each other, women religious began to change many aspects of their lives: the way they dressed, the ways they prayed, the ways they lived in community, and the ways they governed themselves. These, however, were only the external changes; the more important transformations had to take place within the members.

One of the first challenges of renewal was to focus on our own experience of religious life, and ask whether the way we were living was really "psychologically and physically compatible" with the demands of the "apostolate" and the culture and world around us. Paying attention to our own experience was rather new and risky for women in religious congregations.

Self-growth was an early goal of renewal. Reflection on personal experience, interfaced with new ideas about God, deeper understandings of the Scriptures, the nurturing of spirituality and a willingness to share faith, led us to experience growth and maturation in all areas of our lives. This was especially true in the area of personal freedom. For some, it was their first experience of the freedom to "change" what seemed "unchangeable," i.e., some of the "absolutes" of religious life. But if we were called to be mature Christians choosing a gospel life, we had to become mature. For some women this need necessitated going quite rapidly through the stages of growth we had missed because the structures under which we lived did not tend to foster developmental growth.

An essential area of self-development was that of spiritual growth. Daily participation in regulated prayer experiences did not necessarily guarantee spiritual growth, so congregations began to offer opportunities for members to study, to make use of new forms of retreat and prayer experiences, to avail themselves of the opportunity for spiritual guidance or spiritual direction.

For many of us, going through reflective processes focused on self-growth was both affirming and positive. We found that much of religious life was life-giving. A significant number of women in religious communities, however, came to an awareness that the decision to spend one's life in a religious congregation might have not have been the most mature choice for them.

Facing the demands of a new way of relating to church and world required that we be knowledgeable, responsible and accountable. A new emphasis on personal freedom gave us the tools we needed to change and adapt. Growth in these areas wasn't easy for everyone. Individuals had to become more responsible and accountable. In many congregations efforts were made to provide opportunities to help women gain self-knowledge in order to make responsible personal and professional decisions. For some, these new demands were overwhelming. Congregations became aware that the needs of sisters suffering emotional or mental illness and those addicted to substance abuse had to be addressed.

For some of those who had walked with the poor and had experiences of unjust structures, the concentration on the individual sister seemed to be a turn toward individualism and self-centeredness, but congregations realized that if the members were to expand their notion of justice, they had to first experience that justice in their own lives. They recognized that there was an interrelationship between the freedom and responsibility of the individual member and a corporate direction toward mission. Growth in personal freedom would contribute to the development of apostolic responsibility, both individually and corporately.

Freedom is balanced by accountability. Accountability was not new for women religious, but a new theology of religious life suggested a new kind of accountability, one that was built on open communication rather than on requesting permission and responding to orders. Basic to this kind of accountability is the principle of collegiality. Collegiality assumes that the right to grow as a person within a group results from the recognition that each person must participate to the fullest measure of her capacity in moving toward the goal of the group. Her membership in the group, consequently, entitles her to voice opinions, to engage in discussions leading to decisions, to initiate or suggest ideas and programs, to share in activities which flow from decisions, and to benefit from actions affecting the whole group as it moves toward its goal. Collegiality provides an atmosphere that encourages freedom and calls the free person to be accountable, but it requires listening, dialogue and reflection.

The implementation of the principle of collegiality in structures that were, by design and by law, hierarchical was not an easy task. Some early plans for its introduction were: moving from "superior" to "co-ordinators" and then to collegial living in local situations; the introduction of a team concept for leadership at the intermediate level of government, to a regional leadership position supported by a council of the members; some types of leadership councils at the national or international level which included members from regional levels.

Critical analysis or evaluation, an aspect of the new theological paradigm, became a significant tool of renewal. We evaluated everything: our attitudes, our beliefs and understandings, our governmental structures, our finances, our resources and our goals for the future. Today, more than thirty years later, women religious continue to evaluate their ministries and the institutions in which they are exercised in the light of the gospel imperative of justice.

An important value that emerged from an appreciation of the varied contexts out of which we come was that of diversity. Collegiality and diversity foster individual freedom, and they can strengthen corporate commitment. However, there is a natural tension created when both the individual and the corporate body are seen as priorities. It is difficult to honor both diversity and unity. Many religious congregations found they needed to promote the principle of diversity of thought and expression as integral to personal freedom, and yet also affirm a basic unity of spirit in prayer, in communal life, and in apostolic purpose. Establishing policies which affirmed diversity and unity did not automatically eliminate the tension created between those two values.[9]

Doing theology out of a new paradigm had a great impact on the work women religious were doing. Principles of human freedom, maturity, collegiality and diversity began to affect the apostolate. Whereas in the past, members had been assigned to a particular apostolate, in the wake of the new theology that was emerging, women began to realize that to be effective they had to be equipped to do the ministry[10] in which they would be engaged.[11]

---

[9]Early on in renewal, many women realized that the choice for diversity would affect resources significantly. They recognized that as resources diminish, personal choices will be more crucial and that as numbers decrease, the financial resources will become more strained. Crucial questions continue to surface in religious congregations today about how much diversity a group can sustain and still maintain some unity, in what does unity consist, and how can congregations support freedom and diversity and still provide for the future.

[10]Note the shift in language here, from *apostolate* to *ministry*. This will be dealt with in a later chapter 6, "Mission and Ministry."

[11]A good example of this is seen in the move to encourage sisters in foreign countries to study the language and culture of people whom they served. Prior to renewal it was not always encouraged, or even allowed. Often students attending schools staffed by English-speaking Sisters were required to study everything in English.

Women religious began to realize that personal choices of ministerial work, made within the context of church and religious life, require accountability to the Gospel, to the church and to each other. In quite a new way, individuals began to assume responsibility to participate in the church's mission to communicate the Gospel. They also began to understand that one of the steps in maintaining accountability would involve continual evaluation of the work of the ministry as it relates to the call of the Gospel, the mission of the church and the charism of the congregation.

Action that emerged from our doing theology out of a new paradigm was what, in some congregations, was called "open ministry placement." Instead of a major superior deciding who would be "sent" to a particular assignment, each sister was offered the opportunity for self-determination in her choice of ministry placement. This often required gradual phasing into procedures, vocational and academic counseling, investigation of potential new works, coordination of personnel and apostolic opportunities, circulation of ministerial openings, and discernment of choices through continuing dialogue with a major superior. Employers, particularly pastors, who historically had come to depend upon the services of the sisters, had to rethink the staffing of schools. Individuals began to assume responsibility to develop gifts and talents and then, in personal freedom and responsible commitment, to choose, in discernment and dialogue with others, the work they wished to do within the framework and structure of their congregations.

As women began to move into new areas of ministry, they discovered, some perhaps for the first time, that some ministerial endeavors were not considered as appropriate for women; thus their new responsibilities in ministry led them to raise questions about women's role in the church which sent them to further study of the roles of women in ministry. In order to do this effectively, women had to have the opportunity to study Scripture and theology. When they returned to the sources of Scripture and tradition they brought with them their own experience as professionally prepared, competent, mature women willing to serve the church in its mission. They also discovered that the church was not always ready for their participation.

For many of the Catholic laity, the more obvious changes of garb and lifestyle in religious life are the most important changes, and by far, have either a positive or a negative impact on the church today. However, in many cases, these changes have been emblematic of catalysts in the real theological transformations that have occurred among American women religious.

Because religious life in the United States is comprised primarily of a white, middle class population, it was the white feminist, the white civil rights activist, and the white middle class war resister that first captured our attention. Some of us listened to these new voices, and carried the message to our congregations. It took time to "win over the masses." It took much longer for most of us to hear the voices of those within our congregations whose roots were not white middle class—the Hispanic, the African American, the Asian voices, and those among us who had lived and ministered among the poor. Because their experience of religious life in a U.S. congregation was similar to ours, we presumed that the *locus theologicus* of their theology, would be the same, and were shocked to find it was not. It took us a long time to realize that their *experience* of life in a religious congregation was not the same as it was for those of us who were white.[12] Being a member of a U.S. religious congregation and being African American or Hispanic or Asian changed one's experience (Phelps, 43–58).

We now had to ask ourselves, not only how our theology has been "narrow" because of our limited perspective, but also how it has been "flawed" because of the prejudiced worldview that we have inherited.[13] Diversity had to take on a new meaning. We were not just diverse in our choices of ministry and lifestyle but diverse in our deepest vision of what the world created by God ought to be. Our entering fully into a new paradigm of doing theology is leading us to new articulations of truth and new ways of being as women religious. We are constantly experiencing conversion.

Our struggles to find unity within diversity has led us to focus on community in a new way. We strive to build community within the varied living styles of our women, but we also see that our task is to build community in the places where we find ourselves on a daily basis in our ministries. We seek to build our lives today on radical simplicity, a task not easy to achieve in this consumer society. It is easy to get

---

[12]For example, Goizueta explains the difference in the meaning of community between Western culture and the Hispanic experience. In Western thought community is "understood as a voluntary association of atomic individuals," whereas community in the Hispanic culture is "an organic reality in which the relationship between persons is not only extrinsic but, at a more fundamental level, intrinsic as well" (64).

[13]See Phelps (47–52) for a summary of theories that have supported our theological efforts.

caught in the trap laid by advertising and materialism, and we realize that we must work to resist much of it.

It has taken us some time, but we are finally convinced of the need to engage in regular, deliberate study in a variety of areas, supported by the process of theological reflection. This implies that we must not only reflect, but share the fruits of our reflection, our faith with each other. One way to do this is to come together on a regular basis, bringing with us our expertise and knowledge in the many fields in which we find ourselves.

Women have an awakened interest in prophetic preaching, not only because many have the gift for communicating the Scriptures in this way, but because we have learned many things that we need to share with the wider community. We have also learned that our preaching must be grounded in authentic theological reflection, regular prayer and honest study. We have met obstacles that prohibit our preaching and we continually have been able to work creatively around some of the roadblocks.

Above all, many of us have had deep conversion experiences that have led us to be convinced that our action must be that described by the bishops in 1971.

> Action on behalf of justice and participation in the transformation of the world fully appear to us as a constitutive dimension of the preaching of the Gospel, or, in other words, of the Church's mission for the redemption of the human race and its liberation from every oppressive situation. (CU 6)

We have a much broader vision of what that call to justice is today than we had thirty years ago. It is somewhat ironic that the more convinced we become, the less able we are to respond in effective ways because of age and numbers.

Because we have begun to listen to the voices among us who speak from their own experience of being among the poor and the marginalized, we have concluded that we must, in some way, walk in solidarity with the economically poor and most vulnerable of our society, not just to be there, but to struggle with them for their own liberation and self-determination. Thus our study must include becoming aware of the systems and forces that keep some poor and allow others the luxury of wealth. Such awareness has led us also to continual evaluation and critique of our own attitudes, our lifestyles, our ministries, the use of our resources, and the policies that guide our congregations.

Listening to the voices among us, and the prophets who challenge us, has finally, after much personal struggle, led us to the understanding that much of the poverty and oppression, at least in the United States experience, is caused by racism. We have come to understand that religious life has not been exempt from this racism. There is a reason why so few of our numbers are women of color. Our conversion in this area was not an easy one, but our willingness to stay with the painful struggle has led us to new horizons. We are not yet where we need to be, but we are on the way! At least we are beginning to recognize the deep racism we have inherited, to identify the racism within our policies and practices as congregations, and make some changes; and we are starting to take stands against the racist practices in the society within which we live. Our theology must address the dehumanization and marginalization of so many of the peoples in the world in which we live (Phelps, 57). We must be willing to grow into "a new kind of spirituality that is radically on the side of those who are marginalized and oppressed" (Goba, 23).

One of the most valuable ways the shift in theological reflection paradigm has impacted us is to teach us how to reflect on our experience as women. Once we were able to do this, we could begin to hear the experience of other women. At first, our awarenesses came primarily from other women who shared our experience, Roman Catholic women religious. But slowly we expanded our search for truth: we heard Roman Catholic lay women, Protestant women, women of color, poor and marginalized women, battered women, mothers, women theologians. The more voices we heard, the more our reflections led us to stand in solidarity with these women. A point of conversion for many of us was the realization that our attitudes and actions were actually conveying complicity in many oppressive situations. We continue to call ourselves to work for the liberation of all women, in church and in society.

Ecology is an important focus in the world today. As our resources dwindle or are taken over by those able to afford their consumption, the earth gets poorer and the poor suffer more. There are two important catalysts to this kind of consciousness among women religious. First, our interest in women's theology has exposed us to the number of women writing about eco-feminism, revealing the strong link between women's experience and that of the earth, and to creation spirituality. Secondly, our work among the poor has sharpened our awareness that the resources we enjoy so abundantly in the U.S. are not always available, even to those living within the borders of this country.

Religious life has never been a static reality. In the past changes had been small and subtle, and had been seen, perhaps, as unchanging. However, in the last half of the twentieth century, religious life has changed so dramatically and swiftly that it seems to be a totally other reality from what it was.

The paradigm shift that has taken place in theological methodology is not so much a change in the recognition that theological reflection is being done, but a different consciousness of how it is done. I have written of but a few of the radical effects that one paradigm shift can occasion. It is somewhat like the experience of going to the top of a mountain. Our vision changes. We begin to see the other side! We are never the same again!

Conclusion

We women religious have attempted to be faithful to the validity of our own insights as we endeavor to articulate a renewed understanding of religious life. As members of religious congregations we have struggled to express our new awareness in authentic living. Women religious have learned to do theological reflection in a new way. We have come to value our own experience as a source of truth. We had to learn to do theology out of our own context, and to admit that our context is not the whole of the truth.

Some people are quick to point out the downside of this shift in paradigms of theological methodology. The number of incoming women has dropped drastically and many have withdrawn from religious congregations. The future of many religious congregations seems uncertain at best. Many claim that women religious are no longer a sign of what it means to be a truly committed Christian.

On the other hand, the positive results are quite remarkable. Evaluation has taught women religious to be observant and critical in the best sense of these words. It has called into question our belief system and the meaning of tradition in religious life. It has given us a chance to dream and to create a vision for the future.

Probably every congregation has multiple volumes in its archives in which attempts were made to articulate a renewed vision of religious life. However, it was one thing for a congregation to make a statement, but quite another to discover whether or not these statements are actually reflective of the lived experience of the members. It is here that the dilemma arises: do we talk ourselves into new ways of acting, or do we act ourselves into new ways of talking? Or do we engage in real theological reflection and do both?

As we face a new millennium, we cannot rest on the fact that we have done our work, that we have finally articulated a theology of religious life that responds to our own needs and the needs of the world and the church. We are already being bombarded by new questions which, once again we find ourselves inadequately prepared to respond to:

(1) Can the concept of God that has been used by Christians for two thousand years to support the patriarchal exploitation of women, and for centuries to bolster white racism and capitalism, be truly of divine origin? Is such an understanding of God credible?

(2) Can the self-understanding of churches that legitimized sexist, racist, classist, and religious oppression be theologically true? Do women need a male-dominated church for their sanctification and salvation? Do blacks need a white church? Does the proletariat need a bourgeois church? Do believers in other religions need the Christian churches to know God?

(3) What, then, is salvation? What is mission? What is liberation? When do sacraments confer grace? When do they legitimize, at least implicitly, the different forms of oppression supported by white male-dominated churches and most third world churches?

(4) What is to be thought of the Bible and its interpretation when it has been so long utilized to justify dominative sexism, racism, classism, and myopic Christian chauvinism? Is Scripture normative of faith? Who can interpret it correctly and how?

(5) How are we to appreciate the historical Jesus whose whole life and message are being rediscovered in our times principally due to the reflections of those who suffer under oppression legitimized by churches?

(6) How is Christ—the recapitulation of all persons and things—to be thought of in relation to the suppression of women, the poor, oppressed ethnic groupings, despised cultures, and marginalized religions? How can such a Christ—the life of the world—be the motivation of a church in relation to dictatorships, militarism, and nuclear armaments? (Fabella and Torres, 202)

These are only a few of the questions we face within our church experience. What about the critical questions that are already present in American society: health care, the possibility of cloning, assisted suicide, welfare reform, the growing chasm between the rich and the poor. How will we address these in meaningful ways that will be signs to our world? These, and many others yet to be raised, are questions we must face for a new millennium. The task of theological reflection is never done!

Works Cited

Cone, James H. *A Black Theology of Liberation*. 2nd ed. Maryknoll, N.Y.: Orbis Press, 1987.

Fabella, Virginia and Torres, Sergio, eds. *Doing Theology in a Divided World*. Maryknoll, N.Y.: Orbis Books, 1985.

Galot, Jean SJ, "Why Religious Life?" *Review for Religious* 24 (July 1965): 505–17.

Goizueta, Roberto S. *We Are a People: Initiatives in Hispanic American Theology*. Minneapolis: Fortress Press, 1992.

Killen, Patricia O'Connell and de Beer, John. *The Art of Theological Reflection*. New York: Crossroad, 1994.

Lonergan, Bernard. *Method in Theology*. New York: Herder & Herder, 1972.

Phelps, Jamie T., OP "African American Culture: Source and Context of Black Catholic Theology and Church Mission." *Journal of Hispanic/Latino Theology* 3, 3 (February 1996): 53ff.

Schillebeeckx, Edward. *Jesus: An Experiment in Christology*. Trans. Hubert Hoskins. New York: The Seabury Press, 1979.

Sobrino, Jon. *Spirituality of Liberation: Toward Political Holiness*. Maryknoll, N.Y.: Orbis Press, 1990.

Thistlethwaite, Susan Brooks and Engel, Mary Potter, eds. *Lift Every Voice: Constructing Christian Theologies from the Underside*. San Francisco: Harper & Row, 1990.

Tillard, J. M. R. OP, "Religious Life, Sign of the Eschatological Church." *Review for Religious* 23 (March, 1964): 197–206.

Young, Frances. *Can These Dry Bones Live? An Introduction to Christian Theology*. Cleveland: The Pilgrim Press, 1993.

3.

◆

The study of Scripture led to an understanding of God as a God of *kenosis*. Old images and understandings of God as exacting and demanding had many pervasive influences on religious life in the past. Harsh and restrictive practices often had the effect of diminishing the person's self-perception in relation to God. Spirituality was often a question of fulfilling obligations, rather than of developing a relationship with God. The discovery of the God in Jesus who is caring and compassionate and who inspires inner freedom and responsibility transformed the spirituality of women religious both personally and apostolically.

◆

Meeting a God of Kenosis

Carol Johannes, OP

Who, though he was in the form of God, did not regard equality with God something to be grasped. Rather, he emptied himself, taking the form of a slave, coming in human likeness; and found human in appearance, he humbled himself, becoming obedient to death, even death on a cross. (Phil. 2:6–8)

Perhaps the most helpful point of departure for a reflection upon developments in spirituality over the past several decades is the wave of renewal that has occurred in Christology. Somehow the church's official teaching that Jesus is fully human and fully divine tended always to result in a subordination of the human to the divine. The humanity of Jesus seemed more an added on dimension or something so profoundly conditioned by his divinity that it didn't have much reality of its own.

The statement in *Gaudium et spes* that addressed this mistaken subordination contributed to a reclaiming and an enhanced appreciation of the genuine humanity of Jesus:

Human nature, by the very fact that it was assumed, not absorbed
. . . He worked with human hands, he thought with a human mind.
He acted with a human will, and with a human heart he lived.
Born of the Virgin Mary, he has truly been made one of us, like
to us in all things except sin. (22)

This reclaiming and enhanced appreciation has influenced our spirituality in deeply significant ways. It created a new sense of the dignity
and sacredness of every human person, indeed of all things human. With
the coming of Jesus what used to be disparaged as "merely human" was
no longer divisible into categories of sacred and profane. All that is
human began to be seen as sacred. All human experience became, implicitly at least, faith experience.

New reverence for the human brought with it a changed perception
of the nature of asceticism and a more positive anthropology. Our basic
anthropology prior to Vatican II came down to us from a flawed interpretation of Genesis 2 which focused more on Adam and Eve's punish-
ment than on their redemption. This interpretation was reinforced in
Augustine's conviction of limited salvation and made its way into the
Council of Trent's articulation of original sin and the human condition.
Humankind was fallen from grace, weakened in will and prone to evil,
subject to the control of the devil, and condemned to a life of hardship
and suffering by an angry, punishing God (Johnson, 31–32).

This was not, of course, the exclusive attitude toward the lot of humankind prior to Vatican Council II. It was always tempered by belief
in God's love and mercy. But a residue of negative anthropology lingered
in the tradition and distorted both our image of God and our image of
humankind.

With the coming of Vatican II this vestige of negative anthropology
gave way to a renewed emphasis upon the assertion of Thomas Aquinas
that every human person has a natural desire for God because every
human person was made by God in order that God might be Self-gift.
This suggests that every human person is gifted by *nature* (not super-
nature) with the offer of grace. In other words, there is a sense in which
we are all graced by nature.

Though humankind has a history of sin as well as grace, and that
history of sin will always be a current pulling us away from God, nevertheless, prior to and deeper than any sinfulness or blindness or resistance to God, is the movement in us of grace toward God, toward love,
toward divine Self-gift (McDermott).

Looking upon the fully divine and the fully human Jesus as the medium through whom God became Self-gift in human history has tended to transform our image of God. Indeed Albert Nolan insists in *Jesus Before Christianity* that our deepened awareness of the implications of the full humanity of Jesus, a humanity not subordinated to the full divinity of Jesus, must transform our image of God if we wish to discover the true God of revelation.

> By his words and his praxis, Jesus himself changed the content of the word "God." If we do not allow him to change our image of God, we will not be able to say that *he* is our Lord and our God. To choose him as our God is to make him the source of our information about divinity and to refuse to superimpose upon him our own ideas of divinity. (166)

Nolan suggests that we have had a tendency to deduce the characteristics of Jesus from what we thought we knew about the characteristics of God. He asserts that we need to proceed in precisely the opposite direction, deducing everything about God from what we do know about Jesus. According to Nolan, confessing that Jesus is divine changes, not our understanding of Jesus, but our understanding of divinity. He speaks of the need to turn away from all our old images of God so that we can truly find our God in Jesus and what Jesus stood for:

> We have seen what Jesus was like. If we now wish to treat him as our God, we would have to conclude that our God does not want to be served by us, but wants to serve us; God does not want to be given the highest possible rank and status in our society, but wants to take the lowest place and to be without any rank and status; God does not want to be feared and obeyed, but wants to be recognized in the sufferings of the poor and the weak; God is not supremely indifferent and detached, but is irrevocably committed to the liberation of humankind, for God has chosen to be identified with all people in a spirit of solidarity and compassion. If this is not a true picture of God, then Jesus is not divine. If this is a true picture of God, then God is more truly human, more thoroughly humane, than any human being. God is, what Schillebeeckx has called, a *Deus humanissimus*, a supremely human God. (Nolan, 166–67)

Nolan's description of a supremely human God revealed in the fully human, fully divine, Jesus is not reductionist but is a concrete spelling out of the implications of the passage from Philippians known as the kenosis passage, from the Greek word *kenosis* meaning "self-emptying" (Brown 546–49). Paul helps us to discover that God is Self-gifting through our discovery of Jesus who is self-emptying:

> though he was in the form of God, (he) did not regard equality with God something to be grasped. Rather he emptied himself . . . becoming obedient to death, even death on a cross. (Phil. 2:6–8)

Clearly it is God's desire that every human person enjoy fullness of life. And God effects this fullness of life for humankind in kenosis, in self-emptying. The Jesus of the kenosis hymn above recognizes that being equal with God means most profoundly to be one who is non-grasping. "The self-emptying of Jesus unto death—and death on the cross—is the revelation that to be God is to be unselfishness itself" (Richard 22).

There is a way to look at this that suggests that what makes God most divine and what makes humankind most human as well as most God-like is self-emptying, self-gifting love. God's giving God's Self away to us does not leave God diminished. Rather, self-emptying love is what constitutes God as God. Neither does self-emptying love leave human-kind diminished. Rather it makes us most fully who we are. It is this truth that makes the Gospel paradox most clear. When we are over-protective, guarded, and cautious about giving ourselves to God, we die. Something in us shrivels up. When we generously give ourselves away for Jesus and for the sake of the Gospel, however, we find life (Mark 8: 34–35). We are not impoverished or swallowed up; rather we find our deepest and most authentic identity.

The theology of kenosis has generated in us a spirituality that can help us to worship and relate to God in an increasingly mature and confident way. If God is so thoroughly *for* us, if God's love for us is so great that there are no human terms to describe it accurately, then we can trust God fully; we can entrust the deepest secrets of our hearts to God; we can be absolutely honest and transparent with God and claim an intimate friendship with God that can gift us with deep peace and equanimity.

There are two particular emphases in the theology of kenosis that have had an especially transforming effect upon our spirituality. The first is the emphasis upon God as Divine Compassion, and the second, the way in which the all powerful God lays aside power.

In his study of kenotic theology, Lucien Richard speaks of the centrality of compassion as a core attribute of God. From the earliest development of the tradition in Israel through the ministry of Jesus, God has always revealed God-self as a compassionate God. Richard recalls that God is revealed in the history of Israel as both a compassionate father and a compassionate mother. He sees that the intimacy and the loving attachment with which God relates to Israel are associated with the womb. Divine Compassion not only gives new life but also restores life when it has been diminished or lost (Richard, 188). One of the most moving and poignant texts of the Hebrew Scriptures in which God reveals God-self as a compassionate restorer of life appears in Exodus during the account of the call of Moses:

> But the Lord said, "I have witnessed the affliction of my people in Egypt and have heard their cry of complaint against their slave drivers, so I know well they are suffering. Therefore I have come down to rescue them from the hands of the Egyptians." (Exod. 3: 7–8)

For centuries Israel awaited the establishment of the reign of her compassionate God. The inbreaking of that compassionate reign occurred with the coming of Jesus, especially through his miracles. Again and again his heart went out to those suffering brokenness and desolation and he was moved to restore them to wholeness and peace (Richard, 188). Perhaps the most difficult challenge of living the Christian life is that of coming to terms with human suffering, our own and that of others, especially the suffering of the innocent, children, the poor, the vulnerable. In speaking of the sorrow of God, Gerald Vann describes the world as "drenched in pain" (Vann, 78).

That strain of the tradition that regarded suffering as part of God's plan for us or as part of God's permissive will has given way to a different sense of how God is involved in our suffering. The God of compassion does not will suffering and does not visit suffering upon us but has promised to be with us in our pain, and is, in fact, a genius in bringing good out of evil and suffering. But God does not want us to suffer. Today there are even those who suggest that when we grieve over our own suffering, and especially over the anguish of others, our grief is really a sharing in God's own affect, in God's own compassionate sorrow for us (Barry, 842–43).

The fact that Jesus is the perfect revelation of a God of compassion puts the divine exercise of power in perspective. Through Jesus we know that the All Powerful chooses to lay power aside. Richard observes that power that has been filtered through kenosis never dominates or controls or breaks in from above or from outside. God's creative power never takes on any of the destructive elements of the human exercising of power. Rather, it is a power *with*, "a power of love that challenges, releases, gives life" (187).

Richard sees the life and ministry of Jesus through the lens of kenotic Christology in much the same way as Nolan. The former goes so far as to describe the messianic program of Jesus as "subverting" the nature of power. The Messiah's life and ministry transform power into service. That Jesus subverts the nature of power is clear from the way that he uses the metaphor of the Kingdom of God to make known God's gracious presence. Richard describes the use that Jesus makes of the metaphor of a kingdom in his parables as "iconoclastic" because he reverses the ordering of the metaphor so that those who find themselves at the bottom of the pyramid become the first in the kingdom of God (Mark 10:14; Matt. 19:30). Those without status who are normally ignored or dismissed become privileged members of God's kingdom (186).

Richard describes power according to the paschal mystery as essentially relational and self-sacrificing envisioning both mutuality and reciprocity. This power "does not either directly or indirectly intend to control 'the other'; it intends the enlargement of freedom; it is a commitment to the relational 'us,' to mutuality" (186).

For women and women religious in today's culture and church, the God of kenosis, by manifesting compassion and exercising power, forms us and informs our relationship to God, the dominant culture, and the church. For we experience ourselves as called to be, not only agents of God's spreading compassionate love to all we meet, but also as objects of that compassionate love. Generally speaking, women are still at the bottom of the pyramid without significant status, and as such are invited by God to be privileged members of the kingdom. Jesus made it clear throughout his ministry that oppression, injustice, disempowerment and inequality are not of God. He wished to lift the bonds of oppression, empower the weak and vulnerable, and establish God's reign of justice and peace for all time. It seems quite apparent that God is at work within us today effecting this liberation and empowerment. Oppressive structures are still alive and well in our experience. But a spirituality derived from a theology of kenosis is likely to generate in us an inner freedom and confidence in our own equality and infinite value as human persons that will no longer leave us vulnerable to internalizing oppressive and dismissive messages. Indeed, our internalizing of this spirituality has led us to see that the tradition itself and the culture within which it flourishes are in need of critique, of enlightenment, of healing.

This series of essays is the work of members of a religious congregation of women, the Adrian Dominican Sisters, formed in the Dominican tradition. Providing a cultural critique is not a new activity for members of the Dominican Order. Timothy Radcliffe, OP, currently Master of the Order, reflected recently that, "every culture builds a home in which the Gospel may be welcomed, but the Gospel both embraces and criticizes any culture it encounters" (McGreal).

In the thirteenth century St. Dominic himself was called to critique his ecclesiastical culture through laying aside the trappings of wealth and power that had come to be associated with it. Thus he could touch the hearts of the heretics and preach the Gospel of compassion. Though our times are unlike those of Dominic, he provides an enduring model for the contemporary church of a follower of the Jesus in the kenosis passage who consistently sought to deal with his power by laying it aside. Significant decisions regarding the lives of the friars were always made together in community. Oppressive power was something foreign to Dominic's mode of governance, and Dominican men seem to have been reasonably successful in preserving Dominic's strong instinct that to be true to the vision of Jesus, power needs always to be exercised *with*, not over, others.

With the passage of many centuries, however, Dominican congregations of women were mandated by canon law to govern themselves in a hierarchical model according to which it was impossible to be faithful to Dominic's original mode of governance. Among the most significant fruits of the renewal of religious life for Dominican women was their congregations' movement to retrieve Dominic's vision of how power was to be regarded in the Dominican Order. Power is a gift given to be shared, to serve, to support, to free, to challenge all to an ever more faithful Gospel life.

As a case in point, the Constitutions of the Adrian Dominican Congregation assert:

From Jesus, proclaimed in the Gospel, the authority of the Adrian Dominican Congregation, mediated and affirmed through the Church, resides in the communion of its members according to their respective roles as given in this Constitution and Statutes. . . . Our government is participatory, lived in the spirit of freedom and trust given to the Order by Dominic. . . . We govern ourselves in keeping with the principles of collaboration and subsidiarity at every level of the Congregation so that each Sister may exercise coresponsibility. (Adrian Dominican Constitutions and Statutes 1989, 42, 44)

And in the Foundational Statement of the General Chapter of 1992 we read:

> We Adrian Dominicans urged by the creative Wisdom of God who brings forth the earth and all who dwell in it in mutual relationships for the common good and responsive to the hungers of peoples and planet resolve, through the next six years to preach and to help shape a community among ourselves and in our world that witnesses to the healing, liberating and empowering truth of God's design.

Women religious in general, and Dominican women religious in particular, have lived through the demanding process of the renewal of religious life in response to the directives of Vatican Council II. They have experienced a movement in their respective congregations from hierarchical authority as *power over*, to shared authority as *power with*. This movement has resulted in greater inner freedom but also in a considerably deepened sense of responsibility for making the personal and communal choices that enhance their living of the Gospel. In this process, they have come to see that fidelity to the Jesus of the kenosis passage and to the spirit of his disciple, Dominic, demands of all, in all aspects of life and ministry, a relinquishing of the exercise of authority as *power over* in favor of its exercise as *power with*.

Furthermore, they have too often experienced the reluctance of the church to engage in this relinquishment. There is still a hope and resolve in women that the church striving to mediate a God of kenosis may someday become a kenotic church which "manifests a transformation of hierarchical into relational power" (Richard, 187). So long as any individual or group remains in a domination-subjugation position, it is fair to say that the mind and heart of Jesus have not yet been absorbed by the Church.

As for women themselves, their moral sensibilities tell them that their new asceticism involves claiming their true God-given identity within the culture in general and the ecclesiastical culture in particular. This resolve alone will move the church a little farther along the continuum of recognizing its call to kenosis in its service of a kenotic God.

Works Cited

Adrian Dominican Sisters. *Adrian Dominican Constitutions and Statutes.* Adrian, Mich.: General Chapter 1989.

Adrian Dominican Sisters. *Vision Statements of General Chapter.* Adrian, Mich.: General Chapter 1992.

Barry, W. A. "God's Sorrow: Another Source of Resistance?" *Review for Religious* 48 (1989): 842–43.

Brown, Colin, ed. *The New International Dictionary of New Testament Theology.* Vol. 1. Grand Rapids, Mich.: Zondervann, 1975.

Johnson, Elizabeth A. *Consider Jesus.* New York: Crossroad, 1994.

McDermott, Brian. Unpublished Lecture. Cambridge, Mass., 1975.

McGreal, Nona. Unpublished Lecture. Caleruega, Spain, 1997.

Nolan, Albert. *Jesus before Christianity.* Maryknoll, N.Y.: Orbis Press, 1992.

Richard, Lucien. *Christ the Self-Emptying of God.* New York: Paulist Press, 1997.

Suenens, Leon Joseph. *The Nun in the World: New Dimensions and Modern Apostolates.* Trans. Geoffrey Stevens. Westminster, Md.: Newman Press, 1952.

Vann, Gerald. *The Pain of Christ and the Sorrow of God.* 3rd ed. London: Blackfriars, 1952.

4.

◆

Exploration into the nature of religious life in light of church teaching and communal reflection led to a new sense of what religious life is in and for the church. Pope Paul VI was the first to speak of religious life as charism and to associate it with the influence of the Holy Spirit in the life of the people of God. Through reflection on this teaching women religious began to see that they were not a "layer" within a hierarchical ordering, but were outside of it as a free grace for the church. This was an insight that prompted serious reflection on ecclesial identity and questions on how to be both true to that identity as well as responsible within the church.

◆

Religious Life as Charism
Nadine Foley, OP

The charism of religious life, far from being an impulse born of "flesh and blood," or one derived from a mentality which conforms itself to the modern world, is the fruit of the Holy Spirit, who is always at work within the Church. (ET 11)

As women religious responded to the directive to return to the original inspiration of their founder(s), they turned to the long revered histories and traditions rooted in their beginnings. In their origins, religious congregations more often then not arose from the experience and vision of holy women and men who responded to the needs of their times and brought into being religious institutes designed for the apostolic needs that confronted them. Adrian Dominican women who reflected on their origin in the inspiration of Dominic in the thirteenth century, on the apostolic design of the order, its commission for preaching to address the heresies rampant in that time, its mode of governance to support that mission, and Dominic's unique desire to insure freedom and responsibility for the members, found excitement about the possibilities of claiming these qualities of the order in a new way. They, and other apostolic women religious of the present time, are different from the contemplative nuns from whom many took their beginnings. Yet women religious in general had been living, with some modifications, according to customs that had developed among the contemplative nuns of various traditions. Their customs and practices continued to be incorporated into the canon law for religious without differentiation. As women religious began to internalize their original inspirations anew, they found themselves with questions about their identity within the church, particularly as apostolically oriented institutes of religious life. Turning to the documents from Vatican Council II for clarification, they discovered even more fundamental questions about the place of religious life itself within the church.

The Dogmatic Constitution on the Church *(Lumen gentium),* far from clarifying the issues, only offered ambiguity. First, it defined the church as hierarchical from its beginnings and according to the intention of Jesus. That hierarchy was designated as bishops, clergy, and laity. Accordingly, nonclerical religious would be fundamentally laity. The document stated further that religious life is not a "middle way between the clerical and lay conditions of life" (43). In other words it is a form of life to which some clerical and some lay Christians are called. In the chapter on the laity, however, the laity are defined as "all the faithful except those in Holy Orders and those who belong to a religious state approved by the Church" (31). Together those two official positions place nonclerical religious life in an apparent ecclesial "limbo." When the disparity was first noticed, it was a cause for dismay that nonclerical religious—sisters and brothers—had been overlooked by those who had developed this important constitution on the church.

But reflection brought into focus a second inference that could be drawn. Religious life exists apart from the hierarchical ordering, a free, graced life within the church understood as the "people of God," and a gift to the church in that reality. This insight is not only theoretical, it reflects the experience of nonclerical religious whose ministries for the most part have not been within ordained ecclesial roles or church structures but in direct contact with the people whom they have served. "Ecclesial" when applied to women religious can only pertain to the model of the church as "people of God" among and with whom they have ministered for many years. In the quest for ecclesial identity, women religious and religious brothers looked with new awareness to the meaning of "charism" first put forth by Pope Paul VI as expressing the nature of religious life (ET 11). That identity of religious life has continued to appear in authoritative writings. The document *Mutuae relationes*, from the Sacred Congregation for Religious and for Secular Institutes (now CICLSAL) said in reference to religious institutes,

> Every authentic charism implies a certain element of genuine orig- inality and of special initiative for the spiritual life of the Church. In its surroundings it may appear troublesome and may even cause difficulties, since it is not always and immediately easy to recognize it as coming from the Spirit. (12)

These words introduce a section on "signs of a genuine charism." These are identified as: fidelity to the Lord, docility to His Spirit, intel- ligent attention to circumstances and an outlook cautiously directed to the signs of the times, the will to be part of the church, the awareness of subordination to the sacred hierarchy, boldness of initiatives, con- stancy in the giving of self and humility in bearing with adversities. "Awareness of subordination to the sacred hierarchy" is the one feature of this description that bears interpretation, lest it deny the very nature of charism itself. Yet that there is a necessary relationship between the hierarchical and charismatic elements within the church is indisputable. But "subordination" seems an inappropriate word with which to de- scribe that relationship.

Pope John Paul II, in the 1996 Synod document on religious life, *Vita consecrata*, speaks more frequently of *consecration* than of *charism*. Nonetheless, in the introduction he says that "the many charisms of spiritual and apostolic life bestowed on them [women and men religious] by the Holy Spirit, . . . have helped to make the mystery and mission of the Church shine forth, and in doing so have contributed to the renewal of society" (1). And again, "Communion in the Church is not unifor- mity, but a gift of the Spirit who is present in the variety of charisms and states of life. These will be all the more helpful to the Church and her mission the more their specific identity is respected" (4). He speaks further of the unceasing work of the Holy Spirit, who "in every age shows forth the richness of the practice of the evangelical counsels through a multiplicity of charisms" (5). Historically, charism has been understood in a variety of ways. From a pragmatic viewpoint, it has been applied to special works, special ministries. It has been used to describe personalities and movements in an attributed way that is not helpful for expressing the character of religious life. Charism also is associated with the contemporary "charismatic movement" in the church. But, as official teaching since Pope Paul illustrates, "charism" also has a meaning within the theology of the Holy Spirit that has emerged with growing clarity for those exploring the identity of religious life since Vatican Council II. The understanding of charism, as an effect of the indwelling of the Holy Spirit, has been most influential in the ongoing reflection about religious life in which members have engaged.

Women religious have come to understand, from returning to the original inspirations of their institutes, that the many forms of religious life appeared historically as manifestations of the Holy Spirit acting within and for the people of God. The Holy Spirit acts uniquely within those who constitute apostolic or ministerial religious communities in virtue of the covenant into which they have been drawn in a common faith and commitment for the sake of the mission of the gospel. They know experientially that the initial call and response to religious life as charism for the people of God is an effect of the abiding presence and moving impulse of the Spirit of God. Again Pope Paul VI touched upon this theme:

> The interior impulse which is the response to God's call stirs up in the depth of one's being certain fundamental options. Fidelity to the exigencies of these fundamental options is the touchstone of authenticity in religious life. (ET 12)

Such a realization has called women religious to greater attentiveness to the Spirit of God and increased awareness of their responsibility to respond to the signs of the times through communal discernment.

The religious congregation incorporates uniquely the biblical theme of covenant. The idea that God entered into a covenant relationship with the chosen people was an inspired biblical innovation. And it persists into the teaching of Jesus, inaugurator of the New Covenant, according to the author of Hebrews (9:15). Like the covenant that preceded it, this one offers liberation and promise through Jesus. It is extended in a free act of God through him and is sustained by the presence of the Spirit. It carries God's promise of fidelity by the indwelling of the Spirit. It forms a people, an *ecclesia*, purchased through the blood of Jesus the Christ. And so the people of the New Covenant, the Church, came into being in order to pursue the mission entrusted to them by Jesus.

Religious congregations are unique expressions of the *ecclesia* as covenanted communities. They are born in the faith commitment of individual persons under the influence of the Holy Spirit, and the individual persons come together in communities of what the institutional church has called "consecrated life." This kind of origin is an important realization insofar as very few religious institutes have come into being through direct action by members of the hierarchy. Because of their origin from the impulse of the Holy Spirit, and the approval granted by the church, religious institutes are endowed with a certain authority to preserve the characters of their institutes and the authenticity of their mission. This fact is implicit in the directives for renewal given in the wake of Vatican Council II. An internal authority functions through the communal discernment among the members at times such as general chapters. While this principle may not be explicit in the directives issued to religious congregations after Vatican Council II, it is surely implicit. Such authority derives uniquely from the lived experience of the members reflected upon communally in light of the Gospel and of the congregation's founding inspirations.

The process of reflection initiated by Vatican directives involved a comprehensive examination of traditional religious life in ministry in relation to the lived experience of the members. What occurred was further advanced in communal experience that reflected what Edward Schillebeeckx describes:

Experience means learning through "direct" contact with people and things. It is the ability to assimilate perceptions. It is of the nature of this process of learning by experience that the new experience is always related to the knowledge that we have already gained. This gives rise to a reciprocal effect. The discoveries about reality that we have already made and put into words open up new perspectives: they direct perception in our experience to something particular; they select and demarcate, they guide our attention. In this way they become the framework within which we interpret new experiences, while at the same time this already given framework of interpretation is exposed to criticism and corrected, changed or renewed by new experiences. Experience is gained in a dialectical fashion: through an interplay between perception and thought, thought and perception. The function of experience is not to find room for constantly new material in existing patterns of thought which are taken as unalterable, and which are constantly confirmed as a result—though there are also experiences which bring confirmation. No, the connection between experience and thought is rather that the constantly unforeseen content of new experiences keeps forcing us to think again. On the one hand, thought makes experience possible, while on the other, it is experience that makes new thinking necessary. Our thinking remains empty if it does not constantly refer back to living experience. (31–32)

While the experience of women religious is not new in one sense, what was new was the congregation-wide reflection upon the origin, initial inspiration, mission, and charism of the institutes. It was further a new experience to write updated constitutions to fit the reality and the challenges that emerged from the broad consultations that were mandated. For the first time religious in active institutes could write a constitution that corresponded to the kinds of communities in mission they had become. In general those aspects of religious observance that stemmed from a prior enclosed contemplative life were either discarded or altered to fit apostolic religious life. What women religious particularly have accomplished in revising constitutions to fit their reality and experience has involved the claim to an inner authority under the guidance of the Holy Spirit. They exercise such authority through communal prayer and discernment, not in opposition to hierarchical authority, but in courageous fidelity to the Spirit of God. The two cannot be in opposition, although what many congregations of women religious experienced is reflected in another observation of Schillebeeckx.

It can hardly be denied that authoritarian institutions and conformist groups often show as it were innate mistrust of new experiences, of "experience" *tout simple*. They instinctively feel that in experiences an authority can present itself which is a criticism of the normativeness of the factual and of any authority which would merely assert itself as contingent facticity and thus as power. That they must nevertheless acknowledge the critical and productive force—the authority—of experiences emerges from the fact that they often seek to manipulate new experiences. (37)

One of the areas in which differences arose was in the identification of religious life as either essentially consisting in "consecration" or in "mission." While in the documents of many religious institutes charism had often been interpreted as specific works, such as education or healthcare, the deeper reflection of the contemporary period led members to see that particular works were carried out as aspects of the mission in which all Christians are baptized. It followed that, for women and men religious, baptized into mission, the intensification of their baptismal commitment lay in the strength of their commitment to mission, which has been and is considerable. Biblical reflection supported the insight that "consecration" and "mission" were not opposed concepts, but rather uniquely compatible.

Most religious communities of women are ministerial communities or, as some prefer, apostolic communities, whose consecration consists uniquely in what may be called "consecration for mission." As I have had occasion to say at an earlier time (Foley, 1989) our kind of consecration derives from the words of Jesus as recorded in the Gospel of John:

> Consecrate them in the truth. Your word is truth. As you sent me into the world, so I sent them into the world. And I consecrate myself for them, so that they also may be consecrated in truth. (17: 17–19)

At first glance this text might appear to pertain exclusively to the apostles and their successors, but biblical scholars expand the application, for example:

> When Christ prays for his disciples that they may be sanctified and consecrated in the truth, John is probably not thinking of a select few who will be ministerial priests and sacrificial victims, but of a consecration to his own mission by all disciples. (Wijngaards 265)

A religious congregation stands among the people of God marked by commitment to Gospel mission defined for us by the founders of our congregations and by the manner in which it has been extended in our congregational histories. Consecration for mission is central to the kind of covenant relationship with God and with one another that defines our institutes (cf. VC 72). And that covenant must be cherished, guarded, and developed by those, the members of the institute, who have entered into it. They, attentive to the Holy Spirit, who is at work in the church, must be trusted to fulfill that obligation faithfully and responsibly. For religious to forsake that responsibility by turning it over to the hierarchical church is to deny the Holy Spirit and the graced freedom to which the Spirit gives birth.

While some might read such a statement as implying a confrontational stance within the church, that is not the inference to be drawn. Charisms by their very definition must have a range of freedom within which to be true to their identity as gift for the church. History bears out how religious life has been an agent of ecclesial transformation at critical times. Once granted approval by church authority, the members of the institute must be trusted to remain true to the ministerial purposes for which they have been founded. Periodic review by competent external authority is certainly appropriate and even necessary but, for apostolic or ministerial communities, the criterion for such review should be fidelity to the mission, not to established forms that may have outworn their applicability to new situations.

The carrying out of mission is the work of the Holy Spirit whom Jesus promised when he said to his disciples, and therefore to us:

> But I tell you the truth, it is better for you that I go. For if I do not go, the Advocate will not come to you. But if I go, I will send him to you. And when he comes he will convict the world in regard to sin and righteousness and condemnation: sin, because they do not believe in me; righteousness, because I am going to the Father and you will no longer see me; condemnation, because the ruler of this world has been condemned. (John 16:7–11)

This text, along with others here and there in the last discourse of Jesus, set forth the essential role of the Holy Spirit in the economy of salvation. They lead to the account of the Pentecost event in which the *ecclesia* is born. David Power's description of the believing community, and surely the religious community is one, expresses what that community ideally is.

> The Spirit is God's eschatological gift. Its sending is the realization of covenant promise and its presence keeps promise and hope alive. The coming together of the believing community in proclamation, prayer, symbol, and covenant commitment occurs within the communion of the Spirit, and it is in the life of the Spirit that Jesus is recognized in his suffering as the one who brings the promise of God's freedom to those who suffer . . . Where a community in virtue of its remembrance of Jesus Christ engages in freedom and life-giving practice and service, this can only be in the power of the Spirit. There is the inner testimony of freedom to listen, to hear, to accept challenge, to live within a new horizon. There is the outer testimony of service in a love modeled on the foot-washing of Christ. (302)

Church documents have been quite explicit in setting forth some of these themes in relation to religious life. The Holy Spirit, as the document *Mutuae relationes* (1978) reminds us, is the life and vitality of the people of God and the principle of unity in its communion. Further, the Holy Spirit is the vigor of its mission, the source of its multiple gifts, the bond of its marvelous unity, the light and beauty of its creative power, the flame of its love. And religious life in its many manifestations has born witness to those characteristics of the divine in-spiriting through the centuries. The history of each religious institute records the manner in which the Spirit of God has acted within it.

If in fact, then, religious institutes are an effect of the Spirit's indwelling among the people of God, a charism in that respect, the members must insure that the possibility for the freedom of the Spirit to act in and through them is sustained. Over time the proliferation of institutes of apostolic life extended the ministerial service of the church in broad strokes to the poor, the sick, the uneducated, the imprisoned, and all suffering people on the underside of societies. Today's women and men religious are the offspring of these innovators who responded to the Spirit of God calling them forward to a form of life that had not existed before them. They were sisters, brothers and priests. In a particular way they have expressed the diaconal identity of the church after the manner of the first deacons of apostolic times who were commissioned to look to the needs of the poor and suffering on behalf of their communities of faith. It is to such service that the Spirit of God led founders and successors down to the present time.

While the mission itself remains constant, the particular ways in which the ministerial needs are present in each new time and place continually call for modifications according to the signs of the times. Through their dialogue and discernment under the guidance of the Holy Spirit, religious institutes must be trusted to make the responses that they deem possible and appropriate for them. For so many today this responsibility has resulted, not only in addressing the human needs as they present themselves, but in looking to the societal forces that have created the problems. Various forms of social and political action have in a number of instances been the result. Such responses have been made by women and men religious who have internalized the social teachings of the church and found ways in which to apply them.

Past history shows that religious life has been prophetic particularly at major turning points in church history. Some, both within religious life and outside of it, like to ascribe the character of prophecy to religious life and perhaps would regard it as contributing to its ecclesial identity. There is a respect in which this notion has validity but only within a theology of the Holy Spirit. Those who were called to be prophets, both in biblical times and in later history did not seek or claim the role as a personal prerogative. They were called by God and they responded, some very reluctantly. But as people in later times looked back at what they said and did, they could say, "Indeed these were prophets." They were prophets because they could read the signs of their times and respond in ways that were needed. Karl Rahner speaks of prophecy in this way:

> Charismatic prophecy in the Church helps to make the message of Jesus new, relevant and actual in each changing age. It does not matter whether the representatives of this charismatic prophecy in the Church—the authors of religious renewal, the critics of the Church and the society of their day, the discoverers of new tasks for the Church and the faithful—are called prophets or are given other names. . . . If such [persons] do not merely reaffirm general principles and apply them to new cases, but display in their message something creative and incalculable, with the force of historic turning-points, so that they are legitimate and effective in the Church, we may say that the Church has had a "major" or a "minor" prophet. (1286)

These words are consonant with a line from *Mutuae relationes:* "a responsiveness rich in creative initiative is eminently compatible with the charismatic nature of the religious life" (19). *Vita consecrata* expands upon the theme.

> The consecrated life has the prophetic task of recalling and serving the divine plan for humanity, as it is announced in Scripture and as it emerges from an attentive reading of the signs of God's providential action in history. This is the plan for the salvation and reconciliation of humanity (cf. Col. 2:20–22). To carry out this service appropriately, consecrated persons must have a profound experience of God and be aware of the challenges of their time, understanding the profound theological meaning of these challenges through a discernment made with the help of the Spirit. In fact, it is often through historical events that we discern God's hidden call to work according to his plan by active and effective involvement in the events of our time. (73)

If the religious life at this particular point in time will one day be judged prophetic, it will be because today's women and men religious can see how God is working in the present moment and because they will be responsive to the degree that they can. If we are not just reaffirming general principles and applying them to new cases, and if we are offering in our message something creative and incalculable according to the divine plan for humanity, in time to come we may be judged to have been prophetic for our church and our world. And it will be because we are in tune with the Spirit of God from whom our way of life has taken its origin.

The charism of religious life as free gift of grace, as diaconal in ministerial service, and as prophetic comes from the Spirit of God. Religious life is the social manifestation of grace offered and grace received. Because that is so, and because charism belongs to the very identity of religious life, members need a continuing consciousness of the presence of the Holy Spirit as the formative influence in their lives. They need permanent forms of governance that are designed to facilitate the consciousness, discernment and dialogue of the members, particularly at the critical times of general chapters.

Our understanding of the Holy Spirit as the one bequeathed to the church after the ascension of Jesus is emerging with new urgency today. In her book *God with Us,* Catherine LaCugna has written an exhaustive study of the Trinity and Christian life. It is impossible to capture the depth of this work in a few quotations, but for anyone interested in religious life there are many texts worthy of reflection. For example,

The communion of persons in the Spirit does not entail a leveling to the lowest common denominator. *Koinonia* does not swallow up the individual, nor obscure his or her uniqueness and unique contribution, nor take away individual freedom by assimilating it into a collective will. The goal of Christian community, constituted by the Spirit in union with Jesus Christ, is to provide a place in which everyone is accepted as an ineffable, unique and unrepeatable image of God, irrespective of how the dignity of a person might otherwise be determined: level of intelligence, political correctness, physical beauty, monetary value. The communion of persons, however, remains the context of personhood. The community of Jesus Christ is the one gathering place in which persons are to be accepted and valued unconditionally, as equal partners in the divine dance. The equality of persons derives from the fact that all are equally companions in the mystery of divine-human communion. The roles of persons in community will always differ, as will their gifts and talents, their needs and demands. The *koinonia* of the Spirit leads to *diakonia* on the part of all, not just some, of the members of the community constituted by the Spirit. At the same time, differences cannot be made the basis for inequality or subordination. Least of all can differences be appealed to as the justification for vaunting some persons over other persons. (299–300)

This quotation can be read in the context of the often asserted idea that religious congregations are microcosms of the church. In the past that meant that the organization of the religious institute was patterned on the imperial paradigm that had over time been modeled by the hierarchical church. Religious congregations were structured in an authority pattern that reflected this kind of organization, but not as one of the "levels" of the hierarchy. Unfortunately, they were not usually experienced as places particularly susceptible to the Holy Spirit as divine receptivity. Structures more often than not impeded such receptivity. The members were held in place, so to speak, through a particular interpretation of the vow of obedience. Neither the church as a whole, nor the religious congregations, exemplified well the community of persons in the Holy Spirit that Catherine LaCugna describes. Yet in the last thirty years, as women religious have engaged in renewal, many have made changes that draw us closer to the ideal. Perhaps for the first time in our histories we have been able to exemplify what we were intended to be as a charismatic dimension of the *ecclesia*. An important aspect of ecclesial identity today is to show forth the possibility of a different model of the *ecclesia*, one more sensitive to the Holy Spirit in pursuing the economy of salvation for all of those who lie in wait for the redemption won for them by Jesus.

Leonardo Boff too has reflected on charism in and for the church. His insights only further the relevance of charism to the unique ecclesial identity of religious life. He says:

It is not enough that charism comes from the Spirit, thus guaranteeing its vertical dimension. It comes from God for humanity; charism is meant to build up the community, its horizontal dimension. (162)

The ministerial nonclerical religious life has always been one of *diakonia*, or service for the people of God, and in the graced interplay between those who have served and those served there has been growth and enrichment. In that sense the ecclesial identity of apostolic religious has been diaconal. It has the possibility within it to be prophetic if it is faithful and sensitive to the movement of the Holy Spirit calling the people of God to newness. In our time also, by claiming and preserving an inner authority, it has emerged as an image of a renewed church, a microcosm of what the church can be. As community in mission it is exemplary of the koinonial identity of the people of God.

Today many women religious strive to hold the Spirit of God in the mainstream of consciousness, as the life giving impulse toward community, the originator of our bonds in covenant relationship, the inspirer of our movements in ministry, and the creator of our capacity for love, compassion and mercy in all that we do. At a critical time such as ours we need renewed fidelity to the Holy Spirit, the author of charism and prophecy. We need that consciousness in our personal prayer, in our ritual celebrations and in the carrying out of our mission because it is the Holy Spirit who authors all these things. We need a constant attentiveness to the abiding presence of the Holy Spirit in our personal lives, and particularly when we come together. We have come to realize that we cannot have such attentiveness if we are apprehensive and fearful, and in a state of worry about the future of religious life. We know in faith that the Spirit of God continues to abide and will bring forth things both surprising and new. Our fundamental fidelity to the Holy Spirit will inspire peace and confidence in that certainty.

For religious life, as we women are experiencing it and hoping for it, is a vital symbol of the *ecclesia* as community in mission in and for the people of God. Perhaps in time to come we will be judged prophetic for having held on to that conviction.

Works Cited

Boff, Leonardo. *Charism and Power*. Trans. John W. Diercksmeier. New York: Crossroad, 1990.

Foley, Nadine. "The Nature and Future of Religious Life." *Origins* 19, no. 13. (1989): pp. 209–14.

LaCugna, Catherine. *God for Us. The Trinity and Christian Life*. San Francisco: HarperCollins, 1992.

Power, David. *The Eucharistic Mystery. Revitalizing the Tradition*. New York: Crossroad, 1992.

Rahner, Karl. "Prophetism." *Encyclopedia of Theology: The Concise Sacramentum Mundi*. New York: The Seabury Press, 1975.

Schillebeeckx, Edward. *Christ. The Experience of Jesus as Lord.* New York: The Seabury Press, 1980.

Wijngaards, J. *The Gospel of John and His Letters.* Wilmington: Michael Glazier, 1986.

5.

◆

Relation to the church is a value of supreme importance to women religious. What that relationship is and should be has been set forth in a considerable record of church teaching. Contemporary writers have added new insights to traditional teaching, much of which resonates with the experience of women religious. Active congregations have been viewed as a kind of "work force" for the church, but exploration into gospel mission and the nature of religious life calls this identity into question. The probing of the issues is ongoing but a consensus on the implications of religious life as charism is growing.

◆

Religious Life in Its Ecclesial Context

Patricia Walter, OP

Experts in communion, religious are, therefore, called to be an ecclesial community in the Church and in the world, witnesses and architects of the plan for unity which is the crowning point of human history in God's design. (RHP 24)

Introduction

One of the great ironies of the lectionary is found in the readings for the twenty-first Sunday of the year, Cycle B. The second reading contains the injunction "wives should be subordinate to their husbands" (Eph. 5:22). The Gospel then begins with the disciples of Jesus saying, "This saying is hard; who can accept it?" The passage continues to say that many of the disciples left Jesus. Jesus asks the Twelve if they, too, wish to leave. Peter responds "Master, to whom shall we go? You have the words of eternal life. We have come to believe and are convinced that you are the Holy One of God" (John 6:60–69).

The Gospel passage is a part of the Bread of Life discourse. In that context, the "hard talk" refers to the Johannine community's understanding of Jesus' presence in the Eucharist, presented as the words of Jesus himself. Yet the stumbling block for many disciples today is not the presence of Jesus in the Eucharist but the issue of right relationships within the Eucharistic community. It is the words of the letter to the Ephesians, not the words of Jesus, that are hard to endure.

The irony was poignantly underscored for me several years ago, when I participated in Sunday Eucharist with my four younger sisters. Two of them had ended abusive marriages with very difficult divorces. One of them still experienced great guilt because she firmly believed in the church's teaching on the sanctity and permanence of marriage. It was the twenty-first Sunday of the year; the readings were from Cycle B. There was an eloquent homily on the Real Presence; nothing was said to interpret Ephesians. Afterward, my sisters were distraught, trying to understand what to do with the "Word of God." I suggested they speak to the presider. My youngest sister found him and said, "Father, I have no difficulty with Eucharist. It is the saying that wives should be subordinate to their husbands that is hard to endure. Like the disciples, I do not want to leave. Can you help me?"

The issue of right relationships is posed in somewhat different contexts and nuances for women religious than it is for our married sisters. Yet we share their concerns for the need for equality, mutuality, and partnership in personal relationships as well as in civic and ecclesial spheres.

The past three decades have been both exciting and difficult for women religious. In the years prior to renewal, we were church women par excellence, highly visible and revered. Our dedication and commitment were unquestioned, our ministries known and valued. Along with the parish priests, we were at the heart of parish life: church, school, rectory, and convent were the physical nucleus of each local faith community.

Despite romanticization and selective memories, however, those were not halcyon days. The archives of most congregations hold correspondence with pastors who were not paying the sisters even the most meager stipends, with principals concerned about the strain placed on women whose classes sometimes held over sixty students, with superiors trying to find the money to send young sisters to summer school, with members living in unhealthy situations or in assignments for which they were not suited. There have always been tensions.

American women religious responded obediently to the council's mandate to renew their institutes, themselves. In the process, we have questioned and been questioned about our role and identity in the broader ecclesial community. In response to church teaching, our study and experience, and the insights of feminist and other liberation theologies, our self-understanding has shifted. We struggle to be faithful to our call, to the Gospel, to ourselves, for we have come to believe that the good news of the Gospel is a word of liberation and not diminishment.

Since the appearance of Cardinal Suenens's groundbreaking book, *The Nun in the World*, there has been a steady flow of books and articles dealing with religious life and its relationship with the broader ecclesial community. The diverse descriptions spring not simply from different experiences or contexts; they often have their origins in divergent ecclesiologies. The debates of Vatican Council II frequently centered on competing paradigms: church as institution, as christomonistic communion, or as trinitarian community. These debates continue today on many fronts and on multiple issues. They naturally have implications for religious life as an ecclesial reality. Interventions at the recent Synod on Consecrated Life (*Vita consecrata*, October 1994) demonstrated that there are not only complementary but also conflicting understandings of religious life, and that these interpretations are closely linked with the ecclesiologies of the speakers. For religious life is one particular expression of Christian life. Therefore, every theological interpretation of this historical phenomenon depends on certain anthropological, soteriological, and ecclesiological presuppositions.

Preconciliar Theology of Religious Life

The dominant preconciliar ecclesiology, expressed in the 1917 Code of Canon Law, was that of the church as institution. According to this thinking, the church, like the state, was a perfect (self-sufficient) society with its own proper end and all the means necessary to attain that end. These means included the authority to direct the members and to foster both individual and common good. Dioceses (and, in some respects, exempt religious institutes) were constitutive parts of the church.[14] Non-exempt religious institutes (among them, all communities of women religious) fell into the category of nonconstitutive groups or imperfect societies. Imperfect societies emerged from natural bonds (such as families) or from voluntary, contractual arrangements. These societies had their own private ends not directly identifiable with the common good and needed the larger church to attain their spiritual ends. Within these groups, there was a private exercise of authority.

This approach accorded well with the belief that the purpose of religious life was the pursuit of individual perfection. The preconciliar constitutions of many apostolic institutes of women religious began with a description of their general end in language such as this: the general purpose of this institute is the glory of God and the sanctification of its members through the observance of the vows, rule, and constitutions. This description was followed by a statement on the special end, or the specific purpose of the apostolates for which the institute was founded.

Such a rather privatized understanding of apostolic religious life continued throughout the twentieth century until the Second Vatican Council, despite the fact that communities of lay religious acquired some degree of public status through canonical recognition and that the vows of apostolic nonclerical groups were recognized by the 1917 Code as public vows.

In the period preceding the council, religious institutes inhabited the same paradigm as the broader Catholic Church. Like the church, religious institutes were generally closed societies with clear norms and rules. In church and in religious life, there were close ties of relationships, rich symbolic systems informing mundane activities with ultimate meaning, and a strong sense of group identity. Both religious institutes and the church had a coherent system of beliefs and distinctive practices. Unfortunately, the self-understanding of religious and other Catholics was often essentialist and somewhat elitist: religious were consecrated women and men living in the state of perfection; Catholics were members of the one true church. The internal structures of most religious

---

[14]Superiors of exempt religious institutes were clerics with jurisdiction over the members of their institutes. See *Lumen gentium* 45; *Christus dominus* 35; *Ecclesiae sanctae* 1, 25–40; *Evangelii nuntiandi* 69; *Evangelica testificatio* 50 and *Mutuae relationes* 22 for statements on exemption. See also the discussion by Richard A. Hill, SJ, "Autonomy of Life," *Review for Religious* 46 (January/February 1987): 137–41 and John W. O'Malley, SJ, in *Tradition and Transition*, Wilmington, Del.: Michael Glazier, 1989.

groups also mirrored the hierarchical and monarchical structure of the Roman Catholic Church. Just as there were clergy and laity, so there were superiors and subjects. Clergy and superiors bore the responsibility for insuring that those in their care lived out the rules.

Official Conciliar and Postconciliar Theology

Life always precedes and exceeds reflection. This is true of religious life. Official teaching on religious life, in its attention to the global reality, loses much of the vibrancy of the lived experience of individual groups and suppresses the lure and coherence of the different charisms. Furthermore, the tendency to make religious life a subset of consecrated life and the fact that no women religious participate in developing the magisterium are critical handicaps in this teaching. Given all this, there is nonetheless a remarkable development in the official theology of religious life from *Lumen gentium* through *Vita consecrata*.

Lumen gentium posits the divine, rather than ecclesiastical, origin of religious life. The document states that religious life belongs inseparably to the life and holiness of the church, although not to the hierarchical structure (LG 44). Religious life is no longer presented as the state of perfection but as one way in which believers can grow in love and holiness. It is linked "in a special way to the church and its mystery" through this growth in love.

In *Perfectae caritatis*, religious life is presented in terms of the following of Christ, which is "the ultimate norm of the religious life" and the "supreme rule for all religious communities" (PC 2a). This *sequela Christi* links religious with the "work of redemption and the spread of the reign of God" (PC 2a). Thus religious life is an integral component of the life and mission of the church.

Evangelica testificatio (1971) contained significant advances in the theology of religious life. Religious are a "concrete sign" and "privileged witness" of a continual quest for God and of total commitment to the extension of God's reign. Such witness serves the entire church and keeps present "the salvific paradox of the Gospel" (ET 3). Public commitment to following Christ more intensely identifies religious more explicitly with the mission of Christ and therefore of the church. This mission is interpreted as service of the reign of God (ET 23, 50). The vows are also for the sake of the reign of God, which Pope Paul VI presents as the concrete expression of God's presence in *this* world rather than an event which will occur in some other realm.

For the first time in official teaching, the vows are described as prophetic critiques of and alternatives to social sin rather than simply as ascetical practices (ET 13, 16–22, 25). The "eschatological witness" of religious life is not to some heavenly, acorporeal state, but to a way of life whose social arrangements witness to deep faith that all humanity shares a common origin and destiny, that each person is a beloved child and an image of the one God. For the first time, religious life is called a charism (ET 11). The Spirit is active not only in the founding of a religious community, but also in the process of renewal, which is intended to lead religious "to the freedom of the sons [and daughters] of God" (ET 6; cf. 51).

Mutuae relationes (1978) extends and develops the description of religious life as a charismatic phenomenon. Each religious institute has a unique experience of the Spirit, which is incarnated as its charism. The Spirit moves women and men religious "to devise new, ingenious, and courageous ecclesial experiments" in response to the changing needs of the world and, in particular, of "the little ones and the poor" (MR 19, 23ff.).

The *sequela Christi* is linked explicitly with the prophetic mission of Jesus in Religious and Human Promotion (1978). This document presents Jesus' mission as one of the forming of a new community through the gift of the Spirit (RHP 24). Since his mission of evangelization involved both conversion and liberation, the mission of the church also links evangelization and human promotion. So, too, religious life is both "charismatic and prophetic" (RHP 27), a radical response to the radical demands of the Beatitudes (RHP 4a, 15, 22). It announces, anticipates and helps shape human community which corresponds to God's intent, community built on and building just and loving relationships (RHP 19; cf. 15, 18, 22, 33b). Life in communion is the core of the religious vocation and mission: "Experts in communion, religious are, therefore, called to be ecclesial community in the Church and in the world, witnesses and architects of the plan for unity which is the crowning point of human history in God's design" (RHP 24). Religious institutes make visible the mystery of the church as communities formed out of love of God and living in communion with God, one another and the world.

Redemptionis donum (1983), an apostolic exhortation to religious by Pope John Paul II, returns to a theology of consecration to describe religious life. As the church is rooted in the mystery of redemption, so religious respond to the redeeming love of Christ with a redeeming and spousal love which expresses in a particular way the love of the church for Christ. The vows are a way of transforming the relationship of women and men to the world.

Vita consecrata (1994) is an apostolic exhortation by the Pope that follows the Synod on Consecrated Life held in October, 1994. The document calls consecrated life "a precious and necessary gift for the present and future of the people of God, since it is an intimate part of [the church's] life, her holiness and her mission" (VC 3). Through its life of service, consecrated life shows "the inseparable link between love of God and love of neighbor." The text treats consecrated life under the three dimensions of consecration, communion, and mission (VC 13).

Vita consecrata claims that consecrated life "expresses in a particularly vivid way the Trinitarian nature of the Christian life, and it anticipates in a certain way that eschatological fulfillment toward which the whole Church is tending" (VC 14). The document develops the trinitarian dimension of consecrated life both in reference to the works attributed to the three Persons of the Trinity and in reference to intra-trinitarian life. Thus chastity is a reflection of the love of the divine Persons for each other, poverty is an expression of the total self-donation of each divine Person to the others, obedience becomes an historical reflection of the loving harmony of the Trinity, and communal life is a witness of the unity desired and effected by the Persons of the Trinity (21). So *Vita consecrata* asserts, "the consecrated life thus becomes a confession and sign of the Trinity, whose mystery is held up to the church as the model and source of every form of Christian life" (21).

Mission, which is foundational to the identity of the church and "at the heart of every form of consecrated life" (35), is connected with hope or eschatological expectation. *Vita consecrata* does at times use a thoroughly future eschatology, locating the reign of God in some future age or transcendent state. Other passages exhibit a realized eschatology, linking the reign of God with historical expressions of justice, love, and peace. So eschatological expectation "expresses itself in work and mission, that the kingdom may become present here and now through the spirit of the Beatitudes, a spirit capable of giving rise in human society to effective aspirations for justice, peace, solidarity, and forgiveness" (27).

Vita consecrata returns frequently to an ecclesiology of communion, presenting the church as "a mystery of communion," a mystery which takes "shape as a human community in which the Trinity dwells, in order to extend in history the gifts of communion proper to the three divine Persons" (41). The fraternal and sororal life of religious is "an eloquent sign of ecclesial communion" (42). So, citing Religious and Human Promotion, "consecrated persons are asked to be true experts of communion and to practice the spirituality of communion as 'witnesses and architects of the plan for unity which is the crowning point of human history in God's design' " (46). In this practice, loving dialogue plays a key part.

Consecrated life also has a prophetic character, a special share in the prophetic office. This character results from the radical commitment to following Christ (84). Prophetic witness requires consistency in word and deed. "It is also expressed through the denunciation of all that is contrary to the divine will and through the exploration of new ways to apply the Gospel in history" (84).

Some Insights from Contemporary Writers

In a letter to his province of Dominican friars, Donald Goergen, OP, offers a superb analysis of the relationship between religious life and the church, using the core idea of the Gospel. He points out that Gospel requires church, a structured community of believers, yet the church can never fully embody the Gospel. Goergen asserts that religious life exists for the sake of the Gospel, not the church. It emerges from "attentiveness to the surplus in the Gospel" (Goergen, 140). He concludes that "religious life, while essential to the church, is not structurally central in the church, but rather peripheral to the basic structures of the church" (141). All Christians are called to live for the sake of the Gospel. What gives religious life its raison d'être is precisely its concern for the surplus.

John O'Malley, SJ, presents a similar idea in his chapter on priesthood, ministry, and religious life in *Tradition and Transition*. He observes that the exemption granted to the mendicant orders from the thirteenth century onward "created in effect a church order (or several church orders) within the greater church order, and it did this for the reality to which church order primarily looks—ministry" (O'Malley 144). He points out the pluralism that has existed in church order. O'Malley underscores the fact that the ministry of religious institutes has usually focused on those not reached by the stable structures of parish and diocese: orphans, prostitutes, those of other faiths, the "unchurched." He observes that there are two traditions in church ministry and order, with different vocabularies and concerns.

On the one hand, words like "office" and "parish" recur, while on the other we find "need" and "mission." "Hierarchy" predominates in one whereas "fraternity" or its equivalent is found in the other. For the one, "apostolic" indicates a conduit of authority; for the other, it suggests a style of life and ministry. (O'Malley, 169)

From the perspective of a women's monastic community, Joan Chittister, OSB, makes a similar point. She describes religious life as "an alternate form of Christian life" distinctive in its communal dimensions (3). The primary contribution of religious communities is not so much what they do as who they are:

The fact is that religious life was never meant simply to be a labor force in the church; it was meant to be a searing presence, a paradigm of search, a mark of human soul and a catalyst to conscience in the society in which it emerged. . . . Religious simply did what was not being done so that others would see the need to do it too. (2)

According to Hugo Echegaray, Jesus' vision of the reign, or household, of God shaped his practice with a particular logic. In his life and teaching, Jesus left the disciples "the basic principles of an alternative practice that was critical of the system: the practice of the kingdom, which is the basis for a common life as an *ecclesia*" (94). Echegaray sees the logic of the reign of God as permeating, linking, and transforming the economic, political, and social dimensions of reality. On the economic level, the practice of Jesus (and his disciples) follows the logic of gift, solidarity with the poor, and abundance. These economic arrangements are opposed to the practice of the empire, which is based on a logic of hoarding and scarcity. On the political level, messianic practice entails service, equality, and truth in contrast to the practice of domination, class, and deceit. Finally, on the social level, the practice of Jesus and his followers involves freedom, love and the priority of the household of God, while the empire lives from fear, greed and individualism, and the priority of the empire. The logic of the reign of God is in direct opposition to the logic of the empire, whatever the specific empire might be. Practice of the household of God set Jesus and the early Christian communities in conflict with the powers that existed. It is forgetfulness of this practice that creates such pain in the church today and weakens the witness of church and religious life. All Christians are to base their lives on the logic of Jesus' messianic practice. It is not simply an injunction to women and men religious. Yet every level of practice involves a communal existence and could in some way be correlated with one of the vows traditionally professed by religious. The prophetic nature of religious life lies in the communal dimension of our life together, a communal existence explicitly and intentionally committed to the messianic practice (cf. Echegaray 93–102). To paraphrase Gandhi, we attempt to "be the change we wish to see in the world."

Current Realities

Many tensions surface today between religious and other segments of the ecclesial community. These emerge from the concrete realities of ecclesial life. A few of these conflictual areas will be identified here.

There is all too often a minimal exchange of information and a lack of consultation and coordination between dioceses and religious institutes. Diocesan high schools and retreat centers are built in close proximity to those sponsored by religious communities; pastoral and diocesan planning and programming proceed in a parallel, rather than interconnected, fashion with the planning done by religious institutes ministering in the diocese; projects are initiated or discontinued by religious without prior consultation with bishops or appropriate diocesan officials. Coordination and consultation are particularly challenging when the religious institute is not diocesan.

Religious institutes have been understood as carrying out the work of the church through their ministries of education and health care. The rapid and complex changes in higher education and health care bring challenges regarding the viability of many institutions, with ensuing conflicts over the meaning of Catholic identity, the nature of ecclesiastical property, the respective roles of lay boards, religious sponsors and local bishops. Although there may be agreement on the priority of serving the poor, there are limits to the ability of a religious institute or a hospital system to subsidize a particular institution. Many a diocese does not have the resources to assume fiscal and governance responsibilities for an institution in difficulty, yet the bishop may limit the ability of the institute or system to insure the continuance of the ministry because of his definition of what makes an institution Catholic. From the perspective of a hospital system that covers many dioceses, it is a delicate balancing act to have systemwide policies and financial obligations at the same time the system attempts to come to agreement with each local bishop. Although all parties may agree to the importance of a university's Catholic identity, the American legal tradition of academic freedom, significant differences among bishops in their understandings of the role of theologians and of the legitimate pluralism of theological approaches can create a minefield which must be cautiously negotiated in attempts to reach common ground.

In the wake of Vatican II, many women religious moved into the new fields of religious education and then pastoral ministry as pastoral assistants and now parish administrators. Their places in Catholic schools were taken by competent laity whom they had educated. In parishes and dioceses, sisters have usually been the first people entrusted with new ministries or ministries formerly reserved to clergy. They have performed a service in helping ecclesial communities become accustomed to women serving competently in new roles. At the same time, women religious have begun to ask ourselves the same types of questions that our ordained brother religious have been asking. Are we being parochialized and absorbed by and into parish or diocesan structures? What is the relationship between this type of ministry and our charism? Are religious called to minister in places and positions where there are qualified lay people to do so or are we called to respond to needs yet unmet, on the fringes or growing edges of church and society? Where do the loyalties of religious belong when parochial/diocesan events and congregational meetings are scheduled at the same time? The increasing expectation that women will be admitted to the permanent diaconate raises a unique field of dilemmas for women religious. Ordination to the diaconate would recognize sacramentally and canonically the diaconal ministry rendered by many women religious. Would it be at the cost of introducing some clericalism into lay religious communities? What obedience would be due the elected leader of the religious community and what would be due the ordaining bishop? Would those ordained deacons expect to be the regular leaders of prayer within their religious communities?

The diminishing number of active religious, the mobility of members of pontifical institutes, the fact that fewer and fewer institutes agree to commit a specific number of religious over a given length of time to specific ministries, the inability or unwillingness of institutes to make corporate commitments, perhaps because members choose their own ministries in dialogue with those serving in authority, cause some bishops to say that they prefer working with laity, since they cannot "count on" the religious to be in the diocese permanently. Obviously these factors do present challenges to both diocesan and congregational planning. One response to the challenge might be multiyear contracts. Neglected in this observation is the wealth of experience and new ideas that religious bring with them as they move into, as well as out of, parochial and diocesan ministries. Official documents on religious life repeatedly stress the help that religious institutes, particularly international communities, can give local churches in developing a sense of their communion with other local churches in the Church universal.

Women and men continue to enter religious life in the United States. Nonetheless, there is a reality of aging and declining numbers in most communities. Despite the repeated, lovely and clear statements in official texts about the priority of being over doing and about the intrinsic value of religious life, ageism and utilitarianism corrode the attitudes of many religious, clergy and hierarchy. The move from full-time to part-time or volunteer ministry is a difficult one for many religious and requires both gentleness and honesty on the part of their ministerial supervisors and major superiors. Because of conversations with priests and bishops and statements published in the Catholic press, religious sometimes feel dismissed and discarded, no longer valued because their usefulness as an underpaid workforce in the church is seen as coming to an end.

Another sometimes frustrating issue is that of convents. In contrast to the practice in many other areas of the world, women religious in the United States lived primarily in housing provided by parishes rather than in convents which their institutes built and owned. Many convents emptied as women religious moved into smaller communities or new ministries; many have been reclaimed for use as parish offices and gathering spaces. Traditionally, dioceses have set the rent rates. Low rents have often led to low maintenance. It is not just for parishes to absorb the costs of heating and maintaining large convents in which two or three sisters live. Women religious have difficulty finding suitable space for four or more adult women to live together. They are willing to pay reasonable rent or perhaps even to contribute to the cost of refurbishing and repainting adequate residences, but leasing arrangements are often whimsical at best, often depending on the tenure of the pastor. There are often assumptions on the part of priest and people that the sisters residing in a parish convent serve in the parish in some way, even though some of the sisters may be in full-time ministry elsewhere and paying rent to the parish to live in the convent.

Just compensation is another thorny issue. In order to be in solidarity with their lay counterparts, educate new members, care for frail and fully retired members, support their ministries in this country and globally, give just wages to their employees, and prepare sisters for new ministries, many congregations have adopted a policy of requesting wages and benefits on a par with those given lay people employed in similar positions in the church. The model of a set stipend for all religious in the diocese or a stipend based on the stipulated needs of a congregation no longer seems adequate. A sister serving in a parish may receive a stipend higher than a lay person in that same parish doing the same or more demanding work, while a sister in a diocesan position may receive far less than her lay counterpart. This arrangement does not seem just to many laity, priests, and religious. There is resistance on the part of some priests and bishops to the idea of a policy of adopting a single salary scale. This resistance arises at times out of concern for the financial implications, at other times out of a misunderstanding of the vow of poverty. The vow of poverty has never been identified theologically or canonically with an individual's level of income. Canon law is quite clear that everything a member earns belongs to her congregation. Sisters ministering as heads of universities or hospitals, doctors or therapists may receive high levels of compensation. The vow of poverty directs the use of that money: it is part of the common fund; all members no matter what their income or lack thereof are to live simply, sharing with one another and the poor; the congregation is to be a good steward of its resources.

There is an array of injustices experienced by women religious in church ministries that has affected members and their communities, often leading the women to find ways of ministering outside church structures. Far too many women have lost their positions soon after the arrival of a new pastor. Occasionally the sister may no longer be capable of fulfilling her ministry. More often the pastor wants to bring in his own team, or is jealous of the sister's relationships with the people, or is a misogynist. There is often no or a poor process, with little or no recourse. The experience of suddenly losing a ministry unjustly is often devastating, entailing as it does ruptured relationships with parishioners. The sister may need therapy to deal with her anger and grief. She may need to move from her local community to find new employment; at times the loss of her share of the rent means the whole local community must relocate. So there are further upheavals of relationships. Instead of receiving the sister's financial contribution, the congregation needs to support her until she is able to find new ministry.

In most dioceses, religious are not covered by worker's compensation, so their congregations must support them if they are disabled while ministering. In some dioceses, women pastoral administrators, no matter how effective, know that they may be replaced at any time by a priest or deacon.

Meanwhile, the astonishingly slow process of eliminating sexist language from approved translations of Scripture and from liturgical texts strains the patience of theologically educated and conscienticized communities of women. These communities find it makes no sense in their worship to use "horizontal" language that renders them invisible nor "vertical" language that absolutizes only male images of the God in whose image they are made.

Conclusion

Throughout the history of the church there has been a dialectical relationship between religious movements and the hierarchy with respect to reform and renewal. At times when religious institutes have grown lax or become corrupt in the accumulation of wealth, church officials and great reformers have acted to rekindle the fervor of the religious. At other times, religious orders and institutes have led the way in following the impulse of the Spirit to a deeper or new response to the needs of the time. At all times and on all parts, there remains a duty to discern what is necessary innovation, inculturation, or fidelity to a charism and what is ossified cultural expression or unthinking accommodation to a particular culture. This discernment requires careful listening, honest dialogue, mutual and respectful engagement in the search for truth, and openness to conversion.

The recurring tension between religious institutes and the broader ecclesial community is perhaps best understood by Goergen's image of the "surplus of the Gospel." It is not in the end helpful simply to set hierarchical and charismatic elements in opposition. Governance and leadership are charisms. Some form of institutionalization is necessary if the action of the Spirit is to be more than an evanescent and ephemeral impulse. To identify hierarchical elements in the church with the work of Jesus and charismatic elements with the Spirit sunders the unity between Jesus and the Spirit. It nullifies our confession of faith that Jesus is risen in the power of the Spirit and that we are all filled with the Spirit of the Risen One.

The study, processes and experiences we have had in the past thirty years have made us ever more acutely aware of and committed to right relationships with God, with one another, with all people and with all of creation. In response to the mandate of Vatican Council II, we returned to the gospel and the inspiration of our founders and foundresses, evangelized our structures and way of life, involved all members in prayer, study and discussion. We have faced and continue to address topics we fear to talk about. We have shared in the hopes and fears of humanity. In these processes, we have experienced the Paschal mystery and have come to a deeper level of communion with God, one another and the world. To the broader ecclesial community we offer the results of our renewal, models for structuring relationships based in faith and transformed by the gospel.

Religious life, like the church of which it is an essential part, is a reality both graced and sinful. Religious life is a sacrament of the mystery of the church in its form of life constituted by relationships organized according to messianic practices. Religious communities at their best are harbingers and experimental outposts of the household of God.

Works Cited

Chittister, Joan. *The Fire in These Ashes*. Kansas City, Mo.: Sheed and Ward, 1995.

Echegaray, Hugo. *The Practice of Jesus*. Trans. Matthew J. O'Connell. Maryknoll, NY: Orbis Books, 1980.

Goergen, Donald J., OP. *Letters to My Brothers and Sisters*. Dublin: Dominican Publications, 1996.

O'Malley, John. *Tradition and Transition*. Wilmington, Del.: Michael Glazier, 1989.

Suenens, Leon Joseph. *The Nun in the World: New Dimensions and Modern Apostolates*. Trans. Geoffrey Steven. Westminster, Md.: Newman Press, 1952.

6.

◆

Theological reflection led to considerations of who women religious are in light of a theology of baptism. That all are baptized into mission became an organizing principle. While earlier it seemed that the identification of particular religious congregations lay in the works to which they were dedicated, it now seemed clear that through their baptism individual members, and the congregations as a whole, were called to an intensification of their commitment to mission. Ministries were the special ways in which groups chose to carry out gospel mission. In many ways such terms provided a new vocabulary, as well as a new development in self-identity.

◆

Mission and Ministry

The Task of Discipleship
Anneliese Sinnott, OP

The church . . . is interested in one thing only—to carry on the work of Christ under the guidance of the Holy Spirit, who came into the world to bear witness to the truth, to save and not to judge, to serve and not to be served. (GS 3)

Introduction

Dominic Guzman was a man of the Gospel. Not only did he carry his copy of the Gospel of Matthew with him wherever he traveled, he preached and lived this gospel his entire life. He took seriously the challenge to "make disciples of all nations." Dominic believed that to be a disciple of Jesus one must be in mission—preaching and living the Good

News—and be engaged in ministry—doing whatever is needed to help others learn of God's incredible love for all.

All Christians are called to discipleship. As Dominicans, followers of Dominic, we are surely called to be women of the Gospel. We, too, are to be in mission and engaged in ministry. Despite the fact that such a living out of the call to follow Jesus has been part of the Dominican heritage, the last thirty years have presented to us an incredible opportunity for a renewed understanding of this way of discipleship. We have learned, too, that it is not uniquely Dominican.

The words mission and ministry are so commonplace in Catholic vocabulary today that it is difficult to remember that these terms seemed to have had very different meanings prior to the Second Vatican Council. At that time the word "ministry" was usually related to the Protestant experience,[15] while the word "mission" almost always was used in the Catholic understanding to refer to the work of the church in overseas lands. By the late 1960s the language of the church and its theology had changed, a transformation that has had an incalculable effect, not only on Dominicans, but on all religious. In this chapter, I will explore the impact of this significant shift on the life of American Catholics in general and on American women religious in particular. In addition, I want to raise two additional questions. What are the unresolved issues that have emerged out of our new understanding and theology of mission and ministry? What are the challenges for us as American women religious in terms of mission and ministry as we move into the future? I don't pretend to be able to answer these questions fully, but perhaps I can shed some light for the reader through these reflections. My comments flow out of the context of American religious life, and specifically from my experience in the Adrian Dominican Congregation. I realize that the experience of other women religious might be quite different.

Change in the Church

By 1960 people all over the Western World were experiencing the rapid expansion of the post World War II years. It was a time of rebuilding and significant change. It is certainly not coincidental that these years

---

[15]This was even true in the Dominican order. Although we referred to our apostolic assignments as being sent "on mission," Dominicans used the language of "apostolate" for "ministry."

also saw ferment in the church. The call for a new world order was reinforced by the theology emerging from the Second Vatican Council. This theology, especially in the area of ecclesiology, forced radical new thinking.

The ecclesiology of Vatican II focused attention not so much on the church as institution, but on church as community, the people of God. In fact, in the final ordering of the chapters of the Pastoral Constitution on the Church, *Lumen gentium*, chapter 1, "The Mystery of the Church," is followed immediately by chapter 2, "The People of God." This placement in itself was a significant modification from the original proposal, which suggested that chapter 2 should be entitled "The Hierarchy."

Vatican II emphatically restated the Christian belief that God's salvation has been made known fully in the person of Jesus Christ, and so those who believe and follow Jesus come together in a community of believers as Church. The council recalled the New Testament witness and the tradition of the church that baptism symbolizes the gift of God which makes believers into the image of the saving Jesus (1 Cor. 12:27) and signifies their membership into the Church as the body of Christ. All the baptized are defined as being one with Christ (Col. 2:12; Eph. 2:1, 4–6). Thus, *Lumen gentium* claims that

[a]ll are called to holiness and have obtained an equal privilege of faith through the justice of God. (LG 32)

This ecclesiology underlines the lack of distinctions in the call to discipleship. Baptism enables all to share in the call to full Christian life.

In other places in the Vatican II documents we find that, as the people of God, the church inherits the mission of Jesus (LG 5). Jesus came to spread the news of God's salvation, *shalom*. Jesus called disciples to continue the task not only of proclaiming, but also of concretizing the transforming power of the Reign of God through their words and deeds, so that the effects of God's shalom would be evident in history. The mission of the members of the church is the mission given by Jesus to his disciples. The Church is to be the incarnational prolongation of the mission of Jesus. The task of disciples is to do for their world what Jesus did for his world: proclaim the Good News (LG 5; GS 41,15), bring all people to truth (GS 3), and participate in bringing about the reign of God through service to others (LG 5, 9; GS 3, 40, 45). To carry out the mission, the church is to turn its face "to the world," not away from it (GS 1).

The Christian vocation to discipleship, by its very nature, is not only a call to holiness (LG 41), but a vocation to service (AA 1, 2, 3).[16] *Lumen gentium* 11 issued a strong mandate to all the baptized to active participation in the mission by confessing and practicing the faith with which they have been gifted.

Mission is so essential to the nature of the Church that some theologians claim that the Church is Church only to the extent that it engages in the mission of Jesus Christ. Roger Haight suggests that mission is the raison d'être for membership in the Church.

> The Church finds its ground of being in the event of Christ as a "mission" and revelation from God to the world in history. A continuing response to God through Jesus Christ is therefore essential and constitutive of the Church, but in this conception it is not an end in itself; for what is at stake is precisely the quality of that response to God through Christ. To be Christian and to be Church means to be "chosen for service to continue the work of Christ in the world." (Haight, 635)

The Church's mission is fulfilled through the apostolic activity of all the members (AA 3). The words "mission" and "ministry" (or service) are inextricably linked. Ministry is the actualization of the mission. This seems to be a clear mandate to ministry for all, but another statement in *Lumen gentium* clouds the clarity of that call.

> It is therefore quite clear that *all* Christians *in whatever state or walk in life* are called to *the fullness of christian life* and to the perfection of charity. (LG 40) (Emphasis added.)

In this statement the fact that Christians seem to be already divided into categories raises some serious questions. Does the understanding of *"state or walk in life"* alter or conflict with the call of all *"to the fullness of Christian life?"* How does a perception of different states affect the way we live out our call to mission and ministry? Must baptism be completed by orders or public vows to carry with it the full responsibility for Christian life? Or, alternatively, does baptism even call one to do so?

---

[16]I use the word "service" here instead of "ministry" because the Vatican II documents reserve the word *ministeria* to clerics. The word "apostolate" is used by Vatican II to describe the active engagement of the laity in the mission. However, in the North American experience the word "ministry" emerged as the term for service done by both clerics and laity.

It might seem at first glance that, even though we find ourselves in different "states of life," all of us can achieve the fullness of Christian life by whatever path we choose. However, as we examine other texts in the documents we find a somewhat different conclusion. For example, in the chapter of *Lumen gentium* on "Religious" we read:

True, as baptized Christians they (religious) are dead to sin and consecrated to God; but in order to draw still *more abundant fruit* from the grace of their Baptism, they make profession of the evangelical counsels in the church. (LG 44) (Emphasis added.)

Although all the baptized are incorporated into Christ (LG 7,11), and called to the fullness of Christian life, paragraph 44 suggests that all walks of life do not equally lead to that "fullness." Although all are called to an "equal privilege of faith," (LG 32), one must, in fact, choose a particular way of life truly to achieve it. One must do something different to follow Christ "more fully" (PC 1).[17] The theology of such texts seems to be based on a belief that Christians are "equal before God but not necessarily before each other."

The call to all Christians to take an active part in the mission of the Church proved to have greater impact on Catholics, however, than the effect of the ambiguity in the documents. In the years immediately following the Second Vatican Council, service by and to church members began to expand from the narrow sense of church work done by clergy and religious (the few laity that did church work did it by way of exception; they often were hired when no clergy or religious could be found) to include service as broad as the world and as comprehensive as the needs of human beings and could be done by any believer.

The spirit of Vatican II gave the impetus for new experience, and with new experience came a change in language. Sometime before 1970 the language of "engaging in the apostolate" gave way to "living out the mission through one's ministry," and the meaning of ministry changed from church work to the work of the church. In what seemed to be a rather sudden change,[18] the words "mission" and "ministry" took on

---

[17] This is the language that has been consistently used in documents on religious life issued by the Vatican in the last decade. See also, for example, Synod of Bishops, "Consecrated Life's Role in the Church and the World," 1994 Working Paper.

[18] There are no entries that refer to Roman Catholic ministry in theological dictionaries such as *Sacramentum Mundi* or in reference works such as the *New Catholic Encyclopedia* (New York: McGraw-Hill Book Company, 1967). (NCE has one entry listed as "Ministry, Protestant".) The first major theological work with such an entry is *Dictionnaire de spiritualité: ascétique et mystique. Doctrine et histoire.* The article "ministères" in this work

new meaning. Despite the fact that the word ministry in the Vatican II documents refers only to the "ordained," "lay" people began to do the work of the church, and began to call it ministry and claim for themselves a title of minister.[19] Moving away from a model which imagined only the ordained or consecrated as actively engaged in the apostolate, members of the Catholic Church began to experience, not only clergy and religious, but many others sharing in the ministry of the church. In a very short time, the possibility of those who could do ministry expanded to include anyone in the church, and the understanding of ministry embraced many things that were previously thought to be "secular."[20]

Some theologians have attempted to "define" ministry in this new sense. In *The Westminster Dictionary of Christian Theology*, Edward Kilmartin suggests:

Christian ministry is a ministry of salvation in the service of the world. It originates in the charge given by Christ to the church to carry on his ministry. All baptized are called to share in this service in accord with their states of life, special gifts and roles within the social structure of stable Christian communities.[21] (369)

However, new definitions of ministry did not necessarily clear up some of the key problems in the ambiguity of the church's language. Although many theologians could agree, for example, on the words used in Kilmartin's definition, the interpretation of phrases like "charge given by Christ to the church," "all baptized are called to share," "in accord with their states of life," "special gifts and roles," "within the social structure," and "stable Christian communities," can vary considerably and lead to quite different conclusions.

---

states that in the year 1969 the *Bibliographie internationale sur le sacerdoce et le ministère* lists close to 7,000 titles.

[19]Several times in the past twenty years the U.S. bishops have attempted to reserve the word ministry for those in orders. This has not been such a struggle in other countries, for in many languages there are separate words for "ordained" ministry and "unordained" ministry, but in English we have no such distinction, and thus must use words like "ordained" and "unordained," "priestly" and "lay" as adjectives in modification of the noun ministry.

[20]The division of reality into categories such as "sacred" and "secular" comes from a dualistic worldview. Although the documents of Vatican II do not totally eliminate this kind of language, they do, at least, emphasize the organic unity of the place of the church within the world rather than separate from it. (GS 1, 40)

[21]The inclusion of this understanding in an ecumenical work indicates the impact the change of language in the Catholic Church has had on the various Protestant traditions.

Overall, however, it was clear that Vatican II was calling the church to new awarenesses, and its theology had changed radically from what had been official teaching since the Council of Trent. The impact this change had on religious life, especially in the United States, was profound.

Change in Religious Life

The model of religious life for women in the United States in the early 1960s was one that had developed over the preceding century in response to the historical circumstances of the church in this country. We were, in large majority, "active" rather than "contemplative" in the cloistered sense. Our engagement in the apostolate defined the way we lived out our religious lives. Our apostolates were varied but, in large part, we found ourselves in schools, hospitals, orphanages and other church institutions. Most of us were assigned to a particular apostolate, often without any consideration of our aptitude for the work involved. Although there were always exceptions,[22] historically the apostolate of the majority of the members eventually came to be seen as "traditional works" of our particular congregations.

By the late 1960s the context of our American lives (as well as our ecclesial lives) was shifting dramatically! The years of the sixties in the United States were marked by the civil rights movement, Vietnam and its effect on American society, the restlessness of huge numbers of baby boomers, the sexual revolution and enormous economic shifts. For the first time in many of our lives we reflected on what it meant to be Catholic and American, the meaning of racial segregation, whether there was such a thing as a "just war," and the face of poverty in the United States and around the world.

A particular catalyst for change in religious life was the rise of the women's movement. The situation of women in American society was changing rapidly. Some women were working earnestly for liberation and equality, especially in the workplace. Although at first, we women religious, for the most part, still viewed ourselves as separated from other women, the women's movement did encourage us to begin to reflect and take seriously our experience as women, and raise questions about our

---

[22]See Foley (211) for a brief history of the development of women's apostolates in this country.

place in church and society. This was but the beginning of a long, fruitful journey for us (cf. Riley, ch. 13).

Another significant factor that influenced the way we understood our apostolate was the emerging crisis in the Roman Catholic priesthood in the early 1970s: decline in numbers, fewer seminary students, shift in theological understanding of the meaning of "ordination," problems with mandatory celibacy.[23] These factors coupled with the increasing demand for service on the part of the church membership forced work formerly done exclusively by ordained priests to be taken on by others. The obvious cadre of already trained workers waiting in the wings were women religious. In many instances we were not ready as yet to "share" our ministry with the laity.

It was in the midst of all these societal and ecclesial changes that American women religious took on the tasks set forth for them by Vatican II: to look at the signs of the time in the light of the gospel; to re-examine their founding charisms; and to reflect on the implications of these for contemporary religious life. This study and reflection by members of religious congregations eventually caused a radical changeover in the way we thought about and talked about our own lives. What members of active religious congregations did became ministry, and their reason for doing it was not so much because it was traditional work of a particular congregation, but because it was linked to the mission of Jesus.

I suspect that our experience as Adrian Dominican women was similar to that of women in many other congregations. The way we thought about our apostolic activity changed because of the new context in which we were living, the experiences we had, and the process in which we engaged. We began to articulate our new theology and to do things differently. We entered into a process of doing theology that would radically change our lives.[24]

It is difficult to determine in retrospect what the exact relationship between experience and the process of theological reflection was in those rapidly changing years. It is true that we began to engage in theological reflection because we were obedient to the church, and that reflection led to an explosion of new insights. But it is also true that our experience was changing just as quickly, and that factor certainly altered our the-

---

[23]See Schillebeeckx (211–36) for a discussion of some of these issues.
[24]The entire process of *theological methodology* is described more fully in chapter 2.

ological reflection! Recalling just a few experiences will give some sense as to the effect on our theological processes.

The initial move by religious congregations into new works, even prior to Vatican II renewal, often was done in obedience to the hierarchy who presented specific apostolic needs to congregations. In the nineteenth century there was a great need in the American Catholic Church to provide educational opportunities for immigrant children because of the strong anti-Catholic feeling in the nation. Bishops in Central and South America saw a need to educate children from privileged families so that they could become leaders in their countries. Hospitals were founded to care for people who were poor.

By the 1960s some of the needs for these services had ceased to exist or had changed significantly, but often women religious had remained in parish schools, in hospitals and in academies for the elite because their congregations had assumed over the years a kind of quasi-ownership position insofar as they felt obliged to provide personnel even when they had none available or saw more valuable placement for their members. The challenge to look at the "signs of the times" brought us to the realization that the institutions in which we found ourselves were not necessarily the best places for us truly to engage in mission.

Those who worked in academies for the elite soon started to see in a new way the needs of the poor and the oppressed that literally surrounded them.[25] Women staffing Catholic schools discovered that the sexual revolution had permeated their classrooms and wondered whether traditional teaching methods worked any longer. Somehow we hadn't been prepared for a new kind of student with new kinds of problems. Small Catholic hospitals began to be part of larger systems that were forced to operate as corporate businesses.

Because of being closely aligned with parishes, we were often the ones given the responsibility by the pastor to "educate" the parish in the liturgical changes that came as a result of Vatican II. This responsibility meant that we integrated the spirit of the council sometimes in ways that the clergy did not.

With the changes in the parish reality, both because of the new demand for service and the emerging crisis in the priesthood, religious

---

[25]Our very presence in mission territories, even if engaged in work that tended to ignore the existing poverty, caused our own consciousness-raising process to progress much more rapidly than it would have had we not been there at all.

women became the first nonclerical pastoral workers by taking over some of the ministerial work formerly connected to ordination. This led to experiences (e.g., being the minister in a nursing home and not being able to anoint the residents when needed, or dealing with people in difficult personal conflicts and not being able to lead them to celebrate reconciliation, or preparing people for baptism and not being a part of that celebration) that caused new reflection on whether women should be able to participate in all ministries (including those of the ordained). Women's status was changing dramatically in many areas, but our place within the church seemed to be static.[26] As we listened to the voices of women in other churches and in society in the light of our own experience, we began to ask ourselves what this meant for us as Roman Catholic ecclesial women.

All of these experiences affected the way we thought about ourselves as sharing the mission of the church and being engaged in ministry. The road to a new theology of mission and ministry, however, has not always been easy. To travel that road we ourselves needed new paradigms.

We began to look seriously at our own experience as women and actually to talk to each other about our lives and sometimes even about our faith! This led us to evaluate our lives, the work in which we were engaged, and the places where we did that work. We began to see that lay women could engage in ministry as effectively as ourselves. We started to see that some of the situations in which we worked were unjust: we were overworked and grossly underpaid for the quality and amount of work we were doing; some of the institutions with which we were affiliated were guilty of racism, classism, and sexism. We became aware that we had enormous contributions to make to both the church and society, but within our present structures we were extremely limited in some ways. Although our numbers were diminishing, we were among the church's most highly educated workers, and yet we could not give fully what we had.

At the same time we were to reexamine our founder's original purpose and the results were quite enlightening! Dominicans, for example, discovered that Dominic was one who saw a need for radical change in the established order of ministry of his day if the problems of the church at that time and in that place were to be addressed. Our challenge as Do-

---

[26]Roman Catholic women were far behind most Protestant women when it came to recognizing the lack of rights for women in the church. See Maria J. Selvidge for a good survey of the latter's work for equal rights for women.

minicans was not to be just like the Dominicans of the thirteenth century, but to do as Dominic had done: to challenge what was ineffective, and dream about what could be for the sake of the mission in our world. It was clear that many things might have to change. Insights like this provided us with the necessary link between Church renewal and religious life renewal. If our primary focus was to be the mission of Jesus, religious life would have to be lived differently.

For Dominicans, the language shift was perhaps a little easier, because we had always thought of ourselves as being missioned. However, we too needed to develop an understanding of ministry that would connect with a Vatican II sense of mission. The process of renewal that resulted in concrete legislative changes in the lives of Adrian Dominicans was the external symbol of a radical invitation to interior conversion, and to renewed commitment to the call of Christian discipleship.

We had to create new structures that would emphasize the universal call to holiness rather than duplicate the hierarchical structure of a pre–Vatican II Church.[27] Changes were needed in the way choices for ministry were made. Congregations had to be willing to have members re-tool or study to prepare for new ministries. A variety of supports had to be put in place for all the members in these difficult times. And we now had to learn how to be partners in the mission with the laity, especially with other women.

Changing Theology

The theology forming the foundation upon which pre–Vatican II religious life had been built could be labeled "consecration for witness." Religious life was a life set apart, a "state" of life incorporated into the church's structure; its primary function was to bear witness to what it really means to be a follower of Christ.

The documents of Vatican II, in some ways, did not challenge this persistent theology. The language of "paths" or "states" of life is used throughout the various decrees.[28] But Vatican II, although it did not in

---

[27] For Dominicans this change would reinforce the collegial style of governance which they had inherited from their founder, Dominic. Dominican women had to struggle with the conflict between the principle of collegiality that was part of Dominic's vision and the hierarchical structure mandated for women religious by the 1917 Code of Canon Law.

[28] Especially troubling is the language that suggests an ontological distinction which sets the ordained person apart from both "the laity" and "consecrated religious" as the Christian par excellence.

any clear way negate such prior theology, presented a challenge to that way of thinking through its articulation of the universal call to holiness. If all are called to the fullness of life, what is so special about religious life or clerical life? If every Christian is called to mission and ministry, why would one choose religious life or priesthood? What is meant by "vocation"?

As we began to answer these questions, we discovered that our theology was indeed changing. This was, perhaps, one of the most challenging tasks that emerged in our religious congregations after Vatican II.

The theology of ministry of the Adrian Dominican Congregation emerged out of a number of foundational beliefs.[29]

1. Ministry Is Rooted in and Symbolized by Baptism

The questions we faced raised some serious issues around baptism. There is not a developed theology of baptism in the documents of Vatican II, but the way we understand baptism has an enormous impact on our understanding of ministry. If baptism is the sign of potential for full human life in Christ, then any believing member of the Christian community should, theoretically at least, be able to live a life of complete discipleship, and consequently, minister fully in whatever way he or she is called and gifted. There might be other limiting factors, but it is not one's Christian "status" that provides an impediment to ministry.

If, however, ministry is not seen as rooted in baptism, or baptism is seen as the sign of only an "ordinary call" to discipleship, when, in fact, an "extraordinary call" to follow Christ more closely is needed for some ministerial functions, or even for ministry itself, then the majority of Christian believers are automatically ruled out of official ministry on the basis of something other than baptism (e.g., femaleness or marital status).

Making ministry an exclusive dimension of one or two states of life is not supported by the New Testament[30] or solid church tradition,[31]

---

[29]This theology is culled from statements in the Adrian Dominican Constitution and Statutes.

[30]There is some discussion whether the word *laity* stems from *laós* which is used in the New Testament to mean "Church" or Christian community (Strathmann, 502) or from *laikos* which does not appear in the New Testament. At any rate, the distinction between clergy and laity is not clearly visible in the apostolic period, but only comes to the surface later (Schweizer, 176).

[31]The present language of the church, e.g., that found in the Rite of Holy Orders, implies that ministry belongs to one state of life, the clerical, and that this state of life raises one

but is an attempt to support current pastoral practice with some theological foundation, usually in the form of "proof texts." Even proof from the past does not do away with the reality that many of the laity are discovering new ministerial roles in the church and in the world.

A theology built upon distinctions of status is narrow and inadequate. Interaction with a changing world calls for new creativity in meeting its ministerial needs, and this will undoubtedly expand rather than narrow the ministerial force. The first priority is the mission of Jesus. The church cannot afford to maintain structures that might work to the detriment of the mission. Trying to claim a principle of equality while at the same time supporting unchangeable distinctions seems to be nothing more than ecclesiastical double-talk.

Fullness of life can be actualized in many different modes, but the idea of predetermined "degrees" of fullness of life is contradictory to an understanding of baptism as the sign of full Christian discipleship. If this is true, then one must be able to grow continually to new depths of Christian discipleship in response to God's call in a manner fashioned by one's free, open, and integrated response. Growth cannot be predetermined or limited by "one's state of life." God is free to call any and all persons to the full potential of human life.

If the priority that Vatican II placed on baptism as a sign of the call to holiness of all is valid, then the basic question here is how ministry can be reserved to a particular state of life or whether it is an essential component of a Christian way of life. Fortunately, as a congregation, our experiences and willingness to engage in the process of theological reflection led us ultimately to make a choice for an "all are called to holiness" theology over that which suggests "rank and status." It is by our baptism that we are consecrated. Religious life, therefore, is seen as an intensification of our baptismal "consecration for mission." (Foley, 212–13)

2. The Call to Discipleship Is a Challenge to Participation in the Mission of Jesus

The mission of the Church is the mission given to it by Jesus. Christians through the centuries continue to reflect on Jesus' words and actions

---

to the highest status possible. Although this understanding reflects a long tradition in the church, it is not, however, the language of the New Testament. Mary Collins points out that the origin of such language is found in the ancient sense of order and cosmology, and no longer reflects present reality (Collins, 261–94).

that they might learn how to carry on the work of building the Reign of God.

A statement of mission is a statement of identity for Dominicans. The Dominican mission to proclaim the Word of God draws its specific character from its foundation in the apostolic life as conceived by Dominic (vowed life in community, contemplative and liturgical communal prayer, study, collegial governance) and from its fruit, a proclamation of the Word lived out in diverse ministries that express and embody that mission. We recognize that we are called to respond, individually and corporately, with each other and with the entire Church, to the task of continuing Jesus' liberating work of salvation in the world.

Participation in the mission of Jesus requires continual formation as a Christian. Formation is the means through which one's own experience and the experience of the human community, past and present, becomes integrated. Formation for Christian discipleship is a process by which one is challenged to grow into full development as a human person in freedom to expand one's understanding of mission. The clearer our understanding becomes of what it means to live a life of mission, the deeper our response can be. We grow in our awareness of the profound implications of a life centered in mission through the processes of conversion and transformation. On the basis of this conviction, we Adrian Dominicans strive to challenge each other to ongoing formation which is grounded in a life of prayer and study.

We also consider the pursuit of justice to be the way in which we responsibly interpret the mission of Jesus. We had to come to realize that, as Christians, mandated to carry on the mission of Jesus, we needed to take seriously the challenge to address the concrete problems of our particular age with the demands of the Gospel. We claim in our constitution that the signs of the Reign of God appear whenever justice, mercy, freedom, love, liberation, and solidarity with others are evident in human society (ADS 1). As members of the church, therefore, we must be reconcilers and liberators. We must enable others to develop as full human persons. Not just because we happen to belong to a religious congregation, but as Christians, we must work for a just world. The Synod of Bishops stated in 1974:

> Action on behalf of justice and participation in the transformation of the world fully appear to us as a constitutive dimension of the preaching of the Gospel, or, in other words, of the Church's mission for the redemption of the human race and its liberation from every oppressive situation (CU 6).

The Church calls all its members to the task of

scrutinizing the signs of the times and of interpreting them in the light of the Gospel. Thus, in language intelligible to every genera-tion, (they) can . . . respond to the every recurring questions which (people) ask about this present life and the life to come, and how it is related to the other (GS 4).

The experience of renewal after Vatican II led us to the awareness that the commitment to mission requires continual conversion. The Reign of God has not yet come fully because the powers of personal and social sin still permeate the world. Personal and communal conversion must be the mark of any Christian life, especially in those "consecrated for mission."

Conversion is before all else a question of consciousness. A move-ment of God's Spirit in our times is a growing consciousness of the ecclesiastical, social, economic, and political structures that per-petuate the oppression and dehumanization of world peoples. In turn, this emerging consciousness demands that we, individually and as church, create lifestyles and structure that fit us to be a leaven of transformation and a witness to the values of Jesus' Gos-pel (LCWR/CMSM 44).

It is the mission that urges us to a new reading of the world and the culture, that calls us to a greater consciousness and deeper reflection on the meaning of experience, that challenges us to be like Jesus, who hears the cries of the poor and the marginalized, that invites us also to become poor and marginalized, that calls us to conversion. It is through the conversion demanded by participation in the mission that our radical interior freedom as a Christian becomes most manifest. We feel com-pelled to align ourselves with Christians all over the world who have seriously accepted the task of bringing justice to the world.

As baptized Christians we are called to testify to God's holiness and compassion towards a world of injustice in which the vic-tims are God's instruments of salvation for all people (LCWR/ CMSM 4).

There was one way in which we saw ourselves as perhaps bearing more responsibility than many of the faithful. We were educated. We had the opportunity to grow, not only in self-understanding, but in our understanding of ourselves as Christians. Not all Christians have had the opportunity to realize fully their role in the mission of Jesus and of the Church. As persons in leadership positions in the church and in the world, we needed to take seriously the church's own challenge for justice in the world, we had to assume some of the responsibility for formation of the membership. We needed to begin to provide for and encourage greater study of the Christian tradition and the world in which it exists. We had to make opportunities available for development in prayer. We challenged ourselves to support those who have immersed themselves in the mission of Jesus and are working to bring about a just world.

If the Church, in all its facets, is to be a sign of God's salvation in the world, it must be a clear sign. If we are to be part of that clear sign, it would require of us some action:

(1) the allocation of resources for the benefit of people in critical areas of need who are least able to support themselves;
(2) the initiation of social change for the alleviation of injustice and the attainment of rights basic to dignified human life;
(3) the involvement of each of our members in an educative process in social justice as an essential element of her Gospel commitment for the purpose of working toward a more just society;
(4) the gospel imperative that inspires and directs our congregation in its education, stewardship and ministries.[32]

Adrian Dominicans believe that the call to mission in this age must be fundamentally linked to efforts to end poverty, oppression, racism, warfare, violence and injustice whenever and wherever they appear. To be disciples we must participate actively in the mission of Jesus.

3. The Meaning of the Term "Ministry"

Most contemporary theologies of ministry maintain that an attitude of service to others is characteristic of an adult faith commitment and is essential to a life of discipleship in a believing community, rather than a responsibility for some only if a shortage of "official" ministers or some other "emergency" exists. Ministry is the way in which God's presence is concretized in the world. It is through ministry that Christian disciples activate their responsibility for the continuation of the mission of Jesus. The Christian disciple continues the mission of Jesus through ministry. People must experience liberation and salvation in the concrete

---

[32]All of the above statements reflect various Chapter Enactments from our General Chapters since 1974.

reality of their lives in this world or these words will remain only abstract ideas. It is within the event of ministry that salvation becomes visible. Ministry is service, but service that enables people to hear the message of the Good News of God's unconditional love. Ministry is a response to the gospel; it is living Christian love.

Ministry can be thought of as a "way of being" in the world (disciples are recognized by their ministerial attitude), or a specific work of service for the building up of the Reign of God (a function or role). Both concepts have long been a part of the Dominican mode of life. Adrian Dominican women have come to define ministry both as an attitude of life lived in response to the Gospel and as specific actions or service to others for the sake of the Reign of God. Often we do not make a clear distinction between the two definitions, but use the term ministry in both ways.

Living a ministerial life is a lifelong task. Although most of us make ministry a full time professional commitment, we believe that all are called to a ministerial way of life. There are times even in the lives of members of religious congregations when they can no longer function as professional ministers, but can continue to live a ministerial life.

4. The Relationship of the Spirit to Ministry

We believe that God's Spirit has a significant role to play in our lives as Christian disciples. It is the power of the Spirit of God that facilitates our growth in freedom so vital to discipleship. The Spirit gives each of us unique gifts to be developed in the journey of life.

The movement of the Spirit emerges, not only in individuals, but primarily within the community. Christian disciples together, as Church, bear the responsibility for discerning the Spirit's call and direction. The Christian community assumes the task of helping individuals to identify and develop their own unique gifts, and to grow in appreciation of the gifts of others.

Women religious, through lives spent in community both with each other and with other members of the human community, try to foster an atmosphere that helps us to be open to the work of the Spirit in recognizing gifts and in discerning direction that will lead to the coming of the Kingdom more fully in this day and age. We believe that the choices we make in ministry are the fruit of the work of the Spirit. It is God's Spirit who calls, God's Spirit who bestows gifts, and God's Spirit who makes the signs of the Reign of God visible through ministry.

5. Relationship of Religious Life to Christian Discipleship

We make our response to the mission of Jesus as members of a religious congregation because of God's unique call which invites each one of us into religious life as a viable way to live out our baptismal commitment. The decision to enter religious life is a choice to join with certain other Christians in a particular expression of mission. A woman enters a particular congregation to participate in the mission of Jesus as it has been and continues to be understood by the membership of the congregation. Each member assumes responsibility for the life of the congregation in mission.

The choice to live as a member of a religious congregation must be motivated by baptismal commitment to the mission of Jesus. Vowed commitment supports and confirms this choice. The vow of obedience challenges each member to listen carefully to the individual and collective voices of the congregation as a *locus* of privileged mediation of God's will (Schneiders, 141–51). Poverty demands simplicity in lifestyle and common life. Celibate chastity is a unique choice that offers one a particular means of affirming the human person's unique capacity to find fulfillment in relationship to God and others.

Community is essentially linked to Adrian Dominican life with its emphasis on mission and ministry. We believe that community is fundamental to the human condition, essential to the mission of Jesus, and integral to the heritage of Dominic, and that shared life and faith are necessary for continued conversion, and enlarge our capacity for service. We are convinced that being together in community is both an expression of mission and a means for mission.

We believe further that the elements of Dominican religious life, vowed commitment, mobility, community, prayer, study, lifelong formation, ministerial activity, and participative government can and should foster a life fully committed to the mission of Jesus through ministry. Profession in the Congregation then is a valid choice as one way to live out God's call of discipleship.

6. Organization for Mission

Adrian Dominican life is governed by structures designed by the membership, not to restrict, but to facilitate their participation in the mission of Jesus. Authority is given and exercised within the context of the mission. Each of us claims the authority to enter into the mission of Jesus as we together interpret it responsibly in this age. The government of the Congregation is built upon participative collegial groups organized at different levels to allow us to exercise both individual authority and responsibility, and to call one another to accountability. Through our organizational structure, we attempt to implement the principles of collegiality, subsidiarity, unity, and diversity.

7. Relationship to the Church

The ministerial activity of any religious congregation is carried on in union with and in dialogue with the church. Like other women religious, Adrian Dominicans claim authority to respond to the mission of Jesus, but recognize at the same time the need to do this as part of the ecclesial community that is church. Membership in the congregation implies the acceptance of the church as a context for living as a Christian disciple within a religious institute. We willingly place ourselves in a posture of listening to the community of the church, knowing that the church too is, for us, a privileged locus of God's will. Such listening is not limited to the teaching of the hierarchy, however, for they are not the whole of the church, but neither does it exclude it. We attempt to listen to the call to mission given by Jesus to the church and respond with the entirety of our lives. We unite ourselves to the church through a study of its teaching, through participation in its liturgical life, and through responsible action in carrying out its mission.

Our relationship with the church, however, also suggests that we, in a mode of collaboration, are not simply listeners. Women religious have rich, valuable and unique experience to contribute to dialogue within the church. Study, discernment, reflection, listening and dialogue are essential for all members of the ecclesial community. When communication moves only in one direction, when there seems to be a predetermined interpretation of God's will or when there is a lack of openness to new avenues of truth, obstacles are placed in the way of true collaboration.

The Spirit's work, while transcendent, appears in and through human experience (Cannon, 7) and in the theological expressions of this experience. Developing official church teaching out of a limited expression of human experience (only male or only Euro-American) can be an obstacle to the work of the Spirit. Disciplines of the church cannot quench the gift of the Spirit, but they can restrict its influence on the community. If the church is to be faithful to its mediating role in regard to the Spirit, it must be open to the Spirit's movement in all the people of God. To fail to do this could lead to entrapment in an ideology.

8. Relationship with the World

The members of the Adrian Dominican Congregation recognize that we must enter into the mission of Jesus through ministry in the world in which we live, with all its difficulties and its benefits. We do not come as bearers only, but as "bearers and recipients" (ADC 6). We come knowing that any ministerial gift that we can offer will be returned many times over. We recognize that we are a part of the world. We try to see the world, not as a necessary evil, but we enter into ministry believing in the world, willing to call it to accountability, daring to share its joys and its hopes, its grief and its anxieties. We realize that we must fashion our response to mission in dialogue with the world.

Dominicans are especially committed to the discovery of truth whenever and wherever it may be uncovered. Listening to a multitude of voices in human history can lead to greater truth. As members of the Order of Preachers, whose motto is truth, we Adrian Dominican women engage in widespread study in many areas, and in processes of theological reflection that allow us both to articulate our new understandings and to act out of them. Through integration of what has been studied and contemplated, we increase our social responsibility and awareness. We recognize our need to be conscious of the global world in which we live, both of its peoples and its resources. In our ministry we seek to be collaborative with those of other Christian communities in our shared concern for the mission of Jesus, and with all others with whom we find common purpose in addressing the needs of people for human development.

Changing Actions

As we made changes in our theology, we also implemented concrete actions that would put that theology into practice. If we allowed our new understanding to emerge out of our own experience and context, we realized that it would produce change: change in the way we dressed, where we worked, how we found employment, where and how we lived, our entire government structure. These would all radically affect our understanding and living out of mission and ministry.

There was common recognition that new direction in ministry meant new professional preparation for many of the members. Although generally the congregation was well-educated (most members except the very young had earned masters' degrees in various educational fields), this education was, for the most part, aimed at preparation for the work of formal education, and, in a few cases, for professional health care. A diversification into other ministries required some retooling. Our congregation needed to provide sisters with the opportunities to choose educational preparation consonant with their native gifts and talents, and to work in areas where this training could best serve the needs of people.

One of the most influential factors in our development of new theology was the promotion of the principle of diversity in the midst of collegiality and unity as integral to our coming together in prayer, in study, in communal life, and in apostolic purpose. Thus, the corporate mission of the congregation could be expressed in terms of the kinds of ministry supported by the congregation rather than as specific works in which individuals in the congregation must engage. Quite quickly the ministries of our congregation expanded to include education; health care; social service; spiritual direction; legal aid; political action; the fine arts; administration; and pastoral care of all kinds, in parishes, hospitals, universities, correctional institutions, nursing homes, hospices, halfway houses, facilities for the developmentally disabled, housing projects, and social action centers.

Over the course of the last thirty years we have tried to help those choices along by developing criteria by which good ministerial choices may be made. These criteria can be summarized as follows:

Selection of Ministry

Ministerial choices ought to be made out of a recognition of one's own gifts and in continual discernment in prayer and with others to determine God's unique and individual call. In addition, we make our choices for ministry from the perspective of membership in the Dominican Order. Adrian women live out their call as Dominicans to preach the Word of God through a word, lifestyle and manner of service. Our baptismal call to ministry allows us the freedom to respond to the call to mission in whatever unique way we discern to be in accordance with God's will for us. This might also free us to leave a certain ministerial commitment knowing others are capable of doing the needed work.

Link to Mission

Ministry is essentially linked to mission. Adrian Dominicans attempt to make this link visible by making the practice of justice a priority in their lives. We call ourselves to minister in response to the actual needs of people. The Gospel call is one that demands sensitivity to the many situations in which people are in need of salvation. This implies that as ministers we must be astute enough to uncover real areas of needed liberation, and must not fall prey to the trap of responding to perceived or traditional concepts of "religious needs" that may no longer be real needs. Institutionalized Christianity has not always been good at assessing true needs but has often had to depend on its more charismatic members who are usually more free to uncover oppression and discover the need for liberation. Historically, religious congregations have frequently been the vehicle for the work of the Spirit in responding with charismatic freedom to new needs.

Ministerial choices must be supportive of congregation goals, which continue to be formulated in the light of our ever-renewing understanding of mission. It is the responsibility of each individual to evaluate regularly, through approved processes and in the light of congregation goals, both the ministerial function in which she is engaged as well as the institution in which it is carried on. The congregation as a whole calls itself to be accountable to these and similar goals:

(1) to pursue adequate compensation and benefits for those employed in congregation-owned or sponsored institutions;
(2) to recognize racism within ourselves and to work for the elimination of institutional racism in all institutions with which we are affiliated;
(3) to be in solidarity with and work for the rights of the poor and oppressed;
(4) to understand and respond to the global impact of its local activities;
(5) cooperate with others in addressing the sources of social sin;
(6) to live lives of radical simplicity;
(7) to stand in communion with the women of the world.

Accountability

Women religious have become aware that they cannot make ministerial choices in isolation, but that these must be made in light of the lives that will be affected by their choices. Ministerial choices made by one Adrian Dominican member, for example, affect the lives of the other members, and so we enter into discernment processes with other members and with leadership to be sure we have considered all the factors that affect our lives together. Issues such as community and salary must be balanced against the needs of people. The need for professional preparation must be weighed against the potential for long-term commitment to a particular ministry.

Competency

It is important that women religious engage in ministry for which they are competent. People have the right to receive ministry from one who is trained for a particular ministerial function. Even the motivation of mission cannot be an excuse for unnecessary lack of preparation on the part of the minister. We are responsible, not only for initial professional preparation for a given ministry, but also for maintaining competency by keeping current the study of Scripture, theology, and such disciplines as are required for personal participation in mission. We need to reflect with others regularly on the signs of the times and their implications for the mission of the Gospel.

Ministry tends to be one of the few professions that has no built-in requirement for continuing education. In spite of this we know that continuing education in one's field is absolutely essential for good ministry. At the time of developing the annual congregational budget, funds are allocated to provide for the ongoing education of our members.

None of the developed criteria is easy to implement; each requires continual discernment and evaluation by the individual member, by her elected leaders and by the congregation. There may be a number of situations when all four of the criteria may not be able to be implemented at the same time. But if each of these criteria is taken seriously, ministry will indeed be a way of living the mission of Jesus.

The crucial question for Adrian Dominicans, and for all ministerial women religious, seems to be not whether a particular kind of work is catalogued as ministry by officials in the church or even within their constitution, or whether certain criteria can be applied for clarity in understanding; but whether the work in which individual sisters are engaged is contributing to the mission of Jesus through the building up of the Reign of God.

Adrian Dominican Theology of Mission and Ministry

How, then would we express our theology of mission and ministry? We have articulated our theology quite simply in our mission statement:

> In the mission of Jesus we Adrian Dominican Sisters discover and identify ourselves as women called together to share faith and life with one another; and sent into our world to be with others bearers and recipients of his love, co-creators of his justice and peace (ADC 6).

The theology of the congregation has as its central theme, mission. We are sent, in mission, as are all Christians, to "make disciples of all peoples." Mission is the core of discipleship, and the raison d'être for religious life and for ministry. Disciples believe in Jesus, follow him, and give service to others because they have experienced salvation and liberation in their own lives and believe in a God who wishes to extend that experience to all people.

It is interesting that nowhere in any Adrian Dominican document is there a separate section entitled ministry. In our *Constitution and Statutes* the word itself is mentioned rarely and, then, used in an ambiguous fashion. The reason for this neglect seems to lie in the essential link between ministry and the mission, a theme which, indeed, permeates that entire document and subsequent chapter mandates.

Questions

In the introduction to this article I raised two questions: What are the unresolved issues that have emerged out of our new understanding and theology? What are the challenges for us as American women religious in terms of mission and ministry as we move into the future? I turn now to these questions.

Unresolved Issues

In spite of the church's history of strong social messages, a tension point has continued to exist among Catholics (and even within religious congregations) concerning the interpretation of the mission. There has not always been agreement on what peace and justice really mean or how they should be addressed or achieved. This ambiguity should not be surprising. There are numerous examples in recent history in which the church is divided in the interpretation of certain political situations,[33] in solutions to poverty and oppression,[34] and whether certain issues are issues of justice.[35] Is there one correct interpretation of mission or the Reign of God, or do we continue to stay in dialogue, learning from each other?

One issue that will need resolution is the struggle over the language and concepts surrounding mission and ministry. As long as there continues to be a chasm between the language used and the reality happening in the church throughout the world, and between the language of the official church and the language of the people, the church will not appear as a clear sign of the mission of Jesus. The laity, especially women, are using too much energy to fight this battle, energy that could be used for the mission. More and more, they are leaving "church" institutions to do the needed ministry elsewhere. How sad it is that we cannot stand proudly and claim our work in the name of the church!

There are some crucial questions that arise over the meaning of the term ministry which affect members of religious congregations who have had "traditional works." If everything done with "a ministerial attitude" is ministry, then how is the term, ministry, really identified? Is all work ministry? Are there any parameters on one's choices for meaningful ministry?

Another controversy that particularly affects women as ministers is the discussion that surrounds the distinction between charism and office. At the present time in the Roman Catholic tradition, women are unable

---

[33]For example, the controversy within the Nicaraguan Church a decade ago over the Sandinista government as described in "Nicaragua: A Divided Church" (Central American Historical Institute, 4–5).

[34]Many situations exist, particularly in the Latin American experience whereby those on the local level believe that the poor must demand their right to a share of the world's resources even if this leads to revolution, and are often opposed on this point by the members of the hierarchy (Boff, 22–31). Boff claims that "The hierarchy does not have a technical responsibility; they do not say *what* to do. They have an ethical responsibility; in the light of the Gospel they may say whether something is just or unjust, whether it favors participation or hinders it" (29).

[35]E.g., the place of women in the church. See Ashe (137–69) for an exploration of the ways in which women in the Roman Catholic Church have attempted to address the issue of sexism within their religious tradition.

to hold most offices in the church.[36] This effectively removes women from the process of discernment of the Spirit's direction within official church dialogue, because that conversation exists only among those holding institutional offices. This situation forces women to dialogue among themselves and with others in the church, and frequently effects sharp divisions between their reading of the Spirit's movement in the world today and that of the official church. It is unfortunate that a very important area for discussion of ministry is hardly found among the writings of women theologians except as it relates to women's ordination. It would be tragic if their voices are not found in the struggle for resolution.

The relationship between "gift" or "charism" and "office" is not clear in the New Testament literature (Miguens, 99), but history has shown the gradual association of "power to minister" with "occupying an office," as well as persistent suspicion of the "charismatic" (Cooke, 198). A crucial question for ministry today centers around this historical tradition. Does all ministry need to be associated with office, or is office only one possible function of ministry? It is clear that those who do hold office have the responsibility of not only ordering the ministry, but recognizing and fostering the development of the different charisms of all baptized Christians. This task is particularly realized in parish ministry, and many women are engaged in it; however, for most, it is in an "unofficial" capacity.

Challenges

Just because we can articulate a theology of ministry for ourselves does not mean we can rest easily. There are enormous challenges that face us as women in religious congregations, who seek to respond to the call of Jesus to mission through ministry. We need to take seriously church teaching:

> We see in the world a set of injustices which constitute the nucleus of today's problems and whose solution requires the undertaking of tasks and functions in every sector of society, and even on the level of the global society towards which we are speeding in this

---

[36]There are a few exceptions to this that appear in canon law. Most exceptions involve administrative positions that are usually not decision-making.

last quarter of the twentieth century. Therefore we must be prepared to take on new functions and new duties in every sector of world society, if justice is really to be put into practice. Our action is to be directed above all at those [people] and nations which because of various forms of oppression and because of the present character of our society are silent, indeed voiceless, victims of injustice. (CU 20)

We must continually take time and invest creativity into listening to our people, especially the poor. For it is they who, out of their frustrations, dreams, and struggles, must lead the way for all of us. Next we must listen to the vast majority of plain people who would not be called poor, but who are not rich, and who increasingly share in the powerlessness of the poor. (LHM 27)

Because Jesus' command to love our neighbor is universal, we hold that the life of each person on this globe is sacred. This commits us to bringing about a just economic order where all, without exception, will be treated with dignity and to working in collaboration with those who share this vision. The world is complex and this may often tempt us to seek simple and self-centered solutions; but as a community of disciples we are called to new hope and to a new vision that we must live without fear and without oversimplification. Not only must we learn more about our moral responsibility for the larger economic issues that touch the daily life of each and every person on this planet, but we also want to help shape the church as a model of social and economic justice. (United States Catholic Conference)

If we are to make "action on behalf of justice constitutive of the preaching of the Gospel," new demands will be placed on us as we approach a new millennium. As we face questions of our own aging and diminishing numbers, we must, at the same time broaden our vision more fully to encompass the global world in which we live. We must continue to listen to the people of the world to hear their need for liberation and salvation. We must try to remain knowledgeable about issues of economics, health care, poverty, racism, sexism, violence, and all those other factors that impact our lives and the lives of those with whom and to whom we minister. We must take concrete action to eliminate injustice and oppression. We must relentlessly call the church and one another to accountability.

The role of the Spirit in the church is crucial. Depending on how the Spirit's direction is discerned, fidelity to the Spirit's movement could lead us to radical conclusions. If we are to be responsible members of the church community, we must be willing to speak our truth, no matter what the cost.

Works Cited

Adrian Dominican Sisters. *Adrian Dominican Mission Statement*. Adrian, Mich.: General Chapter, 1978.

Adrian Dominican Sisters. *Adrian Dominican Constitutions and Statues*. Adrian, Mich.: Adrian Dominican Sisters, 1989.

Ashe, Kaye. *Today's Woman Tomorrow's Church*. Chicago: The Thomas More Press, 1983.

Boff, Leonardo. *Church: Charism and Power: Liberation Theology and the Institutional Church*. Trans. John W. Diercksmeier. New York Crossroad, 1985.

Cannon, Kathleen, OP "Opening Remarks," In *Preaching and the Non-Ordained*. Ed. Nadine Foley. Collegeville: The Liturgical Press, 1983. 7–9.

Central American Historical Institute. "Nicaragua: A Divided Church." *Woodstock Report 9* (March, 1986): 4–5.

Collins, Mary. "The Public Language of Ministry," *The Jurist* 41 (1981): 261–94.

Cooke, Bernard. *Ministry to Word and Sacraments*. Philadelphia: Fortress Press, 1976.

Foley, Nadine, OP "The Nature and Future of Religious Life," Origins 19, no. 13 (1989): 211.

Guttard, A. and M.-G. Bulteau, ed. *Bibliographic internationale sur le sacerdoce et le ministère*. Montreal, 1971.

Haight, Roger D. "Mission: The Symbol for Understanding the Church Today. *Theological Studies* 37 (December 1976): 620–649.

John Paul II. *Vita Consecrata*. Vatican City: Vatican Press, 1996.

Kilmartin, Edward. "Ministry," In *The Westminster Dictionary of Christian Theology*. Ed. Alan Richardson and John Bowden. Philadelphia: The Westminster Press, 1983.

LCWR/CMSM. *Fifth Inter-American Conference on Religious Life: Apostolic Religious Life in a Changing World and Church*. Washington, D.C.: LCWR, 1986. Note: This document was a joint work of the Leadership Conference of Women Religious and the Conference of Major Superiors of Men. It was published by LCWR as indicated.

Lécuyer, Joseph. "Ministères." In *Dictionnaire de spiritualité: asétique et mystique. Doctrine et histoire,* ed. M. Viller, F. Cavallera and J. DeGuibert. Paris: Beauchesne, 1980.

O'Brien, David J. and Thomas A. Shannon, ed. *Renewing the Earth: Catholic Documents On Peace, Justice and Liberation.* Garden City: Doubleday & Company, Inc., 1977.

Rahner, Karl, et al., ed. *Sacramentum Mundi.* New York: Herder and Herder, 1969.

Schillebeeckx, Edward. *Church with a Human Face: A New and Expanded Theology of Ministry.* New York: Crossroad, 1985.

Schneiders, Sandra M., IHM. *New Wineskins: Re-imagining Religious Life Today.* New York: Paulist Press, 1986.

Schweizer, Eduard. *Church Order in the New Testament* Trans. Frank Clark. London: SCM Press Ltd., 1969.

Selvidge, Maria J. *Notorious Voices: Feminist Biblical Interpretation. 1500–1920.* New York: Continuum, 1996.

"Some Questions Regarding Collaboration of Nonordained Faithful in Priests' Sacred Ministry," *Origins* 27, no. 24 (1997): 403.

Strathmann, H. "Laós." In *Theological Dictionary of the New Testament.* Ed. Gerhard Kittel and Gerhard Friedrich. Trans. Geoffrey W. Bromiley. Grand Rapids, Mich.: Eerdmans Publishing Company, 1985: 499–503.

Synod of Bishops. "Consecrated Life's Role in the Church and the World," 1994 Working Paper, *Origins* 24, no. 7 (1992): 116.

United States Catholic Conference. "Economic Justice for All: Catholic Social Teaching and the U.S. Economy." *Origins* 16 (November 27, 1986): 443ff.

7.

◆

If religious life is a charism for the church, where is the locus of its authority? Women religious have come to see that authority lies in the communion of its members. Such a conclusion stems from the nature of charism, from the conclusions of theological reflection carried on in dialogical fashion by the members of the religious institute, and from the historic sense of religious life as a change agent for the church. The institutional church has a role to play in approving forms of religious life and authenticating constitutions. But the institutes themselves have the responsibility for preserving their charisms and determining how those charisms lead them to respond to the signs of the times.

◆

Locus of Authority in the Religious Congregation

Implications of Religious Life as Charism

Nadine Foley, OP

From Jesus, proclaimed in the Gospel, the authority of the Adrian Dominican Congregation, mediated and affirmed through the Church, resides in the communion of the members according to their respective roles as given in this Constitution and Statutes. (ADC 42)

For implementing the Decree on the Adaptation and Renewal of Religious Life *(Perfectae caritatis)*, according to the *Motu proprio* (ES, PC) issued by Pope Paul VI in 1966, religious were directed to hold a general chapter within two, or at most, three years. In preparing for this chapter, one of the provisions was the following:

The general commission in preparing this chapter should suitably provide for full and free consultation of the members and arrange the results of this consultation in time so that the work of the chapter may be helped and directed. (4)

Whatever the intent of Pope Paul in issuing this directive, the results were transformative of the life of women religious beyond anyone's expectations. Earlier general chapters had been highly formalized and controlled and had concentrated upon the election of general superiors. Issues tended to revolve around superficial aspects of practice—extending the hours for the triennial visit to families from 7:00 P.M. to 8:00 P.M., for example, or permitting the wearing of pajamas instead of nightgowns, oxfords instead of high-top shoes, and other such trivialities. But now, for the first time, floodgates opened as all of the members began to raise questions and issues that lay below the surface of what externally looked like an orderly and disciplined facet of traditional ecclesial life. Questions about the very nature of religious life, its place within the church; about appropriate ways in which to engage in gospel mission; about the preparation of members for ministry; about forms of governance consonant with the maturity of adult, highly educated women; about recognition of the talents and experience of individual members. The questions seemed interminable and engaged many congregations for two or three years of general chapter sessions.

The *Motu proprio* had said some things such as: "The most important role in the adaptation and renewal of the Religious life belongs to the institutes themselves . . ." (ES 1); "The cooperation of all superiors and members is necessary to renew Religious life in themselves . . ." (2); "The general commission in preparing this chapter should suitably provide for full and free consultation of the members . . ." (4); and "The general chapter has the right to alter certain norms of the constitutions . . . as long as the purpose, nature and character of the institute are preserved"(6).

There was an implicit message in such statements that the primary motivating force of the "renewal" chapters was to come from the members themselves. But more influential in the ensuing directions taken in the religious congregations was the sense of inner authority that arose from processes of consultation, the experience of speaking and listening to one another in conversations and discernments about the deepest convictions and values that they held in light of all the documents from Vatican Council II. The sisters took to themselves the vision advanced for the whole church, although at least one bishop expressed the opinion that "to become concerned about the implementation of the Decree on the Church in the Modern World will distract the sisters from their assigned area of concentration: the Council Decree addressed to Religious" (Chittister, 73).

The lived experience of apostolic women and some men religious, in close contact with people in ministries of education, health care and social service at home and in so-called missionary settings, had provided new insights and challenging questions that resonated particularly with the Pastoral Constitution on the Church in the Modern World *(Gaudium et spes)* and the Decree on the Church's Missionary Activity *(Ad gentes divinitus)*. The most frequently quoted line from the former, "The joys and the hopes, the grief and the anxieties of the people of our time, especially of those who are poor or afflicted, are the joys and hopes, the grief and anguish of the followers of Christ as well" (1), struck to the hearts of women religious and moved them to response. There could no longer be life as usual. As we considered the needs for change and new directions for community life in mission to respond to the signs of our times one of the persistent areas for questioning pertained to governance. How were we to govern ourselves for mission conceived in a much broader sense than had formerly been the case? And how might we continue to consult all the members in the kind of processes that had begun?

A number of themes engaged the thought and reflection of the members as they struggled with the issue of governance. Among them were the principles of collegiality and subsidiarity enunciated in the official Vatican II documents. While the principle of collegiality was developed in the Dogmatic Constitution on the Church (*Lumen gentium*) in reference to the "college" of bishops and their shared authority with the pope, or bishop of Rome (25), it was readily appropriated by members of religious congregations as pertinent to their reality as a microcosm of the church. The consultation of all the members in preparation for the prescribed general chapter was experienced as an application of collegiality that was to have enduring effects.

The principle of subsidiarity is set forth in the Pastoral Constitution on the Church in the Modern World in relation to the international community and world trade so that "its task [is] to organize economic affairs on a world scale, without transgressing the principle of subsidiarity, so that business will be conducted according to the norms of justice." (GS 86c) In an editor's footnote, Pope Pius XI is quoted from his encyclical letter *Quadragesima anno:*

This supremely important principle of social philosophy, one which cannot be set aside or altered, remains firm and unshaken: Just as it is wrong to withdraw from the individual and commit to the community at large what private enterprise and endeavor can accomplish, so it is likewise unjust and a gravely harmful disturbance of right order to turn over to higher rank functions and services which can be performed by lesser bodies on a lower plane. For a social undertaking of any sort, by its very nature, ought to aid the members of the body social, but never to destroy and absorb them." (AAS 23); also quoted by Pope John XXIII in his encyclical letter *Mater et magistra.* (AAS 53)

The context of "higher rank" and "lower plane" presumes a hierarchical social ordering. But the concept of empowering persons within social institutes to take hold and direct their lives at what might be called the "lowest level" was a stimulating one as issues of governance arose for our religious congregations. How could we organize ourselves so that decisions might be made at the place where the implications of decisions were most directly felt? Adrian Dominicans devised a plan for governance on a circular model that involved local mission groups, regional councils, and a central council. Mission was the organizing principle. In theory issues might arise in any of the units and move in a circular pattern for consideration by all. As communities embraced "mission" (see chapters 6 and 8) we began to see that governance did not exist for its own sake but for the support and furtherance of Gospel mission. This realization was quite clear in the founding of the Dominican Order and Adrian Dominicans claimed it for their contemporary reality in responding to the needs of the times.

In that respect our reflections on governance coalesced with our efforts to return to the original inspiration of the order in the life and times of St. Dominic. The first nuns of the order, converts from the austere Cathari, were gathered into a monastery of contemplative life at Prouille in France. While the Adrian Dominicans trace their origin to one such monastery established later in Regensburg, Bavaria, our subsequent history as apostolic women had involved a number of changes to make the practices of cloistered contemplative life compatible with active ministerial life. Constitutions, written and revised over a period of time, however, had not yet fully articulated the character of apostolic religious life for us nor for other active congregations of women religious as well. Canon law still reflected principles developed for contemplative nuns living in enclosed monasteries. As a result, as we Adrian Dominicans looked for models of governance to support new movements in mission and ministry, we took our inspiration from the model designed by Dominic for the men of the order.

It has been said that the Dominican Order was the first "missionary" order. Certainly, Dominic sent his first recruits out on the preaching mission to combat the dominant heresy of his time. They were on the move. They had to be educated in order to preach. They had to have the freedom born of commitment to make decisions for themselves when they were far removed from Dominic and those who succeeded him. They were expected to be responsible in carrying out the order's unique mandate. They needed a Constitution that fit the mission for which they were brought into being. The principles of governance incorporated by Dominic are well chronicled in the histories of the order (Hinnebusch, 195–250; Mandonnet, 291–354; Vicaire, 301–19). While he retained fundamental observances that defined religious life in the monastic orders of his time, his innovations for the kind of order that he envisioned for mission in his world were remarkable, both then and now. Reflection on them, along with new concepts arising from study of psychological and sociological development of women, gave rise to new models of organization for mission.

Unique to the governance of the Dominican Order was the system of what might be called in later terminology "checks and balances." Government was resident in three types of chapters—the general chapter representing the entire order; the provincial chapter, the province; and the conventual chapter of the priory. They constituted the democratic, communal element of the order. Through them the powers of those who held office were circumscribed and limited. The principle was further delineated by the arrangement of successive general chapters whose composition varied in representations of superiors and members in a rotational plan embracing a threefold cycle. Legislation to be finalized had to be passed by three such chapters (Hinnebusch, 176–77). That these chapters held supreme authority for the order is clear from the fact that its capitulars had almost complete freedom to revise, complete, or interpret existing laws and regulations (Hinnebusch, 139).

Another feature of Dominican governance is the principle of dispensation. Conscious that the demands of his itinerant missionaries would from time to time bring them into conflict with the requirements of conventual and liturgical life, Dominic provided this principle to hold the primacy of mission in the face of competing obligations. It was not dispensation for any and all pretexts. The general chapter of 1220 states quite clearly

the prelate shall have power to dispense the brethren in his priory when it shall seem expedient to him, especially in those things that are seen to impede study, preaching, or the good of souls, since it is known that our Order was especially founded from the beginning for preaching and the salvation of souls. Our study ought to tend principally, ardently, and with the highest endeavor to the end that we might be useful to the souls of our neighbors. (qtd. in Hinnebusch, 84)

Prior to the renewal chapters of the late 1960s and early 1970s such principles of governance were not generally found in the constitutions and statutes of the Dominican Sisters. But now, reflecting upon the primacy of mission (see chapter 6) for their religious institutes, Dominican women found these original inspirations of Dominic remarkably compatible with their ideas about writing new constitutions to fit their reality as a congregation in active mission. It was as a result of reflection upon the original inspiration for governance set forth by Dominic that the Adrian Dominicans, for example, wrote into their constitutions:

From Jesus, proclaimed in the Gospel, the authority of the Adrian Dominican Congregation, mediated and affirmed through the Church, resides in the communion of its members, according to their respective roles as given in this Constitution and Statutes. (ADC 20)

This provision, rooted in the Dominican tradition, also emerged from an inner conviction, drawn from experience over the years, that we were endowed with an "inner authority," evident from reflection upon our history. Within carefully drawn parameters for our apostolic endeavors in fields of education, health care and social service we had exercised an extraordinary degree of self determination and achieved acknowledged success for the mission of the gospel.

Realizations such as these were shared by other women religious who also came to a sense of inner authority. Now with the challenges set before us by Vatican Council II, reflection upon the original inspirations of our founders, and the range of experiences with the people of God accrued through our considerable histories, we began to evoke our inner authority through general chapters to address the needs of people in our times. We internalized the idea that religious congregations were "microcosms of the church" and were entrusted with gospel mission in a manner unique to the character of religious life as we were experiencing it. For the first time we had the opportunity to write constitutions that expressed who we had become.

The principle of consultation of all the members continued in the development of new constitutions. As drafts were prepared they were submitted to the members of the congregations in regional meetings for study, discussion and recommendations. Consultations were arranged in Rome with representatives of the Congregation for Religious and for Secular Institutes in Rome, as it was called when these consultations began. Through these processes the drafts were revised when deemed necessary or appropriate. For members of our congregations the education, reflection, and discernment that engaged all of the members in developing the new constitutions, a process that resulted in "owning" them, was a deeply transformative experience.

Constitutions for pontifical institutes require approval through the renamed Vatican Congregation for Institutes of Consecrated Life and Societies of Apostolic Life (CICLSAL). The affirmation of the constitutions of institutes of religious life by authority vested in the universal Church is important for the authenticity of mission carried out in the name of the Church. It was in consultation with the Vatican congregation for religious, however, that many religious congregations experienced tension between their claim to an inner authority and the claim that traditional concepts of authority always proceed through a hierarchical line of institutionalized ecclesial authority.

In 1983, Sister Mary Linscott, SND, then a member of CICLSAL, published an article in which she set forth her reflections on government as a result of her consultative work with congregations who were writing new constitutions. What follows is a brief summary of her article.

(1) Jesus had an absolute claim to Authority that he conferred upon Peter and Paul for the purposes for which the Church was founded.
(2) This is a distinctly "religious authority," that persists in the Church with unique characteristics: it is a gift of God; it cannot be assumed; it is not an authority that meets only organizational or functional needs.

(3) It is this authority that the Church exercises in conferring religious authority on a religious institute as a microcosm of her own reality. Only the Church can bestow this authority which is not the same thing as organization, responsibility, power or leadership and always involves ecclesial accountability.

(4) Christ did not hesitate to use authority, to speak of it and confer it. Authority is a positive value and is itself a service.

(5) Each institute, in union with the Church, determines what structures best express the value of authority in its own case. Structures are necessary because vowed obedience is more than a disposition of heart. It is that disposition expressed in action within an ecclesially approved framework.

(6) At each level, general, provincial and local, there needs to be a clear locus of authority in someone whose primary responsibility is: to foster the unity for which Christ prayed; to encourage the development of his life in the members; to promote creative fidelity to his mission. Thus religious structures are personal in the sense that they serve a personal authority.

(7) Religious obedience is to individual persons entrusted with authority, and not to groups or documents.

Certain values in this schema of the authority resident within religious congregations are indisputable: the church has a role to play in affirming the authority of a religious congregation; the exercising of authority is a form of service within the congregation; each institute determines the structures that will best serve its purposes; the locus of authority is within persons chosen by the members to preserve and foster their unique charism. There is general acceptance of these principles. Not every movement that arises in the course of time is an authentic expression of gospel mission, as history verifies. There is need for the authenticating role that is carried out by the church through its various auspices.

But at the same time history also shows that the church was more often than not involved in giving approbation to what had already begun in the visions of the inspired founders of religious orders and congregations.

Certainly this was true in the cases of Dominic and Francis in the thirteenth century. The times called for something new in addressing the heresies and scandals of that period. The church responded by recognizing the validity of the mission to be carried out through the mendicant orders and by allowing them to devise the structure of governance that would support the mission. Had the officials insisted that only the existing models of monastic life be honored the subsequent history of the religious orders, and indeed of the church, would have been quite different. It would seem not an over simplification to conclude that the pope of the time, Honorius III, made his response in light of the missionary needs of the church and acknowledged, implicitly at least, that the Spirit of God was in the visions of the founders. Women religious could ask whether or not such an approach was not still possible for congregations that respond to a call for renewal of governance in light of needs for mission in the contemporary world. In consideration of that question the delineation of authority exclusively through the hierarchical line seems not to acknowledge the charismatic nature of religious life and the kind of authority that derives from its uniqueness.

In his Apostolic Exhortation *Evangelica testificatio* Pope Paul VI said the following:

> In reality, the charism of the religious life, far from being an impulse born of flesh and blood or one derived from a mentality which conforms itself to the modern world, is the fruit of the Holy Spirit, who is always at work within the Church. It is precisely here that the dynamism proper to each religious family finds its origin. For while the call of God renews itself and expresses itself in different ways according to changing circumstances of place and time, it nevertheless requires a certain constancy of orientation. The interior impulse which is the response to God's call stirs up in the depth of one's being certain fundamental options. Fidelity to these fundamental options is the touchstone of authenticity in religious life. Let us not forget that every human institution is prone to become set in its ways and is threatened by formalism. It is continually necessary to revitalize external forms with this interior driving force, without which these external forms would very quickly become an excessive burden. (ET 11,12)

These words affirm two convictions that have guided religious congregations of women in the process of renewing forms of governance. First, there are fundamental values of religious observance that are to be preserved—community life, common life, common prayer, and the vows, for example. Second, many external forms had become burdensome and needed revitalization. As the members of the congregations were consulted, the issues of local and congregational governance were raised from all quarters. The "superior/subject" dichotomy was brought into question, both for its nomenclature and for the kind of socialization that it implied. But theory was not the only consideration. Women religious had often experienced governance as oppressive and stultifying to them as persons. They called for new styles of organization for governance to fit their understanding of themselves as mature and competent, endowed with unique talents and abilities, and capable of self determination and responsible living out of their vowed commitment for mission in the contemporary world. In accord with the insight of Pope Paul VI it was time to "revitalize external forms," of governance in this instance, for they had become "an excessive burden."

Biblical insights were invoked to support the view that the superior/subject form of governance was inconsistent with the teaching of Jesus who had said to his disciples, "If anyone wishes to be first, [that one] shall be the last of all and the servant of all" (Mark 9:35), and "whoever wishes to be first among you will be the slave of all. For the Son of Man did not come to be served but to serve and to give his life as a ransom for many" (Mark 10:44–45). In the Gospel of John, Jesus refers to his followers not as slaves but as friends (15:15). Furthermore, the work of women writers on women's ways of knowing and women's modes of decision making resonated with the experience of women religious as they considered new plans for governance (e.g., Belenky et al.; Gilligan).

Associated with the traditional modes of governance were particular interpretations of the vow of obedience. Here again, Adrian Dominicans were aided by their study of their order's beginnings and the meaning of obedience for them. For Dominicans the vow of obedience implied, not a conformity of will to a superior, but a conformity of mind to the discernment of the community. In the words of Herbert McCabe:

What I have called the modern view, which centers on sheer will, and submission of the will, makes an essential division between superior and subject. There is obedience precisely when this division is most marked, when the subject is not following her own mind but doing what the superior wills. In our tradition, on the other hand, which sees obedience as a kind of learning process, a matter of practical intelligence, obedience is something that brings people to share a common mind. For our tradition it matters that the superior should be right. She too has to learn, to be obedient. . . . For our tradition an obedient house is one which has got as near as possible to the truth, in which there is general agreement

about what is to be done, so that the will of the superior hardly
enters into it. The job of the superior is not to make her or his will
prevail, it is to play the central role in an educational process by
which the good for the house becomes clear to everyone, including
her. . . . Obedience for us is not simply a matter of efficiency in
getting something done but of fraternal [sic] unity, and it would
perhaps be better if instead of speaking of a vow of obedience we
spoke of a vow of solidarity for that is what we mean. (283–84)

The current Master of the Dominican Order, Timothy Radcliffe, OP,
has addressed the issue of authority in a recent article. He reaffirms that
in the order authority is granted to all of the members and functions
through the general chapters in a sequence that honors its multifaceted
character.

Superiors enjoy authority in virtue of their office; theologians and
thinkers by virtue of their knowledge; brothers engaged in pastoral
apostolates enjoy authority because of their contact with people in
their struggle to live the faith; the older brothers enjoy authority
because of their experience; younger brethren have an authority
which comes from their knowledge of the contemporary world
with its questions.[37] (142)

Radcliffe's expansion on these insights is consonant with the reflections of Adrian Dominican women on the concept of inner authority
derived from the knowledge and experience of the members of the congregation. He states that good government works well when we acknowledge the authority that each member has and when we refuse to
absolutize any single form of authority. For, he says, the health of our
government depends on allowing the interplay of all the voices that make
up the community. And he extends these principles to the women of the
order.

The nuns have an authority which derives from lives dedicated to
contemplation; our sisters have an authority which comes from
their lives as women with a vast variety of pastoral experience.
Often they can teach us much through their closeness to the people
of God, especially the poor. (142–43)

---

[37] This article was addressed to the men of the order as the masculine references indicate.
But the women of the order regard the principles set forth as applicable to them as well
as to the friars and brothers.

These reflections upon obedience and governance in the Dominican tradition express well the reflection and insights that characterized preparation for the 1968 Adrian Dominican general chapter of renewal. The process of consultation that had preceded the chapter had given the sisters an experience of obedience in this interpretation of the Dominican tradition. Once begun it could not then be discarded. Instead, the agenda became one of devising a system of governance that provided for the possibility of continued dialogue and reflection that would enable the members to come to a common mind about their life in mission. To bring such an organization into being required the exercise of the congregation's inner authority.

The inner authority experienced by women religious as an abiding effect of the indwelling of the Holy Spirit corresponds well with what Edward Schillebeeckx has called "the authority of new experience." In his book *Christ: The Experience of Jesus as Lord,* he says that "the authority of (new) experiences is itself defined by the surprising nature of reality, which continually proves different from what we think"(37). As women religious began to reflect together upon their experience in light of the Scriptures, the original inspirations of their founders, the Documents of Vatican Council II, and contemporary writings from a variety of disciplines, they were confronted with this surprising nature of reality. It raised questions and invited change. The established ways of thinking and acting, when viewed from emerging perspectives, required reformation. In this respect the congregation was seen to be like the church itself. "Christ summons the church, as she goes her pilgrim way, to that continual reformation of which she always has need, insofar as she is a human institution here on earth" (UR 6).

Christian teaching, relying on Aristotelian and Thomistic insights, has long compared the natural authority of the person, resident in the nature of the human being, with social organization and its requirements for patterns of authority. The reflections of women religious, from within their faith tradition and understanding of how the Spirit of God had acted in their individual and communal lives, began to see the pattern differently. As mature women, capable of assuming responsibility for the direction of their lives, they had made a commitment to religious life within a particular congregation. Their own inner authority as persons in this instance acted under the inspiration of the Holy Spirit, a kind of "religious authority," to which they had responded. Through prayer, reflection, community and ministerial response, they aspired to deepen their baptismal commitments and to bond with other women of similar faith experiences.

Through such free choices they opted to join their personal authority with that of other mature Catholic Christian women and, at the same time, to limit it to achieve their common purposes in carrying out gospel mission. In light of its origin and its purposes there emerges a new expression of "religious authority." By this choice under the inspiration of the Holy Spirit the individual women became participants in the authority already resident within the congregation. The sources of this authority are: the gospel; the lived tradition of the church; the original charism and inspiration of the founder(s); the approbation that the congregation or order received from the church as formulated in its constitutions; and its own tradition, constantly reflected upon and reformed according to the needs of the times.

Within the congregations there is an ongoing creative tension between the ministerial experience of the members and the authority that the body claims for itself as it continues to scrutinize the signs of the times and interpret them in the light of the gospel. This creative tension is at the heart of the general chapters of the congregations as they struggle with the constant need to assess how they must respond to the signs of the times in light of their congregational charisms and their more constant directions in mission. The individual sister has placed limitations upon herself in becoming a member of the religious congregation and is called on again and again to respond to the religious authority resident in the group and conferred upon those who have the role of religious leadership. There is a fundamental obedience involved in the process of setting directions for the congregation's life in mission and it has both a communal and a personal dimension. As women religious have reflected upon their inner authority, they have had a strong conviction as acting as "a microcosm of the church," a phrase that has often been used in other contexts. In this schema the authority of those in what we prefer to call "leadership" derives from the group, but those elected to leadership are nonetheless endowed with real authority to move the congregation forward in mission.

The distinction between "leadership" and "authority" in religious congregations has been an ongoing point of discussion among some who have pondered changes in usage. Sister Mary Linscott expresses a prevailing view when she says, "Leadership is a charism, a spiritual reality given freely by God to individuals for some special purpose in a community; authority in religious institutes is a canonical-juridical as well as a spiritual reality. The two, therefore, are not synonymous and not interchangeable" (1996, 151). Yet she notes that there has been a development in the understanding of these terms and concepts over time. "While leadership and religious authority are indeed different and distinct, they do not have to be in conflict, and in fact both are needed for good government" (ibid.). For many women religious this realization is extremely important and is consistent with plans of governance that have been developed in the period of renewal since Vatican Council II. What many of us might add is that authority does not have to be structured in hierarchical patterns.

As new organizations for governance have emerged they have incorporated the claim to an inner authority but have at the same time preserved the enduring values of religious life adapted to the situations and experience of adult, mature, educated and responsible women religious. Their implementation, particularly through their incorporation into new constitutions in a variety of ways by women's congregations, have brought about new vitality and hope for their continuation in the mission of the gospel. They furthermore offer models of ecclesial organization for local parish and diocesan communities and for the church at large. Clearly, what women religious have been about, and continue to assess and evaluate, has been the revitalizing of external form with the interior driving force of the Holy Spirit of which Pope Paul VI spoke. It has been remarkably freeing.

Works Cited

Belenky, Mary Field Belenky, Blythe McVicker Clinchy, Nancy Rule Goldberger and Jill Mattuck Tarule. *Women's Ways of Knowing*. New York: Basic Books, 1986.

Chittister, Joan, Stephanie Cambell, Mary Collins, Ernestine Johann and Johnette Putnam. *Climb along the Cutting Edge*. New York, N.Y.: Paulist Press, 1977.

Gilligan, Carol. *In a Different Voice*. Cambridge, Mass.: Harvard University Press, 1982.

Hinnebusch, William A. *The History of the Dominican Order*. Vol. 1. New York: Alba House, 1965.

Linscott, Mary. "The Service of Authority: Reflection on Government in the Revision of Constitutions." *Review for Religious* (Mar.-Apr. 1983): 197–217.

———. "Leadership, Authority, and Religious Government." *The Church and Consecrated Life. The Best of the Review 5*. Ed. David L. Fleming and Elizabeth McDonough. St. Louis Review for Religious, 1996.

Mandonnet, Pierre. *St. Dominic and His Work.* Trans. Mary Benedicta Larkin. St. Louis: B. Herder Book Co., 1945.

McCabe, Herbert. "Obedience." *New Blackfriars* (June 1984): 280–87.

Radcliffe, Timothy. "Dominican Freedom and Responsibility: Towards a Spirituality of Government." *International Dominican Information* 353 (July-Aug. 1997): 136–60.

Schillebeeckx, Edward. *Christ. The Experience of Jesus as Lord.* Trans. John Bowden. New York: The Seabury Press, 1980.

Vicaire, M-H. *Saint Dominic and His Times.* Trans. Kathleen Pond. Green Bay: Alt Publishing Company, 1964.

8.

◆

The governance of religious congregations was traditionally modeled on a pattern of dominance in hierarchy. But a community of persons drawn together under the inspiration of the Holy Spirit requires governance that reflects their identity as charism. It is one that must embrace collegiality and subsidiarity in order to respect the thought and experience of its members all of whom have some claim on a dimension of leadership. Having a responsibility for mission according to the original inspiration of a congregation implies a form of decision making and accountability that makes mission possible. Mission becomes the organizing principle for an apostolic congregation that recognizes local mission as the basis for the larger missionary activities of the congregation as a whole.

◆

For the Sake of the Mission
Carol Jean McDonnell, OP

We organize ourselves for the sake of the mission in a government structure which calls and challenges us, individually and corporately, to enter into the mission of Jesus as we interpret it responsibly for our times. (ADC 19)

Howard Thorsheim and Bruce Roberts, futurists, were showing some photographic slides from space to a group of second graders. A particularly striking comment came from a seven year old in the class. As a slide of our earth from 100,000 miles in space was shown, the class was asked what they thought. The young girl raised her hand and said, "We draw the lines." When asked what she meant, she said, "Look at the globe over on the library shelf with all the lines between countries, and then look at the earth as it really is. There are no lines on the earth; just on the globe. We draw the lines" (2).

There is something humanly appealing about drawing lines. It may be that it gives us the appearance of order and/or control. Even as young children, when we colored in our coloring books, we were taught to outline the objects first to keep the colors contained, so as not to go outside the lines.

This reflection of one person's experience of the renewal years and beyond will focus on the issues of organizational structure that in a most basic way have to do with "drawing lines." Where do we draw the lines? In what context do we view them? Do they isolate, individuate, separate, or define the connections and contributions a person or group makes to the whole? What of our design is illusion and what is reality? Gareth Morgan reminds us that "The whole history of organization and management theory is based on the idea it is possible to organize, predict and control." He asserts, however, that the order "becomes apparent only with hindsight" (300). We are in a position now to see from that perspective.

When I look back on the past five decades and put religious life in a larger context in America, I see our institutional life very much in line with the others around us. During World War II, people were concentrating on getting the job done. There was little thought for one's personal needs. All played their part to achieve victory. The postwar years were ones of satisfaction and continuation of the work ethic in the belief that it would bring the good life one deserved. Institutions of learning, religion, government and production provided the framework for molding and utilizing the upright citizen, promising reward and security in exchange for abiding by the rules that were clearly drawn. Similarly, institutions of religious life offered a way of perfection for their members and an opportunity to join in the work of saving souls in exchange for abiding by the norms established and playing the roles assigned. Both worlds had answers and few questions were asked.

In the so-called turbulent 1960s, a number of events occurred that evoked questions for which there were no ready answers. Three assassinations, an unpopular war, a civil rights movement and a young generation seemingly uninterested in the dominant values of the times changed forever the American landscape. The lines of identity and purpose seemed terribly blurred. Well into the 1960s, however, within our convent walls, we continued to work together, pray together, play together, and generally share a single worldview. There were boundaries circumscribing all aspects of our lives. Our structure fostered apartness, and depersonalization, and was dependent on each one playing her role.

At the same time, to acquire adequate preparation for the degree of professionalism required in hospitals and schools, the members studied on campuses across the country, bringing home an expanded worldview. Our daily work too brought us into a changing world. So when Vatican Council II called us to revisit our heritage, our nature and mission, and adapt to the modern culture, there were those among us who resonated with the call.

"Renewal" was the buzzword; change was the mandate. When we first began the process, our activity centered around "tearing down" outmoded structures within which we lived, prayed, ministered and separated ourselves from outside contact. Change was most evident in what was taken out of community life. When consulted, the members' responses reflected that we were in a process of deep fundamental change that involved the necessary element of personal choice. For the average member "choice" was not part of her vocabulary. Her value system was well established and clear lines were drawn to sustain her in her beliefs. While she thought her world was safe and secure, the process of renewal collapsed boundaries, often quickly and painfully.

Change in structure had important consequence since the structure supported in many ways the member's perception of herself. Her identity was so intricately connected with the identity of the congregation that challenging the group's mission and structure challenged the basic identity of the person. "In situations of voluntary change the person doing the changing must be in control of the process, for change ultimately hinges on questions of identity and the problematic relation between the me and the not-me" (Morgan, 238).

Having little experience with choice and only each other as role models, we were in a transition period from a mechanistically controlled group with a solid identity and purpose to a new way of interpreting our call and a new way of relating to one another and the world at large. We did not know what would emerge. The immediate task was to create an environment that would allow the work to begin. In this situation, a gift we could give one another was not to "design new boxes and lines," but rather to encourage conditions that would support each person's struggle as well as a community life with lots of questions. Peter Berger discusses this transition:

A traditional society is one in which the great part of human activity is governed by clear-cut prescriptions. Whatever else may be the problems of a traditional society, ambivalence is not one of them . . . [Now] the modern man finds himself [*sic*] confronted not only by multiple options of possible courses of action but also by multiple options of possible ways of thinking about the world. What previously was fate now becomes a set of choices. Or: destiny is transformed into decision. (16–17)

The starting point of government is the mission, i.e., the identity and purpose of the organization. Traditionally that mission was defined as the perfection of the religious and the salvation of souls. The facilitating structure was a set of relationships illustrated by clear lines of authority. Order was seen in a pattern of clear place in life governed by roles and rules. The stripping action, erasing lines that defined our relationships, was an immediate response. We saw it as a way of breaking through our "self-sealing" environment (Morgan, 244) to explore the multiple ways of thinking about ourselves and the world.

We went at the task with a sense of purpose and, though acknowledging that we were in a change process, were confident we could remain in control of our destiny. In retrospect, I believe the theory, expressed by Morgan in his *Images of Organizations,* that change is an "emergent phenomenon." So, however intimately we participate in the process, "even though our actions shape and are shaped by change, we are just part of the evolving pattern" (299–300). Our choices are ours to make, but there are others making choices too. This kind of confidence gave us the impetus to be proactive in the process. Our imagination provided us with a vision of a future for us and created a backdrop for our choices. At that time, I believe this illusion cushioned us from backing off from the challenges presented to us for it was apparent that the process would continue with or without us.

Our agenda turned to deep identity questions, corporate task questions, and mission questions. But it was a different group now in dialogue. With the demise of many of our symbols that defined us, each sister's perception of the nature of the organization underwent a revision. She experienced and witnessed modern society, a pluralistic society with staggering social issues that gave urgency to the gospel. This awareness caused an impact on our total posture and we discovered that the words used to define our purpose no longer seemed adequate. It was important that we structure ourselves so that ongoing dialogue was easily facilitated to gain insight into the differences among us and to encourage the emergence of each in full personhood as we strove to reclaim our fundamental mission.

We identified the membership as our most precious resource. The spotlight moved from the common task to the individual growth of the member. Brian Hall's levels of consciousness (51) gave us some insight into the struggle within and among us as we searched together. He describes four levels: me-self as center, us-self as belonging, I-self as independent, and we-self as lifegiver. Needless to say, the old structure did not accommodate self-centeredness well. Primarily we operated on the us-level, meaning one measured her effectiveness and self-worth in terms of being and doing what was required in her place for the good of the mission. To varying degrees, members' personal identities were wedded to the organization. Now, identity of person and identity of group were being severely challenged. The us-level of being would no longer serve us. With ensuing emphasis on the individual, we were encouraged to "know thyself" as an autonomous human being.

Our challenge was to reclaim the identity and purpose of the congregation in terms that had meaning for each of us. It was a dual discovery process—identity and purpose of individual and group. I would comment here that the member's commitment to a congregation of women religious goes beyond her relationship with the other members. It begins with her relationship to God and with how she perceives God's call for her in this "way of life." A role, a rule, or a ritual may have become the embodiment of that call and so it would be an act of betrayal to let it go. The perceived consequence was an added impetus to hold on to something of such value, especially when it left a void. The congregation's task was to offer new information and provide new experiences that opened the members to different ways of being and acting with God, with each other and others that could retain the core values they cherished.

As my focus is a look back at the evolving structure of the group, a definition is in order. Structure is dynamic so I think of it in terms of what it does rather than what it is. What it does is support the mission by facilitating the relationships among the members. Therefore, structures will change and adapt to meet the demands of the mission in place and time. "Organizational structures emerge in response to these imperatives of identity" (Wheatley and Kellner-Rogers, 85). It must be added here that returning to our basic Dominican heritage required that we develop democratic structures to honor our truth that authority lies in the membership. Dominic thought of himself as "first among equals." This concept has its origins in Roman times where the principal leader is still a "first" but is not the chief. The leader acknowledges that her leadership is among a group of able peers (Greenleaf, 61). Father Timothy Radcliffe, OP, the current Master of the Order, went so far as to describe democracy as "central to our spirituality." He stated further, "Democracy is more than voting to discover what is the will of the majority. It also involves discovering what is the will of God" (145). For such a pursuit, we must be committed to searching for truth while realizing that each member contributes to that search.

In the early phases of renewal, individually and collectively, internally and externally, we found ourselves in a process of discovery. It was necessary to peel back the layers of structure that supported static relationships. Many of us were surprised at the impact the process had on our lives. While it seemed to be one of taking superficial steps, we discovered that, on the contrary, the liberation from restrictive boundaries had a profound effect on each of us. We were taking away something of value in the old and were unsure of what would replace it. On the two extremes, some of us, like deeply rooted trees, refused attempts to venture into the unknown, and others of us, like air plants, wandered freely. Most of us were somewhere in between, testing and experimenting with the idea of personal choice.

At that time we governed ourselves in what appeared to be a loose manner with a large number of persons in leadership regionally so that leadership teams could be in close dialogue with all of the members. Designated house authority was withdrawn leaving the local communities to determine how they were to relate to each other. The usual work continued in schools, hospitals, and elsewhere, but the major work of the group was rebirth. The regional leadership was charged with keeping connected with individuals and communities, encouraging their openness to new ways of being and doing. With a large widespread membership, those in leadership roles faced the daunting task of keeping lines drawn within new parameters. Symbolically they found themselves coaxing the trees to uproot and reining in the air plants. It was no doubt an illusion to think that a new type of control could come about through drawing lines universal to all. The congregation was caught between two attractors both fighting for influence. The challenge was to tip the balance from the old to the new.

Actually it was a time of chaos, but a rich, wonderful chaos. Unfortunately for most of us, we may not have appreciated its merit. This period can be summarized as a transitional situation in which "people frequently need to reflect, think over, feel out and mull through action if a change is to be effective and long-lasting. If the change agent tries to bypass or suppress what is valued, it is almost sure to resurface at a later date" (Morgan, 238). The active listening, the tolerance, the hesitation on the part of leadership to interfere contributed to the disruption as the message was that the limits are no longer clear. The congregation was involved in a search for what was of value and needed to rely on each member to contribute to the choices that would shape the future mode of governance for the sake of the mission.

The image of the energizing organization was one of an open system operating in a nonlinear pattern. The whole world became a part of the system as we opened ourselves to hear its voices, expressing an individual world view and then a collective one. Our identity could not be conceived apart from our relationships. We came to realize that our self-awareness is raised in evolving patterns of activity and insight, positive and negative reflective loops, that bring meaning to our life. Relating is not a one-dimensional process of give and take, or cause and effect, but rather a continual emergence of meaning that affects for good or ill the identity of each of the participants and thus the identity of the group.

What happened to us as a congregation, expressed by Wheatley in her book, *Leadership and the New Science* (88–94), encourages us to see organizations in this light by making a case that such a lens gives recognition to three elements of a system: (1) self-renewing, in that mission and structure engage in a fluid process where the system may evolve to a new order when needed; (2) self-referencing, as the system is autopoietic, its activity is within the bounds of its integrity; and (3) self-organizing, as change is not an enemy. Resiliency, rather than stability, is the important feature.

When we look for order in the chaos of those early years, these elements make the task easy. In that pivotal moment, wrenched from a static way of being, the diverse activity, the multiplicity of individual and group options, the membership spread over a continuum of "personal search for identity" and the seeming lack of common mission and values may have come across as mayhem. Yet we need not have worried since in sorting out what was really valuable and how to express that value, we were in a natural process of chaos seeking order. It was a purposeful search in a way organized by each individual to find meaning in her life. She was trying to make sense of what her "call" was all about. In doing so she was participating in the emergence of a new form of life for the group. This was jarring to the system as it was so accustomed to operating in a uniform manner. In *Shaping the Coming Age of Religious Life*, the authors offer a description of the tension that occurs in that first stage.

> During the time of breakdown and conflict, doubt increasingly pervades all dimensions of the community. In the spiral of doubt, major contradictions or dilemmas begin to reveal themselves. There is a tension between personal freedom and fulfillment and the common good of the community, between transcendent and secular commitments, between personal choices of ministry and the needs of the community and between continuity of traditional works and the responsiveness to new needs. . . . There is a loss of mission and identity. (Cada, 98–99)

The elements named above were our saving grace. For the organization did not encourage sustaining the old notion of who we were but fostered a wider system of relations. The autonomous individual has the capacity to create herself and does this continuously throughout her life forming patterns of being. "Over time, these become boundaries limiting the freedom of self-expression. Who we are becomes an expression of who we decided to be. Our choices become limited as we strive to become consistent with who we already are. We reference a self, and that reference constrains us" (Wheatley and Kellner-Rogers, 48). While the ways of being and acting in a larger world were tested, this new information was reflected back to a self with her own integrity and sense of identity. She did not start at ground zero. Her choices were not arbitrary but were made through a deliberate process in evolving into the person she wanted to be. She and we are much more resilient than we give ourselves credit for being, and, though we could not predict the responses of the individuals and group to the actions of one, we could rely on each other to process new information in a manner that was consistent with ourselves. Uniform lines were not drawn, but each person's unique sense of the group provided its own restraint.

The question is not "how does one keep the system under control?" The question is rather, "what guiding principles can we agree upon to evolve new ways of relating to one another?" Our living in religious community for a number of years programmed our expectations of what constitutes "a good religious." More importantly, our relationships with one another were legislated so that in any given circumstance responses were predictable, even in the way we were taught to relate to God. We do share one faith, but our expression of that faith is lived out in a variety of styles. We were becoming increasingly aware of different options that raised the issue of the nature of religious life itself. The principle of pluralism has been present for a long time, but the idea and acceptance of it is another story. Thomas McDonnell discusses this apparent divergence in an article entitled "A Pragmatic Heresy: Building Community":

> In translating their personal subjective certainties into norms for "building community," there is often the unconscious urge to establish a mystical dictatorship. In other words, they [religious ?] become intolerant of other religious whose graded insights and experiences are different from theirs. The radical root of the Christian community remains the reconciling grace of Christ, diffusing itself as diversely as He wishes. A recognition of the legitimacy of this diversity is pivotal for a theological understanding of Christian community. Though it may be an excruciating experience to translate this idea into actual living circumstances within religious communities (due to the tensions it will cause), the attempt must be made. Above all, a reorientation of our frame of reference will no doubt be required. . . . Pluralism is not a passing fad. Its basic point is that no two of us ever experience and formulate our approach to God in exactly the same way. (McDonnell, 20, 23)

As the members reflected upon themselves, new relationships were evolving with their God, their sisters, and their world. On the congregation's part, the task was to change the context in which the members tested out this new way of living, to give this new attractor a face. The concept of shared responsibility, or collegiality, was introduced. Membership involves choosing to identify one's own call to mission with the mission of the group. This choice calls for full participation. What does that mean? Where do I come in? These were the kinds of questions asked. Instead of interpreting decision making as a saying "yes" or "no" to a proposition, it became more understandable when perceived as a process involving a series of actions with four components: evaluate, recommend, decide, and act consistent with the purpose to which we are committed. As a cycle it keeps repeating itself. So in dealing with an issue, we will at any given time be at one or another of these stages. Since the process is cyclic, there is always a chance to renew it through learning from experience or new information as one goes along. The key to making shared responsibility work is effective participation in the process. Again, going against our ingrained uniform response, we had to learn that often we may each be effective in contributing at different points and in different ways. Recognizing individual experiences, talents, and knowledge in a given situation and acting on those available resources is understanding the corporate effort. The structure facilitates the relationships among the members so that each step has a high level of efficacy. Our organizations are not boxes or charts. "Rather they are a series of relationships in action . . . a series of transactions between individuals" (Janov, 214).

The challenge in the principle of shared responsibility is to resist the pull of "playing her role in group" according to the old way of allowing others to dictate where the member best "fits." In an environment where she is given the message that her personal identity is important, that reaching her full potential is bound up in the mission of the group, she does have a choice: the assigned box or the reality of who she really is. The idea does cause confusion. In an attempt to get everyone into the act, we are sometimes inclined to deny the diversity of talent, experiences and knowledge among us. We require of one another and demand for ourselves the exact same kind of participation.

The outcome of this situation was seen clearly in a number of leaderless groups. Their original goal was to increase everyone's participation and prevent domination by any one person. But lacking any formal structure, no one was sure of where she stood or what she could do. Groups became immobilized or dominated. Here our instinct for order led many groups through this sometimes chaotic process. Their interest in getting the task accomplished enabled them to work out a way to organize in a productive manner. Whether the group has an appointed leader or an evolving leadership, it is important that we know what we wish to accomplish and involve each person in such a way that her gifts are exercised. Louis van der Merwe, in describing a group process without an appointed leader, states well our intended experience and end result:

> The sense of empowerment that is developed in these workshops comes from both exercising choice, and from being heard and seen by the members. People develop what I see as the essence of leadership—the ability to declare a position on an issue but remain open to influence. People start taking responsibility for self within the context of the community, and feel fully accountable for achieving their shared purpose. (428–29)

Power is a gift given by the group to a member to serve the interests of the group. It is the recognition that one has what it takes in this time and place to get the group on its way. An appointed leader, especially, must recognize that potential, and at times, get out of the way of the one who can make a significant contribution in a given situation. Part of the activity of working out relationships is understanding and appreciating the differences in one another, an affirmation of self-reference. Messages are given and received in those reflective loops so, although we may have only ourselves for reference, self is created in the relationships. If the person hears the message often enough, she begins to believe and respond in a manner consistent with how she sees herself. The task of government is to create the environment in which such possibilities flourish.

In addition to working out our means of participation the manner in which a group would come to a decision to act was a paramount consideration. The word used and still used today to describe this process is *consensus*. I would argue that consensus is not a process but rather a point in group decision making when members reach substantial agreement to move, to get into action. It is not "unanimity." "Substantial" here means that the group, in a number of possible ways including an outright vote, can determine that it has permission to act. The method used depends on the nature of the issue, and on the number and diversity of the persons involved. We discovered the need to be flexible in our methods and willing to explore new approaches. A key point here is that all alternatives in the issue should be examined and each person's contribution valued. Only when these conditions have been fulfilled will the group go forward, knowing that it has sufficient support to move and an understanding of where support is lacking and why. These assurances can be factored into the implementation process.

Accountability is another activity that needed a new frame of reference. It had always been carefully spelled out in ritual and rule with prescriptions that made it easy for a member to know that she was doing the right thing. The method and content of reporting was the same for everyone. When the diversity of the group is acknowledged, accountability is seen in a broader context of mutual responsibility and in understanding the interconnection of the actions of the individual and the actions of the group. "I count with the group. The group counts with me. You can count on me and I can count on you" is a succinct definition. If we think of ourselves as organisms making up the whole of the congregation organism, we can say we are in symbiotic relationship with each other. Wheatley reminds us of the geneticist R. C. Lewontin's statement: "Symbiosis, the merging of organisms into new collectives, proves to be a major power of change on earth," and goes on to say that, "Life creates niches not to dominate but to support. Niches are an example of symbiosis" (qtd. in Wheatley and Kellner-Rogers, 35, 42). Each member has a distinctive niche in the group. This new collective then is dependent on each member for its identity and its unique characteristics. The connection is so strong that one cannot analyze the new organism by analyzing its parts. It is in the interactivity that the group is known.

This concept of accountability requires that we find ways to communicate with one another in strong bonds and that we find ways to show we care about one another. A pattern of mutual caring emerges at the point where we understand that respect for personal freedom and the validity of counsel, affirmation, and direction are not mutually exclusive. There seemed to be a lot of liberation activity, but liberation denotes moving away from, while freedom denotes freedom to move toward new meaning, new purpose. I suggest that the first taste of freedom brought each of us to the core question "who am I" and opened up questions of "call." The liberation from a trapped way of thinking allowed this re-examination and some concluded that the nature of her call had changed and that it now lay outside the congregation. It was that same exercise that caused the majority to stay through times that were very confusing. In the absence of a strong group identity, the individual's personal values and vision gave her the framework and impetus to work together with the group to forge a new way of being for herself and the others. It was a free choice and an announcement that in a reconstituted religious life she is most free to fulfill her meaning and purpose.

The life and vitality of the group is highly dependent on the continuing symbiosis among us. The structure must facilitate trusting relationships that evolve new patterns of accountability. Today we have come to expect certain actions of reporting and listening from the leadership, although any overall pattern emerging for the members is less apparent. That is not to say that persons are not accountable. We have found means of communicating our mutual responsibility in a variety of ways. The rigors of the old way left their mark most vividly in this particular area. When the rituals and rules fell by the wayside, it became clear that there were many more air plants than deeply rooted trees in this regard. We were not accustomed to affirming one another and we were reticent to call one another into account. The suppression of individuality accounted for our reluctance and too much submission impaired our sense of common responsibility. Through the years the elected leadership has been responsive when sought out for counsel, encouraging communi-cation in personal decision making and tolerating lapses. If the organi-zation requires more to be effective in its mission, change will emerge from the membership as we become farther removed from repressive practices and recognize how our forward movement benefits from new practices. The practice of accountability is important as it embodies the unique value of the member and our reliance on one another.

In keeping with our commitment to integrate within the structure the principles described above, we developed a system of linking groups. Local houses were decreasing in size. Some members were making min-istry choices that removed them from our geographical centers. The local house as the primary unit of government was no longer viable. Many of our members met in small groups for a variety of reasons. We for-malized this loose configuration into a web of linking groups. Within a year, with some shifting of the original groups and some additions, each member belonged to what we call a "mission group." It is now the pri-mary government unit. We believe these relationships within and among the groups expand one's participation in the education, communication, and decision making necessary to shape a community response to the mission.

We adopted the principle of subsidiarity where decisions are made by those most immediately affected by and obliged to carry them out. Each of us was struggling with the consequences of the impact of a single member, a group or the congregation's decision on our own life. The old attractor of having someone else decide for me was a strong one for some. They found it hard to accept responsibility for a decision, and would rather have anyone to blame other than themselves if an outcome did not prove sound. Our history had also fostered the mentality among official leadership that they ought to go in and "save" a conflictual sit-uation. In this respect the symbiotic relationship of problem generator–problem solver was an unhealthy one. With the establishment of small groups, the members found more opportunity to identify local issues and situations and to find ways to work them out together on the scene. The role of good leaders was to broaden their horizon by bringing insights from a wider perspective and to offer observations on the impact of their choices on the whole. "Self-organization succeeds when the system sup-ports the independent activity of its members by giving them, quite lit-erally, a strong frame of reference" (Wheatley, 95).

The process of choosing brought about a change in our very way of thinking. In a controlled society, decisions seemed clear cut, following the generally accepted three modes of thought: right or wrong, either/ or, and above and below. Putting into practice democratic principles made the relationship of above and below nonexistent. We continued to have elected leadership and interlocking groups, but endorsed the principle that "hierarchy exists only to link the diverse efforts of the group; not to confer status" (Janov, 5). The narrow choices of one or the other also was no longer relevant since encouraging relationships that foster self awareness and personal responsibility opened a wide range of possibilities given the diversity of the group. The situation was often chaotic. "They slosh around in the mess, involve many individuals, encourage discoveries, and move quickly past mistakes. They are learning all the time, engaging everyone in finding what works. The system succeeds because it involves many tinkerers focused on figuring out what's possible" (Wheatley and Kellner-Rogers, 25).

As we became more confident in ourselves, the spotlight now shone on the identity and purpose of the group. The gospel and our Dominican heritage became more visible in the evolution of the autonomous individuals. In a variety of linking groups we brought these insights to the common table. We were able to agree on a statement of mission that resonated with the members and a constitution that laid out the guiding principles. We are now more unified at our core, and we are continuing to become more so. New information and new ways of acting in our world are continually reflected in the circular patterns that change us.

Structures that honor self-referencing, self-renewal, and self-organization aid these natural processes. It is quite the opposite from the theory that we can design order into being. In hindsight, the offering of new ways of relating through shared responsibility and respecting diversity gave us choices. We had a different context to consider in our struggle between ingrained ways of relating and new possibilities: rigidity or flexibility; conformity or pluralism; certainty or resiliency; submission or collegiality; accountability through roles and rules or accountability as a sign of mutual caring, to mention a few.

The congregation can do no more than posit alternatives to the old ways. Which is more attractive? Which rings more true to myself? To have any long-lasting effect these questions can only be answered freely by the member. She will organize her relationships in a way valuable to her. The organization would receive mixed reviews on its actions. Some felt they were wrested from a meaningful life as a search for new meaning was forced upon them. Others felt it was like a weaning process with movement too slow to their liking. Deliberate change, and that it was, is and always will be a delicate course upon which to embark.

We return to where we began, to our fascination with lines and boundaries. What then, is the meaning of boundaries? Where do we draw the lines? In what context do we view them? Do they isolate, individuate, separate, or define the connections and contributions the person or group can make to the whole? "Like skin, a boundary both separates and interacts with the world, keeping some things out, letting other things in. Boundaries can be thick or thin, solid or permeable, fixed or elastic" (Starhawk, 148). It is not boundaries themselves that should be avoided. It is rather, the dogmatic, detailed design of them that should be resisted. We come back to the importance of simple governing principles: mission, vision, values, organizational beliefs, and the few rules individuals need to shape their own behavior. When these messages are embraced by the members, we can trust them to define the characteristics needed for their own, and ultimately the group's, boundary at any given time. Rooted in our identity and purpose, our boundaries simply define us and others in relation to us, and therefore to the infinite possibilities the world has to offer. We understand our niche in the larger scheme of things and can communicate this understanding not in spite of, but because of, the definition. We know and can use what we find at the boundary for our own self-renewal.

The spotlight shines broadly now on the symbiotic relationship between members that define "we-life giver." The biography of the individual and the history of the group intersect at all points. This relationship cannot be controlled but it can be nurtured. Jill Janov's description is apt: "Inventive organizations are based on partnerships of discovery, in which both parties, regardless of job title or function act interdependently to uncover entrenched assumptions that give rise to the current reality . . . align self-interest with common cause . . . create a future of everyone's choosing and unleash the full potential of all We struggled constituents" (214–15). Inventors tinker a lot. They are not afraid to try out new things and they are never satisfied with the product. Soon they are tinkering again to improve upon the last model.

Starhawk in a poem written for a different context has application here. A group is gathered around a fire sharing stories of times past. The young ones say "tell me, old ones, how did you do it? How did you change it?" And they smile and listen, here is what they say to you.

We held out our hands and touched each other.
We remembered to laugh. We went to endless meetings.
We said no. We said yes. We invented. We created.
We walked straight through our fear.

We spoke the truth. We dared to live it.
We remember that time. The time, my children, that is no more. (344)

The story does not end here. Today is a new day. The regrets, hurt, reconciliation, joy and all those emotions and actions that went into forging our new relationships and are still with us, become the insights, understanding and information we need now to shape our relationships of the future. Walter Brueggeman provides a sharp description of the task in the context of ministry: "Prophetic ministry consists of offering an alternate perception of reality and letting people see their own history in the light of God's freedom and his will for justice. The task is to evoke an alternative community that knows it is about different things in different ways" (Brueggeman, 110). The member and the group continuously reflect back on themselves in the context of their evolving relationships with each other and the world, integrating that information with their experience, history and values. In these ways they define their reality and forward the work of their mission.

Works Cited

Berger, Peter. *The Heretical Imperative.* Garden City, New York: Anchor Press/ Doubleday, 1979.

Brueggeman, Walter. *The Prophetic Imagination.* Philadelphia: Fortress Press, 1978.

Cada, Lawrence, SM et al. *Shaping the Coming of Age of Religious Life.* New York: The Seabury Press, 1979.

Greenleaf, Robert K. *Servant Leadership: A Journey into the Nature of Legitimate Power And Greatness.* New York/Mahwah: Paulist Press, 1977

Hall, Brian. *The Development of Consciousness.* New York: Paulist Press, 1976.

Janov, Jill. *The Inventive Organization: Hope and Daring at Work.* San Francisco: Jossey-Bass Inc., 1994.

McDonnell, Thomas. "A Pragmatic Heresy: Community Building." *Sisters Today* 46, no. 2 (1976): 20–28.

Morgan, Gareth. *Images of Organizations.* 2nd ed. Thousand Oaks, Calif.: Sage Publications, 1997.

Radcliffe, Timothy, OP. "Dominican Freedom and Responsibility." *International Dominican Information* 353 (July-Aug. 1997): 136–60.

Starhawk. *Truth or Dare: Encounters with Power, Authority and Mystery.* San Francisco: Harper and Row, 1987.

Thorsheim, Howard I. and Bruce Roberts. *Metaperspectives: The Systems Approach and Its Vision.* Salinas, Calif.: Intersystem Publications, 1984.

van der Merwe, Louis. "Bringing Diverse People to Common Purpose." *The Fifth Discipline Fieldbook.* New York: Doubleday, 1994. 428–29.

Wheately, Margaret. *Leadership and the New Science: Learning about Organizations from an Orderly Universe.* San Francisco: Berrett-Koehler, 1994.

Wheatley, Margaret and Myron Kellner-Rogers. *A Simpler Way.* San Francisco: Berrett-Koehler, 1996.

9.

◆

Forms of governance that respect the ideas and experience of the members require new approaches to leadership. New measures of freedom for the individual member were potential sources of tension in relation to the religious value of community. Leadership that affirmed the individual but at the same time looked to the common good of all was the contemporary need. Resolution of the implied tension is not an easy task. The general chapters of the congregations lay the foundations and directions for mission and ministry during a specified time. Much is demanded of the individual members in embracing and pursuing this direction in concert with the total membership. Leadership is exercised in providing planning, direction, motivation and resources in implementing chapter directives. It is the responsibility of leadership to call the members to accountability and to preserve the common good.

◆

Leadership for the Common Good
Donna J. Markham, OP

Transformation is the organizational search for a better way to be. It is what happens when the environment radically alters such that the old ways of doing business are no longer appropriate or possible, and a new way becomes essential. The alternative is extinction. (Owen, 5)

Introduction

Since the closing of Vatican Council II women religious have experienced marked shifts in the ways in which they have governed themselves. Changes in the language used to articulate understandings of authority, leadership and accountability betray a major revisioning of traditional definitions. For example, in many women's congregations, a movement away from the term "superior" to a word such as "leader" gradually took hold. This occurrence reflected a clear reinterpretation of what was regarded as an essential construct. A "leader" is one entrusted with the responsibility of calling the community to accountability in mission and to fidelity to the directives of chapters. She is vested with authority but, at the same time, is seen as "sister." She is no longer viewed in a maternal context, nor is she acknowledged as "superior" to her sisters. This apparently simple change in language gave expression to significant alterations in underlying constructs related to the locus of authority. No longer did authority reside outside the members, in a person above the individual members. Rather, members grew in their struggle to develop and claim a stronger sense of communal and personal inner authority.

The responsibility truly to "authorize" leadership to act on behalf of the common good—to entrust a member or members, for a time, to hold the group focused and faithful—became a far more tangible obligation of membership in the post–Vatican II congregation. Additionally, while not necessarily abandoning traditional terminology, it became common for terms like "general council" or "provincial council" to be referred to as "leadership teams." Straining to move away from prior models of exercising authority which carried with them more authoritarian patterns, women religious moved toward more collaborative, mutual, and participative language. Some congregations experimented with totally egalitarian teams, with no person identified as the leader, president, or provincial. During the 1970s, for example, the Adrian Dominicans elected teams of "co-provincials" who served in each province of the congregation. It is interesting to note that upon evaluation, however, this model was abandoned in favor of the election of one person who was entrusted to lead the newly defined governmental unit in collaboration with a "mission council." One could surmise that had not the congregation tried the co-provincial model, more creative and healthier ways of exercising collaborative leadership today might not have developed.

Experiences, Insights, and Questions

As with any emergent understandings of old concepts, inevitable tensions surface. How is the common good to be held in balance with the good of the individual member? Over these past thirty-five years, shifts in the manner in which women religious have organized themselves for mission have resulted in significant changes which carry with them a degree of healthy tension. To name a few:

- Religious live in the midst of a continuing escalation of complexity in all institutions and systems within which we minister.
- We have witnessed an increasing diversification of ministries in which members are far more able to utilize their individual creativity and talents in service of the Gospel.
- There is an increasing plurality of expression regarding personal spirituality and relationship with God. There is a clear movement away from participation in those structures and systems that are oppressive and demeaning to women, and a deliberate movement toward engaging in systems that address the needs of the poor, the oppressed, and the abandoned.
- We have deepened our understanding of feminism as this relates to our engagement with our church and our world.
- We see an escalation of questioning about matters of profound meaning and the consequences for our communal life as members of our institutes, not to mention our life as dwellers on this planet.
- We continue to examine models of leadership, modes of participation and decision making, as well as forms of governance, which are faithful to our commitment as Gospel-driven women.
- Leaders continue to experience the pervasive tension between pastoral responsibility and its consequent caregiving obligations, and vision-driven, spiritlinking, connective, and transformational leading.
- Women religious have a far stronger sense of internalized personal identity and individual maturity. At the same time, we struggle to achieve clarity concerning what constitutes corporate, communal identity, and requisites for membership.
- We have deepened our sense of inner authority and self-directedness, yet struggle with how this relates to any congregational ministerial focus and communal accountability.

And, we have witnessed the common good being held hostage at times by malaise and a depletion of communal passion. We have witnessed the common good being compromised by leaders who have become overly preoccupied with the torment of a troubled individual and have diverted their attention from the compelling and potentially transformative task. We have witnessed the common good being co-opted by leaders becoming frightened and paralyzed in the face of an articulate few whose questions and critique of the culture have become inextricably enmeshed with, or superimposed upon, the backdrop of gospel faith which is the bedrock of religious life. At times we have also witnessed leaders—perhaps in misdirected efforts to affirm individuals—failing to critique emergent societal, religious, and cultural movements as these impact on the common good of the congregation.

So what has been learned from these experiences? Women religious have intensified the conviction that pluralism and diversity must be held in tandem with a binding sense of identity and relationality, solidified by strong, systemic core values and concerted goals. We know that interdependence is imperative for our survival as a planet, as nations, as church, and as religious institutes and are clear about the given that all living systems are characterized by networks of relationships. Religious are more aware than ever that everything is somehow connected and has an impact, for good or bad, on everything else. Consequently, we have learned that relational boundaries need to be permeable enough so that openness and bonding to other communities and to the larger global community are possible, and yet that those boundaries must also be clear enough so that identity is not compromised.

Women religious have learned, too, that neither hieratic leadership models nor totally consensual models are effective in this time of rampant change, heightened complexity and anxiety-provoking ambiguity, and we search for new ways to express leadership and exercise authority. We have learned that neither the subordination of individuals to the needs of the community nor the subordination of the common good to the needs of individual members will make for a viable future. We have learned that new expressions of stronger community are being called for, whereby persons exercise true interdependence, participation, and responsibility about matters pertaining to the well-being of all those systems of which we are a part. We know that we need to develop skill in managing conflict and diversity if we are to accomplish this to any successful extent. We have embraced even more deeply our need for ongoing contemplative reflection and conversation about matters of the heart and soul. And we have learned with some trepidation that to the extent profound doubt about the meaning and validity of our founding myths pervades our communities, we flirt with division and dissolution.

Given this situation, we are faced with serious questions: at what point do diversity and escalating plurality within our institutes lead to entropy and organizational dissolution; how will we work with our differences so that the end result is synergy rather than division; how can we, with our members, become more intently engaged in the promotion of a personal communitarianism which recognizes that the dignity of each person is most fully achieved in communion with others; what can we do as committed women of the Gospel to help heal the gender rift, the ideological rift within our church, the racial and economic rift in our country; what deliberate and concerted actions should we be taking as communities of faith to address materialistic individualism and the psychopathic exploitation and mutilation of creation; how will we inspire others to that end; what are the signs of emergent models for leading in a connective era?

In an effort to shed some light on what leaders might do to assist their congregations to address these serious issues, it is important to focus on three areas of skill development: conflict management, guarding against "groupthink" (Wren, 360ff.) and promoting communal efficacious action. By no means intended to be the only skills needed, these are three areas that call for some special attention today. It would be foolhardy also to suggest that the implementation of these skills will, in and of itself, provide any easy answers to the difficult concerns that face congregations of religious today. A leadership team's proficiency in understanding the fundamental principles behind each of these skills, however, can serve to keep the congregation moving forward, and hold open the possibility for the emergence of true synergy. By synergy, I mean the energy-laden, unexpected accord—or communion—that emerges in a group so that momentum can be channeled toward the good that is held in common.

Becoming Comfortable with and Adept at Handling Conflict

Perhaps more than any skill needed by religious leaders today is the ability to manage conflict well. In a real way, this ability short-circuits the likelihood of groupthink setting in and supports the promotion of communal efficacious action. While we all know that conflict is a normal part of any human relationship and an important part of the interaction in any vital group, much of what follows concerning managing conflict will seem somewhat counterintuitive. It flies in the face of our upbringing and our instinctive responses to confrontation. It is probably safe to say that most human beings employ two basic responses to conflictual situations: we tend to shy away from them altogether, take no action, or procrastinate in the hope that the problem goes away; or, we may engage in symmetrical interchange, become defensive, fight back, engage in debate and soon find ourselves in dead-ended stand-offs. With the first strategy we quickly learn that the denial of the possibility of conflict is one of the easiest ways of becoming involved in one. With the second strategy, we find ourselves caught in dualistic thinking that categorizes others as either with us or against us, thus underscoring the proverbial "line in the sand" with rather self-righteous winners and demoralized losers.

To engage a third strategy, that is, to act counterintuitively, we anticipate and deliberately move toward that which is feared in efforts to establish connection. We meet conflict proactively. We anticipate conflict and confrontation and approach the other with the clear, well-articulated intent to dialogue. In so doing, we open the possibility of engaging in a process of ecological relationship-building that provides a context for working through resistance and mutual erroneous assumptions about the other. We do not engage in debate, but rather in dialogue that has been prepared for with rigorous study, prayer and reflection. While debate is predicated upon convincing and winning, dialogue is built on a commitment to listen and learn from the other. Debate encourages dogmatic rigidity and judgment; dialogue encourages the search for insight and truth. If all parties have not prepared for the conversation by disciplined and intensive study, reflection and prayer, then we are not ready to dialogue.

Engaging in dialogue also means that while we are open to listen and to learn, we also know that there are certain group issues about which a group cannot compromise. Such issues include compromise of identity, internal consistency, and core values. A group ceases to exist as itself when these constitutive elements are compromised. For example, religious leaders have a fundamental fiduciary obligation to promote the unity of the congregation. They cannot endorse the compromise of those founding values and principles that have endured over time and that constitute the foundational elements of identity, charism, and mythic history of the community. On the other hand, conversation and dialogue around the contemporary meaning of communal identity—no matter how divergent our understandings may be—is of critical importance and should not be shied away from in spurious hopes that differences will disappear. But to entertain that the fundamental identity of the group is open for negotiation is to promote disunity, disintegration, and ultimate demise. Membership in the group has become meaningless.

A few examples: one can be a part of a group called psychologists and struggle with reformulations and new constructs relative to the study of personality and behavior. But to assert that the study of behavior and personality is no longer relevant to the discipline of psychology is to move oneself outside the identity of being a psychologist. Similarly, Dominicans can struggle with how to enflesh the mandate of the order to preach the gospel of Jesus Christ in today's world, or how they will name and address contemporary heresies, but they cannot say that they will replace the gospel of Jesus Christ as a foundation for that preaching mission with some other construct. To do so would be to move outside the identity of being Dominican. Likewise, when an individual experiences a loss of identity, that person moves into a profound state of confusion and terror. In the most dramatic sense of this phenomenon, the psychotic person has little or no awareness of who she is, what she is to be doing, or what meaning there is to her very existence. This is why the therapist, as an agent of responsive and responsible authority, must take swift action to protect her patient from further disintegration and potential self-destruction.

Likewise, good leaders take clear and directed action to protect the solidarity of the group, its commitment to unity in the face of challenges to its founding purpose, identity and mission. They do so by calling the group to reflection, prayer, and respectful engagement in dialogue. They, with the group, walk toward what is feared and claim their truth in faith and in commitment to the greater good.

Leaders in this era of connection live in the midst of ongoing and predictable diversity and differences (Lipman-Blumen, 8–21). Accordingly, they also live in the midst of the conflicts that arise from plurality of insight and thought. Any successful engagement in conflict between two or more parties must, then, be founded on certain assumptions: that there is a commitment on the part of all involved to learn from one another and to engage together in the search for truth; that there is an agreement to carry out the conversation to its conclusion; that mutual respect among peers is a prevailing value; and that no party will resort to oppressive or vindictive strategies during or after the conversation. Those leaders who will succeed will possess an internal disposition of grace, flexibility, balance, empathy, courage, creativity, as well as a heavy dose of curiosity about the different and unusual. But it is important to reiterate that even these qualities are insufficient if leaders themselves are frightened or unclear about or uncommitted to what constitutes the identity of the group that they have been called to serve.

It is also important to say that without mutual commitment to basic assumptions pertinent to effective conflict management, there is little purpose in devoting time and energy to engagement. There comes a time when evasion, or avoidance, or a direct naming of the lack of benefit in carrying out a discussion any further may, actually, be an effective strategy. Our problem has been that we have often resorted to these strategies prior to attempting to work more proactively with the conflictual situation.

Guarding against Groupthink

The greater the extent of ambiguity in a particular situation, the more likely it is for a leadership group to fall into what some group analysts refer to as "groupthink." This is a dangerous dynamic which arises when, in the face of adversity or perceived danger, a cohesive in-group (for purposes of this discussion, a leadership team) insulates itself from conflict with the out-group, that is, the larger membership. It does this by concurrence-seeking and unquestioning agreeableness among the in-group members. Fundamentally, groupthink interferes with leadership's ability to act on behalf of the common good because it has closed off alternative courses of action. It falls into a tight-knit, closed system in which team members avoid deviating from consensus. The in-group thus shares an illusion of unanimity concerning most of its judgments and positions. In the worst scenario, certain members of the in-group (leadership team) unwittingly assume the role of "mindguards" who protect the leader and other in-group members from adverse information that might break their sense of well-being about the perceived success of their past decisions.

Groupthink results, therefore, from a largely unconscious effort on the part of a leadership group to fortify itself in ambiguous, conflictual times, against perceived threats from the out-group. It is characterized by the in-group feeling a certain invulnerability and over-optimism about the future. This happens because negative feedback has been dismissed as a result of rationalizing and stereotyping the behavior of the disagreeing others as being invalid, irrelevant, erroneous, disloyal or uninformed. The search for truth has thus been compromised both within the leadership group itself and in the aborted possibility of sincere engagement with the out-group. When diversity of thought has been stifled within a leadership group, stagnation, boredom and a lack of internal resilience set in. Underlying this experience is often a misunderstanding of consensus which masquerades as a kind of non-hieratic, more feminist model of managing disagreement and decision making.

Groupthink is especially serious and should not be underestimated. It is a known fact of group analysis that the membership of any large group reflects the deficiencies of its leaders. When diversity of opinion, conflict and serious dialogue find little or no room for expression in the leadership group, the membership will unconsciously respond, mirror or react, ultimately jeopardizing the common good.

In order to counter the unconscious pull toward groupthink, leadership teams may wish to set in place certain safeguards. For example, set in place strategies for critical evaluation of decisions and actions which include evaluators from outside the team itself; probe for alternatives before coming to agreement; encourage processes focused on surfacing different ways of addressing a given dilemma; broaden the decision-making base with consultation from persons from different disciplines and areas of expertise; after a period of time apart, hold a second chance session to readdress the issue; ask the question about too much unanimity.

Promoting Efficacious Communal Action

Leadership teams which manage conflict well and avoid the traps associated with groupthink instill in their communities the belief that it is, indeed, possible for something important and significant to come from concerted communal action directed toward the greater good (Bandura). If a community has little sense that it is making a difference as a group it will experience organizational anxiety, corporate depression and an intensified fear about a danger-filled future. It also will not attract members to join it. On the other hand, leaders who work well with conflict and thereby promote the internal unity of the community model a capacity, through a clear commitment to pursue truth together, to make a difference in this world of ours. They exemplify a certain fearlessness and passion in repeatedly calling the group to fidelity to its identity in mission. It is a proven fact that, if all else is equal, the group that is more unified and clear about its identity and mission will endure beyond the group that is fragmented. In other words, integration and unification contribute to life; disintegration and fragmentation, to demise.

Religious know well that the desire to flourish is not an end in itself. Rather, we choose life as members of religious institutes because we are committed to radical discipleship. We commit ourselves to a vowed life in community in order to make a difference—for the poor, the oppressed, the vulnerable and the abandoned in our world. We believe we can do this better because we are united as sisters and, so, we invite others to walk with us. We do this not simply to bolster our sense of well-being, but because we believe desperately in the mission of Jesus to promote justice and right-relationships among peoples, between individuals and their God, among all who dwell upon this planet. And we know that this work is not finished. We invite others to join us in this connective mission of pursuing what is true, what is just, what is merciful and who ultimately is the One who unites us all.

Most congregations have identified issues critical to the common good of our society today. In numbers of communities across North America there is a remarkable consensus on the issues religious perceive as critical. Whether through chapter acts, vision statements or communal goals, concerns pertaining to the environment, racism, spirituality and the needs of women and the economically poor and oppressed continue to surface. These concerns are cited with deep compassion and the commitment to live the gospel as wholeheartedly as possible.

I was watching in awe as the NASA scientists shared their excitement as they realized they had together accomplished something absolutely awesome. This team of women and men was jubilant as they recognized that their dreams, their hard work and their collaboration offered us earthlings a chance to see another world. They were passionate. They did something fantastic and offered it freely to the world as millions of us plugged into the internet and participated in the unfolding events.

I do not believe for a moment that our dreams and our hard work on behalf of those who are oppressed and abandoned are any less altruistic than those NASA scientists. Why is it, then, that when it comes to addressing these serious needs we seem not to engender that same sense of excitement and passion and corporate accomplishment among ourselves, not to mention, among others? This was the question I found myself pondering—I must admit, with a little tinge of sadness—as I watched the ongoing televised press briefings.

Religious want to make a difference in the mission; we want to see something come of all our hard work. We want to know that we are participating in something that makes a tangible difference in our world. We long for that unimaginable excitement and passion that comes with the knowledge that something important has been achieved as a result of those dreams, those visions, that enormous degree of commitment and hard work. When a group lacks the sense of anything much happening from a colossal output of effort, the group begins to experience itself as not very worthwhile, not very efficacious. What follows is a series of negative corporate consequences: heightened individualism, attrition of membership, loss of meaning and identity, corporate malaise.

While many religious, as individual members, experience a degree of satisfaction in knowing that we are addressing those compelling needs identified through our chapter processes, the query persists: are we perhaps depriving ourselves of the possibility of corporate magnanimous accomplishment? Have congregate individual good works superseded the ability to do something passionately, and concretely, together? What might it mean if we were to specify concretely what we will do together as members of individual congregations, or perhaps as all women religious in concert, to make a monumental contribution to the well-being of the oppressed, to the well-being of mother earth?

Frequently, as religious begin to entertain thoughts of concerted and clearly defined, concrete communal endeavors, we conjure up our worst memories of the past. The urgency of the needs of these times, however, demands that we let go of that history and with new eyes and wonderful imagination begin to tap into our corporate passion in re-visioned effort to address the good that we hold in common.

Religious have the dedication, the commitment, the vision, and a mission that is larger than the NASA team. We are attuned to needs that make a Martian endeavor pale. Oppression and exploitation are no strangers to us. The exploitation of our planet, of the abandoned, of women and children is daily addressed by wonderful women religious all over this continent and beyond. But now is a time for us to come together in ways we have never imagined to make an even greater difference.

John Paul II underscores the significance of the ecological link as a driving force in this communal mission as religious move together toward a future in which we desire to make this difference:

> the earth is ultimately a common heritage, the fruits of which are for the benefit of all. . . . It is manifestly unjust that a privileged few should continue to accumulate excess goods, squandering available resources, while masses of people are living in conditions of misery at the very lowest level of subsistence. Today, the dramatic threat of ecological breakdown is teaching us the extent

to which greed and selfishness—both individual and collective—are contrary to the order of creation, an order which is characterized by mutual interdependence . . . simplicity, moderation and discipline, as well as a spirit of sacrifice, must become part of everyday life, lest all suffer the negative consequences of the careless habits of a few. . . . An education in ecological responsibility is urgent; responsibility for oneself, for others, and for the earth. . . . (466–67)

Engaging together in this efficacious action on behalf of the common good calls each of us to a deeper expression of our personal value and meaning as well as enables us as communities to unleash communal energy toward the promotion of the well-being of all. To lead on behalf of the common good is as exciting as it is heroic. To stay centered on the ultimate vision of unity; to manage conflict in service of what is true, faithful and just; to stand committed to the unfolding meaning of our identity in mission is the substance of leaders who invite conversion and the linking of spirits and hearts at a time when not to do so is, likely, to toy with death.

Steering Clear of Resistance

Finally, a word or two of caution. Temptations to distract attention from the demands of such a ministry of spiritlinking leadership abound. For any leader to allow herself to become caught up in energy-draining endeavors focused on individual need and maintaining the status quo is to entrench herself and her congregation in resistance. It is to deplete energy from individuals and from the community as a whole.

It is tempting to allow time to be captured by individual crises and attention to the aberrant behavior of a few. Leaders can bind anxiety by engaging in seemingly interminable discussions around how to manage crises—many of these deliberations better left to the mental health community or to others who are more expert in resolving the situation expeditiously. Recognizing the difference between getting caught up in crisis management and working with the crisis in order to promote the common good is an art form that requires continual attention and development. Leaders must guard against the enticement to bind our anxiety about the future by distracting ourselves in lengthy preoccupation with maintenance tasks which seemingly lend a temporary sense of concrete accomplishment to a day's work. They also must also guard against a certain emotional and behavioral passivity that simply lulls them into a tolerance of diversity without restraint.

In the end, individual efforts may well be accomplished, but the larger vision of the community's contemporary identity in mission is relegated to some hypothetical time in the future. When the promotion of the unity of the group in its response to the crying needs of the people of God and creation is overshadowed by leadership's over-attention to member's individual self-comfort and personal gratification or the inability to articulate boundaries and limitations on those behaviors which stand to harm the greater good, then something is radically wrong.

Obviously any group has a number of maintenance tasks that need attention. It is questionable, however, what portion of time and energy should be spent on those tasks by those who are entrusted with leading today. Honest self-monitoring and evaluation of the use of team time is an important reality test for a leadership group. Alternative procedures are in continual need of creative redesign in order to free leaders to lead—not simply to manage.

Conclusion

This is a moment when we need leaders to call one another and call our communities to heroism; to call us to risk entering into those conflictual conversations that will connect us in trust and in hope to one another; to lead into the midst of those difficult dialogues that will bring us into deeper and more respectful relationship with all those who long for a church, a society, and a world in which communion in spirit and truth prevail; to risk calling us to concrete corporate ministerial responses; to invite us to passion; to help us to face together the different, the other, the frightening, and the unexpected. We need leaders who call us to discover ever more deeply that the good which we hold in common is nothing less than the participation in the compassionate goodness and mystery of God.

Works Cited

Bandura, A. "Human Agency: The Emperor Does Have Clothes." Keynote Address, Canadian Psychological Association Convention, June 1997.

Bellah, R., et al. *The Good Society*. New York: Alfred A. Knopf, 1991.

Claremont de Castillejo, I. *Knowing Woman, A Feminine Psychology.* New York: Harper Colophon Books, 1974.

Hollenback, D. "The Common Good Revisited." *Theological Studies* 50 (1989): 70–94.

———. "The Catholic University and the Common Good." *Current Issues in Higher Education* 16, no. 1 (1995).

John Paul II. "Peace with All Creation." *Origins* 19, no. 28 (1989): pp. 465–68.

Lipman-Blumen, J. *The Connective Edge: Leading in an Interdependent World.* San Francisco: Jossey Bass, 1996.

Owen, Harrison. *Spirit. Transformation and Development in Organizations.* Potomac, Md.: Abbott Publishing, 1987.

Rivers, F. *The Way of the Owl: Succeeding with Integrity in a Conflicted World.* San Francisco, Harper, 1996.

Roszak, T., M. E. Gomes, and A. D. Kanner, ed. *Ecopsychology: Restoring the Earth, Healing the Mind.* San Francisco: Sierra Club Books, 1995.

Tracy, D. *Plurality and Ambiguity: Hermeneutics, Religion, Hope.* San Francisco: Harper and Row, 1987.

Whyte, D. *The Heart Aroused: Poetry and the Preservation of the Soul in Corporate America.* New York: Currency Doubleday, 1994.

Wren, J. T., ed. *The Leader's Companion: Insights on Leadership through the Ages.* New York: The Free Press, 1995.

10.

◆

The mandate following Vatican Council II to religious congregations to hold renewal chapters within three years and to consult all the members in preparation opened up a Pandora's box of questions about, suggestions for, and negative assessments of religious life as it was being experienced. Central to the issues were the congregations' attitudes toward their individual members. For too long the superior/subject relationships had hindered psychological growth and held the members in states of arrested development. But at the same time they were being highly educated to assume positions of responsibility in schools, health care institutions, and comparable ministries. Early general chapters in the process of renewal addressed the problems and made decisions to enable the members to become full adult women in the freedom with which Christ had made them free.

◆

For the Sake of the Gospel

Virginia O'Reilly, OP

The up-to-date renewal of the religious life comprises both a constant return to the sources of Christian life in general, and to the primitive inspiration of the institutes, and their adaptation to the changed conditions of our time. (PC 2)

Introduction

This article tells the story of the response of one congregation of Dominican sisters to the Vatican II mandate for the renewal of religious life. The mode of life common among sisters at the time was often in conflict with the pressing needs of the people they served. We can now see that the sister's lifestyle at this period was better adapted to earlier cultural norms than to the needs of the people of God in mid-century America. At the time of the renewal chapter in 1968, these issues were confused, nebulous, difficult to identify precisely. It was in the process of renewal that what needed to be done gradually became clear. Now, from the perspective of over thirty years, it is possible to examine the effects of the chapter of renewal on the individual sister as an important help in the effective communication of the gospel to people of a complex society.

The story of this one congregation of women religious is similar in substance to the story of many religious groups who labored to build the church in the United States during the last hundred years. In the establishment of the parochial school system, health care facilities, and social service agencies, emphasis was on the provision of institutions to meet the needs of the immigrant church. The institutions were necessary to serve the faith community in a largely unfriendly Protestant world. The services provided by Catholic sisters were uniquely fitted to the survival needs of the immigrants, as well as to the acceptance of the Catholic community within the larger society.

The effects of this monumental institutional development on the individual sister were often unfortunate. The needs of the institutional ministry were primary; the needs of the individual sister were routinely subsumed to the needs of the institution to which she was assigned. By mid-century, anachronistic practices, and the residuals of the structured mode of operation that had obtained earlier, resulted in increased incidents of role conflict for the individual sister. The ministry of the sister in the early fifties was no longer primarily to European immigrants. The success of earlier efforts meant that many of the immigrants, together with the Catholic Church itself, had become a mainstream social force in the United States. The sister practiced her ministry in the modern postwar Western world, a technically-oriented and highly individualized society. In the Third World, a new consciousness of developing cultures focused ministry on awakening people's sense of their rights as human beings, and in supporting people's efforts to help themselves.

Both forms of ministry required a sister with a positive self-image, articulate, able to make independent decisions at the level of her competencies, confident of her personal worth and the primacy of her mission, clear and unambiguous in her loyalty to the gospel and its values. The challenge of the renewal chapters was to identify and modify those aspects of the religious lifestyle of the period that served as obstacles to such ministry.

Historical Influences

The concentrated effort to *do* things for people struggling to survive in unfamiliar surroundings characteristic of the immigrant period became, in current circumstances, an effort to *enable* persons to do things for themselves. The institutional approach was beginning to be replaced by an individualized approach to ministry more in keeping with the complexities of contemporary society. It would not be an easy transition: the structures of religious life which had sustained the very difficult burden of the past had become familiar and dear to sisters still in active ministry. Women religious in the United States had flourished as a result of their ministry to European immigrants. Cloister practices, maintained long past their utility, were cherished as evidence that in entering religious life, the sister had made a complete break with the world. The people who had benefited from the ministry of the sisters loved them and supported and protected them and their works. The sisters were valued and praised for their service.

But winds of change were blowing both in secular society and in the church. In the early 1960s it became apparent that "a social class system, based on race and ethnicity, long in place, and reinforced by religion" (Neal 1994, 127), no longer met the needs of society. The global reason for this was the demise of colonialism, and the growing awareness among people of Third World countries of their rights.

The declaration of human rights by the United Nations in 1948 affirmed the right to freedom and to the resources for life to all as equal human beings, sharing the same nature and hence the same rights and responsibilities. This declaration affirmed the need for the same education together with others so that peoples might teach and learn from each other. Possession of enormous wealth and power by the few, while many people have less than they need to live with dignity, was recognized by the church as a problem.

A New Understanding of the Mission of the Church

The promulgation of Peace on Earth (*Pacem in terris*) was Pope John XXIII's contribution to the developing awareness of human rights apparent as the twentieth century advanced. The pope recognized that a new world order would result from the United Nations's recognition of human rights. Procedures and norms persisting from other centuries and different understandings of the human condition were still operational in the life of the church. A general restructuring was needed to free the church from flawed assumptions about human inferiority and superiority that undergird socioeconomic structures which served to perpetuate the advantage of some and the misery of others (cf. Neal 1990, 40). John XXIII convened Vatican II in order to eliminate customs and rules that violated contemporary understandings of human rights. "Pope John XXIII had already written about this in *Mater et magistra* in 1961, noting that the Church in Latin America was far too closely linked with oppressive political economies. He further elaborated this theme in *Pacem in terris* (151–56), where he claimed that peace, poverty, and human rights are the concerns of committed Christians everywhere" (Neal 1990). This "opening of the windows" resulted in a new understanding of the mission of the church, an understanding that was the culmination of a hundred years of Vatican teaching, through which the church has explicitly committed itself to the special option for the poor (cf. Dorr; Neal 1990, 40–41).

This change in the church's understanding of its mission led to one of the most influential documents of Vatican II, the Pastoral Constitution on the Church in the Modern World (*Gaudium et spes*) which "invited Christians to review their customs and traditions in order to purge them of sinful structures, that is, of rules that brought death rather than life to suffering multitudes" (Neal 1990, 41).

Several influences earlier in the century had presaged this change in the church's understanding of its mission. Prominent among these was the new and vigorous return to the study of the scriptures, and the acceptance of the centrality of the Word of God in the life of the church. The complexity of moral issues surrounding World War II, especially the Nazi experiment and the use of the atomic bomb to win the war; postwar dilemmas such as those posed by contemporary medical practices, in particular at the beginning and end of human life; the ethical issues regarding the exploitation of underdeveloped peoples; all of these presented the church with new and very difficult challenges. The church's ability to respond to these pressing needs of modern women and men was hampered by the accretions that left certain of its ministries anomalies in contemporary society.

One result of this change in the understanding of the mission of the church was the Vatican II document Decree on the Up-to-Date Renewal of Religious Life (*Perfectae caritatis*). This document mandated that religious adapt and renew every part of their lives. Customs and practices of another time needed to be examined and perhaps abandoned in order for the religious to serve the needs of persons in contemporary society. Pope Paul VI issued the Apostolic Letter *Ecclesia sancta* (ES), which set norms for the implementation of renewal in religious communities. The most important provision of this document was the mandate that every congregation was to hold a special general chapter within three years to determine the lines of its renewal. By renewal two things were meant: first, a return to the sources of a Christian life (the Scriptures), and secondly, a return to the original charism (inspiration) of a congregation. Adaptation was to be the adjustment of the norms and practices of the congregation to facilitate the communication of the gospel message in contemporary society. The purpose of this review of all aspects of life in religious communities was to eliminate naivetés that were standing in the way of the new direction the mission of the church was taking.

In order to carry out the new understanding of the mission of the church, a move away from the prior emphasis on institutional norms in ministry was required. This need presented a difficult challenge. Here in the United States, just at the period when the successful integration of both the church and the descendants of immigrants into the structures of American society was occurring, changes in the society around them as well as new ideas on the church's mission as expressed in the Constitution on the Church in the Modern World (*Lumen gentium*) had marked the end of an era.

American Cultural Experience

The American preference for participation in matters that affect one's life, learned since childhood, involves a belief in the dignity of the individual. This belief made the understanding and application of such Vatican II principles as collegiality and coresponsibility seem reasonable and natural to the American sister. A common experience for many sisters, in the role of teacher, had been active participation in the process of helping young Americans mature as responsible citizens. The ability to differentiate between unity and uniformity, the capacity to accept diversity, to safeguard the rights of all parties, were not only part of a sister's heritage as an American, they were part of her ministry as an American sister. In the effort to make the changes necessary to participate in the new understanding of the mission of the church, the sister listened to the message of Thomas E. Clarke, SJ, with considerable enthusiasm. "Your special call," he said, "is to be a channel by which the distinctly American experience of freedom, and all that is noble and enduring in it, is more fully assimilated into the life of the church all over the world" (CMSW National Assembly 1958: qtd. in Quinonez and Turner 76). This advice was not lost on the delegates to the Adrian Dominican General Chapter of Renewal in 1968.

Professionalism

The postwar development of technology and the emphasis on the individual in first-world nations provided a new and very challenging context for the work of the sisters. Particularly in America, where the demand for professional credentials accelerated between 1920 and 1950, sisters obtained university training during the summers and on weekends, as well as in full-time study in some cases. Since the demand for her services was increasing, and the obligations of the religious life unchanging, a sister was sometimes placed in a difficult set of circumstances as she attempted to fulfill all of her obligations. These and other efforts to prepare women religious to assume professional roles as they engaged in the apostolate had another beneficial aspect:

> The competencies developed by religious in the many secular fields required for their professional ministries had the additional effect of providing them with critical tools of analysis that they began to apply to their own personal development and their social organization as religious institutes. (Foley 1997, 7)

This phenomenon became evident as the delegates to the renewal chapter began their work in the summer of 1968. Of particular interest is the interactive aspect of the delegates' use of their professional competencies. Sister Jeanne O'Laughlin, an expert in futures planning, provided the chapter as a whole with the language that enabled the delegates to clarify the diversity evident in the group's readiness for new ideas. Terms like "early innovator" and "late adapter" on a continuum of change acknowledged the important differences in a sister's readiness for change, and granted respectability and acceptance to diverse positions. This terminology facilitated attentiveness to the unique attitude and experience of the individual sister. The delegates at the renewal chapter were women whose formal education equipped them to work as professional educators, social workers and health care personnel. Sharing their lived experience of almost three hundred diocesan or congregation-owned institutions throughout the United States and in Latin America clarified for them the need for change in their way of life as women religious. The delegates identified interaction among themselves as the most significant factor moving the individual (and thus the group) toward change (Lefebvre, 2).

Role Conflict

The sister, who during the primacy of institutional ministries had been largely invisible, was, in the 1960s, prominent among her professional peers as she exercised her ministry. A sister lawyer competent to plead cases before the Supreme Court of the United States was influential in immigration matters and civic affairs, as well as in the lives of the young women students she mentored. Grant funding was obtained by a sister scientist to further her own research, but in addition, to provide opportunities for her students to participate not only in her research, but in its presentation to her professional peers, both at home and abroad.

In ministry settings, the sisters acted as adults according to the norms of their professional competencies. The sister CEO of a hospital negotiated with state and civic officials, and in addition to running the institution effectively, served as chairperson of the state hospital association in California. The curricula of an elementary public school district was enriched by a sister in dramatic arts, who introduced spontaneous drama as a teaching tool and instructed the public school faculty in this art, which she had learned in England while on a Kellogg Foundation Grant. A high school guidance counselor taught for several summers in a leadership formation program, where she was not only the sole sister, but the only woman who was a staff member. An art teacher did exemplary work in her painting and in her professional exhibits, and became a professor of art at a leading university.

The clash of cultures between ministry and the professional competencies it required, and minutiae of permissions and schedules as they were practiced in traditional convents often produced frustration for the sister minister, as well as moments of comic relief. A high school guidance counselor sometimes had to leave an interaction with a troubled adolescent in order to be on time for the 4:30 P.M. choral recitation of the office. The dramatics arts teacher's professional judgment regarding costumes for a school play was overruled by her superior, who preferred another color for the leading character. A science teacher, whose students had won both state and national awards for the excellence of their science projects, was rebuked by her superior for having her picture in the city newspaper without explicit permission.

This notion of obedience, based on the concept of the submission of the will of the subject to that of the superior, was contrary to the Dominican tradition of consensus in the choice of effective ministerial procedures (McCabe, 282–86). The conflict sometimes experienced by the sister in the pre–Vatican II period resided in the substitution of a superior's judgment, for that of an educated professional woman in the area of her competence. The confusion was the long-held tradition that separated religious life from life in the "world." The ministry of the sister was set in the world. According to this paradigm, the primacy of her religious observance superseded the demands of her ministry. It was not necessary that any conflict should have arisen here, since the custom of dispensation has been one of the earliest traditions of the Dominican Order. These incidents are cited to illustrate how the legalism of "strict observance" of the rules governing the lifestyle of the sister in some cases took precedence over charity and common sense, as well as being contrary to the tradition of the Dominican Order. The most important point to be made, of course, is that such a rigid interpretation interfered with the ministry of the sister.

The delegates who made up the Dominican Life committee for the first session of the Adrian Dominican Renewal Chapter were experientially aware of the conflicting demands made on the time and energies of each sister. Women religious followed a lifestyle where unresolved dichotomies in the relationships between cloister practices and the demands of Christian service were stressful for many sisters. In presenting goals to the chapter in the summer of 1968, the committee declared, "we want to face realistically the concrete situations in which our sisters find themselves, to take care not to offer the community a set of theoretical goals that are impractical and even impossible to aim at, let alone reach. We must be aware of the sisters, who are first of all persons with human needs" (Lefebvre, 54).

The phrase "the sisters, who are first of all persons with human needs" became a guiding principle for the general chapter of renewal. It is evident in the goals set by each committee as the work of the renewal chapter began. The local Adrian group who wrote the spring 1968 proposal to the general chapter recommending that "without neglecting her apostolic duties, a sister be free to act as a responsible adult to combat poverty, racism and war without 'special permission' " (Lefebvre, 3) highlighted the stress under which a sister often worked in her attempts to bridge the gap between her perception of the needs of the people of God and the separation from "the world" then current as proper for women religious.

The traditions of the Dominican Order were quite other. From the beginning of the Order, a democratic, collegial form of government was utilized. The revision of the Code of Canon Law in 1917 had not succeeded in removing some of the historical anachronisms that affected women religious. Sisters' lives, for example, were more minutely regulated than those of male religious. Although the sisters were restricted from the full exercise of the Dominican traditions of coresponsibility and collegiality by the fact that they were women, they were, without formal structures, able to live, by custom, within the spirit of this Dominican tradition. The major areas of conflict continued to be the dichotomy between the professional autonomy appropriate to the exercise of the ministry, and the passive dependency considered appropriate by some for the relationships between a superior and her subjects. This unfortunate dualism between the concept of "the City of God" (the Church and the spiritual life) and the "City of Man" (the world and human endeavor) (Quinonez and Turner, 34) was a legacy from the Greek philosophical roots of early theological writers like Augustine. It is encapsulated, like an insect in amber, in writings about religious life up to the present. Yet it is one view, and not the only view, of religious life. It is a historical remnant of the conditions under which early religious life forms emerged. In the dualistic view, to enter religious life meant to "leave the world." The Decree on the Up-to-Date Renewal of Religious Life said, by way of contrast:

> The manner of life, of prayer and of work should be suited to the physical and psychological conditions of today's religious. It

should also, insofar as this is permitted by an institute's character, be in harmony with the demands of the apostolate, with the requirements of culture and with the social and economic climate, especially in mission territories. The mode of government of the institutes should also be examined using the same criteria. For this reason, constitutions, directories, books of customs, of prayers, of ceremonies and such like should be suitably revised, obsolete prescriptions being suppressed, and should be brought into line with this synod's documents. (PC 3)

For the sister, this decree meant that constructs accepted without question from the earliest days of her religious formation were under evaluation.

The delegates of the 1968 renewal chapter, obedient to the requested examination of every aspect of their lives, eager to restore a structural mode more appropriate to a Dominican Congregation, and attentive to the concerns of the sisters as expressed in over a thousand proposals addressed to the delegates by the congregation at large, deliberated with care for the effect of their decisions on "the sisters, who first of all are persons with human needs." They were ready to make the basic structures of community life more responsive to the needs of the apostolate.

The 1968 general chapter reinstated the tradition of a local community chapter meeting monthly. This enactment made it possible for the sisters to make appropriate ministry decisions at the local level. It was a beginning, and a small one. As its implementation brought it effectively to the local level, the outmoded separation between "convent life" and "apostolate" came under discussion, sometimes heated discussion. It became apparent that new skills were needed: the ability to state opinions, to engage in discussions that led to decisions, to initiate ideas and programs and to share in activities resulting from the decisions. These were the burdens of the emphasis on personal freedom, and for the most part, the sisters responded eagerly, and set about learning the necessary skills. From this beginning would eventually emerge a new model of governance for the entire congregation (General Chapters, 1978 and 1982; cf. Lefebvre, 140–41). This governance plan was adopted later; the role conflict problem was in the process of being solved.

This 1968 decision to make appropriate ministry decisions at the local level was a fundamental change for the Adrian Dominican women. It affected the way in which they lived together in community, the responses they made to ministry, and how they would govern themselves within the congregation. In the best sense of radical, it went to the root of the confusion and stress reported by the sisters. As progress was made toward the development of a functional organization for governance oriented toward collegiality and coresponsibility, it became apparent that a new spirituality, based on concepts of personal and communal discernment, was evolving. Rather than the response to the "voice of authority" so long in vogue, a spirituality of response in obedience to the mission of the church was slowly coming into being. That spirituality was tentative, and still in process, yet clearly central to the new understanding of mission of the Adrian Dominicans and of many other congregations of sisters. For the Adrian sisters, it represents a return to their roots as Dominicans. Don Goergen, OP, clarifies what is involved:

> Spirituality is a particular way of being human. It cannot be imposed from the outside or enforced. Yet Christian spirituality never means "living only for God" while others in our history are given second place. Following Jesus can never be a mere repetition of some earlier form of Christian spirituality, but is rather Christian creativity in a historical context. Spirituality is always new adventure, with Abraham and Sarah as models. "They set out on a journey, not knowing where they were going" (Heb. 11:8). (61)

Participative Process[38]

The participative process adopted by the Adrian Dominicans for use in the pre-chapter period and in the renewal chapter itself was an important element in focusing on the individual sister of this congregation. In her letter of December 2, 1966, Mother Mary Genevieve Weber, prioress of the congregation, reminded the members of the responsibility and privilege to which they were called by mandate of Vatican directives: "It is the duty of each sister to assist in evaluating and contributing her thinking to the very important work we are entering together" (ADA).

No facet of the sisters' lives was to be exempt from scrutiny, no individual's observations or experiences of Adrian Dominican life were to be disregarded as the renewal chapter agenda was prepared. Through

---

[38]Personal interview with Noreen McKeough, OP, a member of the central committee and of the pre-chapter commission who was later elected a general councillor by the renewal chapter of 1968.

Vatican II documents and available commentaries, the concepts of collegiality (the sharing of authority among colleagues) and coresponsibility gradually became better understood and accepted by the sisters. As a consequence, they came to realize the importance of each individual's contribution toward the chapter's agenda. During the years 1965–67, community members in each convent held discussions relating to the Vatican documents and to pertinent articles on the updating of religious life. As these discussions progressed, the need for regional networking was seen to be an important next step. Toward this end, thirteen geographical areas were designated, each one made up of sisters who elected an area representative. Proposals, questions and suggestions from individuals, local communities, or groups in each area were directed to the committee in that area. Committees categorized the submitted materials, which included position papers on topics of special interest to some regions. In 1967, the thirteen area representatives came together to form a central committee, thus bringing the networking process to a new level.

In the summer of 1967, this group was assigned the task of formulating a revised constitution that would incorporate the directives from Rome and reflect more accurately the life of contemporary Adrian Dominican Sisters. Sequestered for six weeks, the central committee worked on a proposed constitution, basing their efforts on the study of Scripture, reflection, and dialogue. After consultation with a canon lawyer, the group finished the proposed document and presented it to the general council, who received it with approval.

Eventually the proposed constitution was rejected by the renewal chapter. Although it had served as a breakthrough from the outdated earlier constitution, the delegates felt that it was premature, since it had been written prior to the renewal chapter. As the central committee communicated with the congregation in the summer of 1967, it became clear that the role of a general chapter was not well understood. This misperception was generally true of religious congregations, as noted by Theodore Vittoria, SSP, in an article on "The Powers of the General Chapter." Vittoria pointed out that the general chapter while in session is the supreme legislative authority in the congregation; the major superior and the councilors are mandated to carry out the enactments of this governing body, according to the constitutions of the institute. The major superior and councilors are, in effect, the administrators or executive body in the congregation (Lefebvre, 23).

One of the first actions of the central committee had been to submit a proposal to the council for the election of a pre–chapter commission.

The final phase of general chapter preparation was identified as the responsibility of this commission. The proposal was accepted. In the July 28, 1967, Central Committee Bulletin for Adrian Dominican Renewal (Lefebvre, 24), the duties of the newly elected pre-chapter commission members were listed as: (1) agenda preparation for the general chapter; (2) preparation for the intelligent voting of the capitulars; (3) involvement of each sister in the study and discussion of provisional documents prepared by the central committee in response to the material submitted by the sisters.

Emphasized in this bulletin was the role of the commission members as communicators. These women were to disseminate information from the regions to the whole congregation and listen carefully to the response of the sisters. The commission was to organize the material resulting from these discussions into a form suitable for use by the chapter delegates. The sisters were reminded very clearly that the chapter delegates could act only on those consequential elements that the individual sister had presented to the commission during the period of concentrated renewal.

During the last period of chapter preparation, two concerns remained at the level of the individual sister. The first of these was to engage in a study/writing/dialogue process centered on the proposed constitution, and the second was group study of issues already raised in the congregation and distributed as study papers by the pre-chapter commission. The sister was asked to recommend actions on these issues through her established representatives.

The participative process used in the pre-chapter preparation period carried over into the conduct of the general chapter itself. The delegates quickly voted the necessary changes to allow any interested sister to witness most sessions. They admitted as full chapter delegates two sisters elected as representatives of the sisters in temporary vows. Although the process used in the Adrian Dominican Congregation has been regarded as an example, every congregation was under the same mandate from Vatican II. The effect of this process on the sisters was remarkable. It made it possible for them to realize that their life in ministry was meant to be life-giving, not just for those they served, but for themselves. A new appreciation of the saying of Saint Irenaeus (second century) developed, "The glory of God is the human person fully alive," as well as a deeper understanding of the work that remained to be done in this area.

Self-Study

The need for a survey of the congregation's personnel and resources was identified by several sisters as basic to the deliberations of the chapter delegates. Legislated during the 1968 summer session of the renewal chapter, the survey was planned to address the task in two ways. A professional organization, Nelson Associates, was engaged to study the sister's ministerial outlook, her works and their effectiveness. The Adrian Synthesis, designed by a committee of delegates, addressed the sister's attitudes on various aspects of her personal life. The individual sister was central to each study. The survey in 1969 was the first attempt to ask every member of the congregation her opinions and feelings about religious life. In order to encourage participation and frank responses, the survey was anonymous. The return rate was 98 percent. Membership in the Congregation at the time of the Synthesis was 2,323.

Evidence of the care taken to involve each sister in this process is seen in the introduction to the Synthesis:

One of the major factors which this questionnaire attempts to investigate, in a number of ways, is *change*, especially to gain some knowledge of the number of sisters who hold a view of the Church, religious life, the congregation, and their own religious life as developing or adaptive. Attitudes toward change would seem to be fundamental determiners of the sisters' readiness to accept efforts in renewal particularly those which affect the apostolic orientation of the congregation. (Foley 1969)

The results of the Synthesis were distributed to the members of the congregation. Each sister was asked to prepare a written response to questions posed by a workshop coordinator in her area. These responses were discussed and analyzed at a regional workshop: the thinking of the sisters in the region was summarized and these regional reports were collated and distributed to the general chapter delegates. The use of consultants assisted the delegates to understand the implications of the Synthesis from the perspectives of sociology, psychology, and theology.

Sociologist William C. McCready noted the concern of some sisters about personal objectives that may or may not correspond to those of the order. He noted strong support for the concept that the proper role of the superior is as a facilitator of collegial decisions (see Radcliffe, 138–47 for a current presentation of this concept). He saw the renewal process as meeting the needs of this group to confront the contemporary world, and the opinion of most sisters that it is moving at a good pace. The question he posed to the delegates was: "to what use will this data be put?"

Psychologist Sister Mary Grace Davis, SND, emphasized that in the past, leaders utilized the information available to them. She noted that at the present time more sophisticated means for getting information is available to assist in the decision-making process. The data indicate that certain choices are imperative: the sisters are hurting. One conflictual area is fear of change: the sister can often see the need for change, but her feelings are against change. Davis saw the clarification of the goal of this group, why it exists, as essential. Some sisters question the validity of religious life if familiar customs are abandoned.

Davis noted that women religious were a product of the very authoritarian culture of the church, and were known for conformity within the church. Personal security for an individual sister came from the approval of superiors. Courage was required to risk rejection because of personal opinions. The temptation to close off those who differ from the general opinion had to be resisted lest the work of the chapter suffer. In the Synthesis, distrust, not only of people in authority, but of each other, came through.

Davis was concerned about the attitude toward failure that surfaced in the Synthesis. The confusion in the minds of some sisters between failure in an activity, and personal failure, were interlocked very closely for many women religious, and this was evident in the Synthesis data. This fear of failure could be seen in the need for approval from authority before any initiative is put into action. Davis felt that women religious should be giving great witness to Christian joy and freedom; often, instead, they were giving witness to fear (8).

Theologian Benedict Ashley, OP, gave another helpful commentary on the Synthesis results. For our purposes, his identification of two broad groups in the congregation, the group professed less than thirty-five years (80 percent) and those professed more than thirty-five years (22 percent) is illustrative. He attributed the disparity between these two broad groups, who were by no means homogeneous, to a cultural lag. "The real cause of the polarization is the fact that the adaptation of religious life to changed cultural conditions was long overdue. Because religious communities failed to change gradually they are now faced with the much harder task of making radical changes all at once" (6). Within the larger group, Ashley identified the sisters professed from five to seventeen years, 37 percent of the total membership at the time, as "those who have felt the need for change, and have experienced the difficulties of a rapid transition more strongly than any other group, because they were formed under the older system without being convinced of its realism or value" (7). This is the group in a "dynamic condition." They are the most discontent, the most questioning, the most confused, the most full of proposals for change. This is the group that furnishes the starkest contrast to the elder sisters of the community.

Ashley noted that the church was reluctantly moving from the post-Reformation stance of "fortress church" to the twentieth century and post–Vatican II stance of "pilgrim church." The difficult transition in religious life was a reflection of this same problem. He saw the historic transition of the whole human family into the age of modern technology as the basic motivating force in these changes.

Among the recommendations that Ashley made to the delegates as "most urgent" was a program of continuing theological education that would permit every sister to understand the reasons behind the changes. He felt this was the only way that older members would see the new spirituality as truly Catholic. From this understanding Ashley felt that older members would appreciate that young people possess spirituality as a deep conviction. Furthermore, he suggested experimentation specifically in the area of the spiritual life. In addition, in accord with the mandates of Vatican II, he recommended that a greater degree of attention be given to the study of the congregation, and of the Dominican Order.

The need to press resolutely ahead was emphasized by Ashley, who felt that faltering at this point would only prolong the struggle. It is true that changes had gone too fast, but they were long overdue. "We must be firm in going to the root of the matter. We must construct a spirituality which is truly viable and livable in this twentieth century and open to the twenty-first, or we will not have been faithful to the Gospel" (1969, 11).

The delegates used the results of the Nelson Associates and Adrian Synthesis studies in the formulation of general chapter policies. One such policy emphasized the individual sister as the congregation's first concern, and placed coresponsibility for the congregation's life and mission as a duty of each sister. Other legislation provided for the continuing religious formation of each sister.

Recognition of the sisters themselves as the Congregation's primary resource led to efforts to develop the spiritual gifts of each sister through the Theology Institute at Siena Heights College (1971–74). A total of 814 Adrian Dominicans participated in these summer theology programs; many sisters returned for a second, third, and fourth summer. In addition to the Theology Institute, efforts were made to offer sisters opportunities for spiritual and psychological growth by workshops, seminars, and weekend retreats at both the generalate and provincial levels.

The Adrian Synthesis revealed a wide diversity among the sisters. The response to this diversity was a policy that stated in part that "diversity of thought and expression is integral to . . . basic unity of spirit in prayer, in communal life, and in apostolic purpose" (EGCR, p. 1, ADA). The form of prayer which became the norm for the local community was "communal prayer rooted in Scripture," and each local group chose the form most acceptable to the sisters.

The choice of residence made by the sisters was supported by congregational officers at the generalate and provincial levels. These choices made a wide diversity of lifestyle possible. Sisters chose to wear either the habit or contemporary garb. The kind and nature of the apostolic ministries chosen by the sisters widened, as a policy for open placement was implemented. The number of local communities increased, and the goals and objectives of each group were determined by the sisters themselves (Lefebvre, 56–57, 97).

In the area of the apostolate one of the first realizations was that the Congregation was overextended in the sense that it had committed itself to more places of service than it had personnel available. After making a study of the parish school commitments, and designating certain ones for the withdrawal of personnel, the directors of the apostolate in each province followed up the study with visits to all the school superintendents involved. They explained the need for the reduction of personnel they could supply to the schools, and the criteria upon which the decision had been based. It was this initial step that paved the way for further implementation of policies related to the individual sister in ministry.

At the time of the formulation of the policy on government in 1969, the renewal chapter sponsored a congregation-wide experience of collegial living. Since structure arises from need, the general council developed a program for discussion in the local community about the needs and expectations of the sisters for leadership on the local, provincial and generalate levels. These discussions of "Structures for Renewal" were influential in the subsequent provincial chapters. Chapters at this level were responsible for providing plans for government at the provincial/

vicariate level. The general chapter session of 1970 ratified each of the plans for governance that was presented. The central administrative level of the congregation emphasized a concept of service that would free the individual sister, the local community, the province and the congregation as a whole to serve the needs of the people of God. The results of both the objective and the subjective phases of the Adrian congregational self-study of 1968–1969 led the general chapter delegation to formulate a written statement of philosophy as consecrated women in celibate community, and to determine their basic objectives in the light of this philosophy.

This 1969 statement was a declaration of the principles at the foundation of Adrian Dominican corporate life and work. By the end of the final session of the general chapter of renewal on August 17, 1970, the Adrian Dominican women had rediscovered through the renewal process that their fundamental unity was indeed in "the love of Jesus Christ that brought them together." Updates of the Adrian Synthesis, broadened to include areas of mission and ministry originally done by the Nelson Associates study, were completed by members of the congregation for the 1972, 1977, and 1981 general chapters, when it was discontinued. By this time, most members had found living and ministry situations that corresponded with their personal talents and expectations and could agree that the congregation had provided a positive environment for diversity (Beres 1982, 26). The congregation owes the adaptation of 1,500 years of tradition in religious lifestyles to our complex and demanding contemporary period to both the sisters of the congregation, who surfaced the hurts, tensions, and difficulties they experienced, and to the delegates of the renewal chapter of 1968–70, who laid the foundation for the new structures. The courage and fortitude shown by all of these women, both in the renewal process and in the painful period of adaptation to new structures, is a testimonial to the obedience they showed to the Vatican mandate.

The renewal chapter of 1968 did not complete this task of adaptation. In a real sense, it is always an ongoing task. The renewal chapter did set in motion processes that enable the individual sister to be the full human person she is called to be by God and, for this reason, facilitated in an extraordinary way the "new sister" called for by the communication of the Gospel message in present-day society. This massive effort to adapt the lifestyle of women religious to a contemporary setting has not only changed the familiar structures to which these women were accustomed, but has required many changes on the part of those they serve. For these people, "the faithful," Vatican Council II has caused an examination of their faith and responsibilities that many found difficult. It is understandable that the response to change in the lives of women religious has been, for some, an added and unwelcome burden. But it is the Holy Spirit who calls both those of us who are women religious and those who have been such loyal and generous supporters of the sisters. Together, we respond to the call of the Spirit to go forward to the unknown future in the freedom of Christ, and in his love.

Psychological Issues

The participative process by means of which the Adrian Dominican Sisters prepared for and implemented the renewal chapter allowed for interaction among sisters regarding the most basic aspects of their religious lifestyle. Issues that had been the exclusive concern of persons in authority were subjected to an intensive analysis and discussion by the individual sisters. In-depth appreciation of the requirements of different geographical locations, as well as the needs of the individual sister in her ministerial responsibilities were shared, often for the first time, as sisters from different regions met and discussed proposals for the general chapter. The American preference for self-determination, largely in abeyance as the sister conformed to the accepted religious lifestyle, reasserted itself and energized the process for the individual sister, and for the group to which she belonged. The rigidity of previous forms of religious discipline sometimes had the unfortunate effect of arresting the sister's personal development at the level at which she had entered religious life, since the experiences that lead to mature adulthood, often involving painful mistakes, were usually not available to her. Since so many of the sisters came directly from high school, or, in some cases, even earlier, few prior opportunities had promoted self-determination or personal initiative. Certainly the pre–Vatican II structures of religious life were inhibiting to the sister's personal growth in many cases.

The heady experience of being consulted and listened to on issues previously unavailable for public examination, and the opportunity to submit proposals regarding these issues to the general chapter delegates enabled the individual sister, in many cases, to bridge the gap between the intellectual acumen she used in her educational and ministry responsibilities, and the passive acceptance of the direction of others sometimes required of her in her conventual life style. After learning in her early formation that her religious life meant that the realm of the sacred and the realm of the secular were distinct, it was revitalizing to realize that the world was an appropriate place for her apostolic involvement (Quinonez and Turner, 39).

Not all the effects of a more liberal approach to religious life were positive, certainly not immediately. For some sisters, the effort to achieve age-appropriate levels of personal development meant some painful choices on the way to greater maturity. Mistakes were made. This was difficult for the individual sister in the process of continued growth, and perhaps, at times, more so for the sisters who lived with her. But progress toward maturity meant a much more effective sister minister, and sisterly charity supported these efforts during the struggle of the sister to grow toward full adulthood. The reward for this sisterly love and concern was the presence of a stronger, steadier, mature woman. But since it is not possible to skip developmental stages, and necessary that each stage be "grown through," for the occasional sister, it took some time, and great patience on the part of all involved.

The development of psychology as a cultural influence in this country and the increase in the importance of the position of guidance counselor in high schools meant that an appreciable number of sisters had professional access to concepts of human and personal development that they were happy to share during the renewal process. As the sisters participated in science and other programs funded by the National Science Foundation, they enjoyed a mobility and access to technology that allowed contact with a variety of people with different norms. They experienced themselves as competent, not only academically, but socially and professionally, not because they were "sisters," but because of who they were as persons. They learned a new basis for group relationships and appreciated the change from authoritarianism to consensus, with the respectful acceptance of diverging views and alternate formulations of complex issues.

While some of the sisters found the renewal process exhilarating, many women religious found it painful and difficult. The dismantling of familiar structures, and their replacement by unfamiliar structures, caused severe stress for many. The speed with which this change process occurred in congregations of women religious increased the experience of stress, especially for older members. Rapid and repeated alterations in the person's environment often results in a loss of the sense of personal identity and a devaluation of cherished life meanings. In the earliest days of renewal, when a win/lose attitude surfaced in some situations, conflictual interactions shook both the "early innovators" and the "late adaptors" as they seemed to see either their bright hopes for newness or their cherished life-projects facing extinction. The Adrian Dominican Sisters attempted to mitigate this "change shock" by allowing a sister to choose both the changes she felt she wished to make and the time at which she wished to make them. Those who felt they could not change were encouraged to continue a lifestyle with which they felt comfortable. The ability of a sister to choose her place of residence as well as her ministry made it possible for like-minded sisters to group together in either old forms of life and ministry, or new forms, as they chose.

The sensitivity of the chapter delegates and the elected leaders was especially evident in the provision of support services at this time. Psychological services, study opportunities, especially in theology, and assistance with ministry placement were helpful to many of the sisters. Programs for sisters in mid-career, termed *Education for Life and Ministry,* as well as assistance with the aging process, called the *Penafort Program* after a Dominican saint famous for his productivity into old age, assisted sisters in special groups to deal with the change processes in a supportive environment among their age-mates. Summers of formation for sisters at stated intervals after profession, such as the fifteen year renewal, gave younger sisters the opportunity to process their own difficulties with change. When it became clear that the individual sister could choose the time and kind of change she felt ready to make, panic subsided.

The acceptance of diversity as a congregational policy eased much of the problem. At the same time, it is difficult to measure the real suffering undergone by a conscientious woman as she strove to comply with the directions of Vatican II. Although the initial response to the mandate of Vatican II for change was enthusiastic among the Adrian Dominican Sisters, the theoretical aspects of change (what should be changed, and why) and the incarnational aspects (i.e., doing it at the day-to-day level) did not enjoy the same welcome. As Davis commented in her report on the Adrian Synthesis, there was a preference for affiliation over the choice of structural change for many sisters (Davis, 6). There was evidence that the need for affiliation common to groups of women religious made it difficult for some of the Adrian Dominican women to change if such change meant a weakening of affiliative bonds.

Another concern identified by Davis was fear of rejection. Conformity was a strong influence in pre–Vatican II community life. Some sisters found it too difficult to face possible rejection if they failed to conform to the norms prevailing in their living and work environments. That this reluctance may have been the result of certain practices the mandate from Vatican II was attempting to change was probable. Early in the renewal process, the Adrian Synthesis was reporting attitudes that existed prior to the later structural changes. We do not have accepted psychological measures for the sisters before 1973. In her report on the Adrian Synthesis Update (April 1973), in which a modified Authoritarianism Scale (Beres 1976, 237) was included, Beres noted a relationship between an authoritarian need structure and more support for the pre-change norms of the congregation. The other end of the scale is less consistent with the pre-change norms, and more indicative of a democratic need structure. Small groups of sisters were in three studies (Keeley 1977; O'Reilly 1977; Kowalski 1984) that were carried out later in the renewal process. On these measures sisters compared well with norms on the California Psychological Inventory (Keeley; O'Reilly) and the Personal Orientation Inventory (O'Reilly; Kowalski), suggesting basic psychological health. However, all three studies noted that on the Rotter Internal/External Locus of Control Scale the Adrian Dominican women in these studies showed a tendency toward external control, somewhat unusual for the age levels of the sisters in the studies, as compared with other norms. This tendency may have been an effect of the centralized authority structure in which these sisters had lived throughout their lives.

Ashley's theological commentary on the Adrian Synthesis Update notes "There is an increasing satisfaction with community life, its openness, collegiality, interrelatedness and vitality. At the same time, there does not seem to be an obliteration of divergent opinions. On most questions there remains a wide spectrum of opinions, often a considerable group of 'undecideds,' and dissenting minorities, which are not always the same people. Thus I believe that we can conclude that while polarity is decreasing, it is not in the direction of uniformity or the triumph of one faction over another" (1973, 6).

The psychologist Marian Yaeger, OP, noted the problems of conformity, fear of rejection, and fear of failure that continued to surface in the Adrian Synthesis Update (1973). Davis had been concerned with these issues earlier, especially with the evidence that personal security for many sisters came from the approval of superiors, rather than from development as a mature person. Another area of concern for Davis was the amount of distrust of authority, and of one another present in the Synthesis results. Although changes in governance structures had lessened these responses somewhat on the Synthesis Update (1973), Yaeger emphasized that such attitudes may act as a detriment to change and to the acceptance of diversity in the renewal process for those sisters who hold them. She suggested a focus on the inner transformation and freedom that enable a sister to choose behavior that indicates true renewal. While external changes in governance and ministry provide a favorable climate, it is the responsibility of the individual sister to create for herself a deep sense of personal identity. This requires courageous commitment in the face of risk. "Identity is one's witness to the truth in one's life" (Yaeger, 2). The issue of authentic identity in the choice and living of one's religious life in one's own person was, she felt, the truest guarantee of a healthy relationship with one's sisters. One must have arrived at a mature identity and basic self-respect before one can respect another in her own authentic reality. Yaeger goes on to note that "one's own *authentic* and personal beliefs and *convictions,* based on experience of oneself as a person, experience of one's ability to choose or reject even good things which are not relevant to one's life" constitute the "witness to the truth in one's life" that is authentic identity (ibid.).

The tendency to rely on external control mentioned above is consistent with the Syntheses' reports on conformity and related issues. Yaeger offers the remedy of attention to growth in personal identity as a way of developing an inner locus of control appropriate to a mature adult. This development reverses the tendency to rely on the group for a sense of identity and offers instead respect for one's own and for others' authentic identity, and therefore respect for the group.

Sociologist Roberta Keane, commenting on the Adrian Synthesis Update, found that the data revealed rather dramatic shifts in the attitudes and experience of the sisters between 1969 and 1972. The overall patterns indicated optimism for the future, a great deal more satisfaction with community life and for the opportunities available for the development of talents, and a growing sense of the change-oriented nature of religious life. She pointed out that "Areas that have some potential for tension in the community are conflict between individual goals and congregational goals, and the goals of the Church hierarchy" (3). She indicated some of the pitfalls inherent in decisions made by majority rule, concluding that participatory government has its own hazards, but the problems are capable of resolution. "Unity of life and purpose is possible amidst diversity of expression" (9).

Many Adrian Dominican Sisters would identify maximizing the involvement of each sister in ministry planning as the area in which they can identify positive psychological effects. These possibilities available due to changes in governance exemplify the effort of the congregation to reverse harmful effects that may have persisted from prior practice. The general chapter of 1972 outlined the following goals:

(1) to provide opportunities for spiritual growth and personal development of the sister-minister;
(2) to replace autocratic decision-making with a process that would maximize the involvement of each sister in ministry planning;
(3) to abandon merely responding to requests for service received from external sources in favor of creative searching initiated at all levels of the congregation;
(4) to expand ministry exercised only among Catholics into ministry penetrating all segments of society;
(5) to move from a position of isolation of congregation efforts into a coresponsible relationship groups in society working to meet similar needs (General Chapter Enactments 1972, ADA).

By the time these goals were formulated, it was clear that this one congregation could not meet all the needs of contemporary society, but needed instead, to utilize its resources in such a way that its stewardship was both prudent and oriented toward gospel mandates. A notable change was the effort to place basic responsibility on the sister to discern and utilize her God-given talents in ministry, as opposed to assigning a sister to fill an institutional slot, as had often occurred in former times. This did not mean the sister was an independent agent. It meant rather both individual and communal discernment as to how the gift she made of herself to the religious order and to the Church could be utilized for the glory of God, as well as for her own maximal development as a spiritual person.

Movement on from 1968 to 1972

The complexity of moral issues in the latter half of this century has been recognized more clearly by Roman Catholics, and many others, since Vatican Council II. The recognition that justice was linked to systemic change was a lesson learned from the civil rights and peace movements of the 1960s. New ministries, such as advocacy for the poor, the use of political power to lobby for social justice, responsible investments, joint efforts with other religious groups to promote nuclear disarmament and efforts toward the promotion of peace attracted many sisters. This concern with unjust structures changed the focus of ministry. Challenge to the historical structures of church and society that are primarily patriarchal seemed a necessary concomitant to evangelization. Especially in countries of the Third World, it is essential that the church work for justice by transforming the unjust structures of modern society in order to assist in making changes for the better in people's lives.

> The resulting growing awareness that health, education and subsistence services are finally being recognized as human rights, to be provided for by common wealth and global resources, explains the new concern of sisters to share in transforming work with poor people (Neal 1990, 35).

As Adrian Dominican Sisters expanded their intellectual and ministry horizons, they came, one by one, into direct experience of violations of human rights and the oppression of developing peoples. Work in the Dominican Republic in the 1950s, including witness to a revolution; compliance with the request of the Holy See to increase personnel in Latin America, leading to the foundation of missions in Peru in the early 1960s; assisting in the formation of a new congregation of women religious in the Philippines in 1965. Such experiences served to educate Adrian Dominican women in the dreary alphabet of immoral exploitation of the helpless poor on a global scale.

Very close to home, the civil rights movement brought into consciousness the inequities that custom had institutionalized in our own American culture. Sisters whose ministry was located in the Detroit or Chicago areas had firsthand experience of the violence that erupted as efforts to remedy the situation met resistance. Sisters in the Los Angeles area saw firsthand the brutality that was used to control a people's march to freedom. The unpopularity of the Vietnam War, and the many relatives and friends of the sisters involved in it, raised questions in the minds of many about the immoral use of power for motives other than the defense of our freedoms. Continued dedication of vast amounts of money and material to the proliferation of nuclear arms, when so many people globally lacked the basic necessities for life, was an ongoing concern, a scandal at the heart of the most prosperous nation on earth.

Not every sister participated in the awareness of the urgent concern for action felt by the sister who had personal experience of global moral crises. The openness to others' experience that had characterized the pre-chapter preparations made all the sisters sensitive to individual needs in this area. Many sisters gained an understanding of these issues by experiencing them through the communications media.

The preparation for the hundredth anniversary of On the Conditions of the Working Class (*Rerum novarum*) in 1991 enabled many church personnel to realize that the concern for the rights of workers in the late nineteenth century had extended to those of all poor peoples of the earth by 1991 (See On Christianity and Social Progress, *Mater et magistra*) and that seeking to eliminate sinful social structures of power and wealth had become a function of evangelization by 1971 (OA 1971; Neal 1990, 40–41). As a result of the renewal efforts in their response to the mandates of Vatican II, sisters were prepared for the challenges involved in such an evangelization.

The Synodal document on Justice in the World (*Convenientes et universo*) "expressed the clearest in the statement of the new direction of the Church's option for the poor" (Neal, 41).

> Action on behalf of justice and participation in the transformation of the world fully appear to us as a constitutive element of the preaching of the Gospel, or in other words, of the Church's mission for the redemption of the human race and its liberation from every oppressive situation. (CU 6)

Pope Paul VI provided an original contribution to the church's own understanding when he wrote, "Development is the new name for peace" (PP 87; Goergen 70). On the twentieth anniversary of this encyclical, Pope John Paul II wrote On Social Concerns (*Sollicitudo rei socialis* 1987). "By maintaining continuity with the concerns of On the Development of Peoples (*Populorum progresso)* and by a social analysis of the world twenty years later, John Paul II renews Catholic social teaching by his contribution of a theology of solidarity as a Christian virtue" (SR 72).

> Today, furthermore, given the worldwide dimensions which the social question has assumed, this love of preference for the poor, and the decisions which it has inspired in us cannot but embrace the immense multitudes of the hungry, the needy, the homeless, those without hope for a better future. It is impossible not to take into account the existence of these realities. To ignore them would mean becoming like the "rich man" who pretended not to know the beggar Lazarus lying at his gate. (See Luke 16:19–31) (SR 42)

The changes in religious life in the last thirty years have been for the purpose of enabling the sister to understand and to participate in the mission of the church as defined by its highest teaching authority.

Summary

We have seen the success of the efforts that the sisters made during the last century to meet the needs of the poor, uneducated European immigrants. We have noted the effects that an apostolate limited to institutional ministry had on some of the sisters in this effort. We have looked at the changes in both the surrounding cultures and the church that required a new understanding of the church's mission. We have examined the reasons for the church's call to renewal and the generous response of the sisters. We have considered the psychological impact that the attempts of the sisters to meet the needs of persons in a complex contemporary society, while encumbered by outmoded customs and rules, had on the life, health, and ministry of the sisters. The time of renewal was one of great hope and promise. Adrian Dominican Sisters made monumental efforts to adapt their lifestyle to the needs of the times, and to the original inspirations of the Dominican Order. Whatever the consequences of our human restructuring, we acknowledge that the first principle for the renewal of our religious life is our fidelity to the Gospel.

Works Cited

Ashley, Benedict, OP. "A Theological Analysis of the Adrian Synthesis 1969." Adrian Dominican Chapter of Renewal. August 1969. ADA.

———. "A Theological Analysis of the Adrian Synthesis Update 1973." Adrian Synthesis Workshop. July 1973. ADA.

Beres, Mary Elizabeth, OP. "An Organizational Analysis of the Adrian Synthesis." Adrian Synthesis Workshop. July 1973. ADA.

———. "Change in a Women's Religious Organization: the Impact of Individual Differences, Power, and the Environment." Ph.D. diss., Northwestern University, 1976. Abstract in *Dissertation Abstracts International* (1977): 1211.

———. "Attitudes and Feelings of Adrian Dominicans: A Preliminary Report Based on the Adrian Synthesis Surveys." January 1982. ADA.

Davis, Sister Mary Grace, SND. "A Psychological Report on the 1969 Adrian Synthesis." Adrian Dominican Chapter of Renewal. 1969. ADA.

Dorr, Donal. *Option for the Poor: A Hundred Years of Vatican Social Teaching.* Maryknoll, N.Y: Orbis Books, 1983.

Foley, Nadine, OP, ed. "Orientation to the Instrument: Adrian Synthesis 1969." ts. 1969. ADA.

———. "The Ambiguity of Religious Life: Does it Evolve?" *Review for Religious* 56, no. 1 (Jan.-Feb. 1997): 6–13.

Goergen, Donald, OP. *Letters to My Brothers and Sisters.* Dublin: Dominican Publications, 1996.

Keane, Roberta. "Unity, Diversity and Change: Issues That Concern Adrian Dominican Sisters." Adrian Synthesis Workshop. July 1973. ADA.

Keeley, M. Jean, OP. "Personality Corrrelates (CPI and I-E) of Vocational Satisfaction and Commitment for Professional Religious Women." Master's thesis, Loyola University, 1977.

Kowalski, Joan, OP. "The Relationship Between Self-Actualization and Congregation-sponsored Growth Programs for Women Within the Adrian Dominican Congregation (I-E, POI)." Ph.D. diss., United States International University, 1984.

Lefebvre, Jeanne, OP. *A Decade of Change: 1968–1978.* Unpublished manuscript, ADA 1986.

McCabe, Herbert, OP. "Obedience." *New Blackfriars.* Vol. 65, no. 772 (June, 1984): 280–87.

McCready, William C. "A Survey Abstract: Adrian Synthesis." Adrian Dominican Chapter of Renewal. August, 1969. ADA.

McKeough, Noreen, OP. Personal interview. August 8, 1997.

Neal, Marie Augusta, SND de N. *From Nuns to Sisters: An Expanding Vocation.* Mystic, Conn.: Twenty-Third Publications, 1990.

———. "Meeting the Challenges of the New Century: Through the Eye of the Needle." In *Religious Life: The Challenge for Tomorrow.* Ed. Cassian J. Yuhaus, CP. New York: Paulist Press, 1994: 127–42.

Nolan, Albert. *Jesus Before Christianity.* Maryknoll, NY: Orbis, 1992.

O'Reilly, Virginia, OP. "Self-Actualization and Perceived Locus of Control in Three Groups of Professional Women (CPI, I-E, POI)." Ph.D. diss., California School of Professional Psychology. Abstract in *Dissertation Abstracts International* (1977): 27604.

Quinonez, Lora Ann and Mary Daniel Turner. *The Transformation of American Catholic Sisters.* Philadelphia: Temple University Press, 1992.

Radcliffe, Timothy, OP. "Dominican Freedom and Responsibility: Towards a Spirituality of Government." *International Dominican Information* 353 (July-August, 1997):136–60.

Yaeger, Marian, OP. "Adrian Identity: Wholeness-Humanness and Holiness." Adrian Synthesis Workshop. July 1973. ADA.

11.

◆

The sense of personal responsibility for pursuing gospel values by active congregations of women religious has led to new movements in ministry. One of these stems from the realization that living in a democratic society where decisions with life-altering consequences are made by elected representatives places an onus upon those committed to gospel ministry. Engaging in the political process in a collaborative effort among many religious congregations of women gave rise to NETWORK. It is a prime example of the emerging consciousness that active congregations of religious have a responsibility to the world in which they live.

◆

Women Religious Engage the Political Process

Working for Social Justice from the 1960s to the 1990s

Carol Coston, OP

My heart is moved by all I cannot save
so much has been destroyed.
I have to cast my lot with those
who age after age
with no extraordinary power
reconstitute the world. (Rich, 67)

Thirty years ago, in 1967, I was teaching at Tampa Catholic High School during the school year and working on a master's degree during the summers. Both the ongoing civil rights struggles and the Vietnam War were major outside influences, as well as the internal renewal process in my religious congregation. My master's thesis was going to be on "Black Theater in the 1960s," and I made writings and speeches by African Americans a major part of my classes in speech and religion.

Today, in 1999, I am the director of Partners for the Common Good 2000, an alternative loan fund whose ninety-nine investors are religious congregations, predominantly Catholic sisters; eight Catholic health care systems; and three Protestant organizations. The nearly eight million dollars invested in the fund is loaned out to groups doing low-income housing or small business development throughout the United States and internationally in Central and South America, and in South Africa. The fund also places low-interest deposits in low-income credit unions, which serve ethnic and racial minority groups, many of which have been underserved by traditional financial institutions.

I now live at Sisterfarm, on seven acres of land in the Texas Hill Country, forty miles northwest of San Antonio. So far this morning I have spent time in prayer and reflection, put out the dogs, played with the cats, set our fifty tomato, tomatillo, and squash transplants on the deck, adjusted the grow lamp on the indoor seedlings, brought the dogs back in because I remembered our neighbor called and complained that they were chasing her lambs, moved the computer back inside because it was too bright to see the screen outside, and put the tray of broccoli and edible chrysanthemums next to the dining room window to get the morning sun. (Any reluctant writer will recognize these delaying tactics.)

These two ministries, in 1967 living in a city convent with Adrian Dominicans and teaching high school, and in 1999 living in a rural area managing the investments of ninety-eight other congregations, form a personal framework for some of the transitions and transformations that have influenced me, but also delineate similar movements that have taken place in religious life, particularly in the area of social responsibility. Another framework is the following set of quotations:

> My heart is moved by all I cannot save
>   so much has been destroyed.
> I have to cast my lot with those
>   who age after age
> with no extraordinary power
>   reconstitute the world. (Rich, 67)

This is what Yahweh asks of you
> only this:
To act justly, to love tenderly,
> to walk humbly before your God. (Micah 6:8)

Can we be like drops of water
> falling on the stone
Splashing, breaking, dispersing in air
> Weaker than the stone by far, but be aware? . . .
As time goes by, the rock will wear away.
(Holly Near and Meg Christian, adapted from
> > a Vietnamese poem)

Action on behalf of justice . . . is a constitutive dimension of the preaching of the Gospel. (CU, 34)

This is a strange assortment of authors: a Jewish feminist, a prophet of the Hebrew Scriptures, two lesbian feminist singers, and the Synod of Catholic Bishops. Yet each quotation resonates with influences felt by Catholic sisters in the turmoil, excitement, and challenges of the late 1960s through the 1990s.

After some intense and painful years of renewal following Vatican Council II, during which all aspects of religious life came under review, many women religious felt a personal call to political activism and corporate responsibility and looked for ways to channel their frustration and dismay at injustice in the political, social, ecclesial, and economic arenas into a focused and constructive, they hoped, response. These women began to see the need for a more systemic approach to social change.

In this article I will focus on one Catholic organization in which women religious became politically active, NETWORK: a national Catholic social justice lobby that recently celebrated its twenty-fifth anniversary.

I write this remembrance from personal involvement, as well as from the perspective of a particular congregation, the Adrian Dominican Sisters, who actively participated in forming this organization. This approach offers the advantage of direct experience, as well as the inherent biases and limitations of the writer. However, I also have incorporated the memories and experiences of many other sisters from different congregations in the telling of these stories.

Hearts Moved by the Civil Rights Struggle

During the 1960s, many United States religious were moved by the images on television of police brutality against peaceful marchers in Alabama, of courageous black students being dragged from white-owned restaurants in North Carolina, of the bodies of innocent black children killed in an African American church. Their horror at these blatant injustices, as well as subtler forms of racial discrimination, led to a variety of responses by sisters nationwide. Several of the sisters who attended the 1971 organizing meeting that founded NETWORK had already become activists in this arena. Among them were:

- Kathryn McDonnell and Alice McDonnell, members of the Religious of the Sacred Heart of Jesus, were then living in a low-income, predominantly African American housing project in Washington, D.C. Kate worked on Section 235 Housing, a program of the Department of Housing and Urban Development (HUD) to encourage home ownership, and Alice walked the inner-city neighborhoods as a community health nurse.
- Josephine Dunne, SHCJ, was missioned to Rosemont College in Pennsylvania in 1969. Kate and Alice visited the college to intercede on behalf of Jo so that she could be released to work with them and Monsignor Geno Baroni on inner-city problems. By 1971 Jo was working for the Campaign for Human Development at the national office in Washington, D.C.
- Claire Dugan, SSJ, and sixty-four other sisters in Providence, Rhode Island, spent the summer of 1970 living in housing projects among the poor white and black residents. This led Claire to become Director of Sisters for Urban Improvement.
- Marjorie Tuite, a Columbus Dominican, went to Chicago after spending twelve years working in Harlem. She joined the Urban Training Institute in 1968 to help the civil rights movement by training organizers from the South to be prepared better to confront racial injustice.
- Kathleen Gannon and Carol Coston, both Adrian Dominican Sisters, were active in 1971 in Ft. Lauderdale, Florida, trying to get the county commissioners to pass an open-housing ordinance so that African Americans could live wherever they wished. Carol then worked as an administrator for Neighborhood Youth Corps 2, a Department of Labor program for high-school dropouts,

most of whom were single-parent, African American young women. Kathy worked in religious education for the Miami Archdiocese.

- Mary Hayes, SND, a history professor at Trinity College in Washington, D.C., whose notes provided much of the above data, told me that she, too, was moved to social action by the civil rights movement. She said that this movement was a major motivation for many of the other proactive sisters she interviewed and who founded or helped shape NETWORK over the years.

Called to Act Justly through Political Action

According to Mary Hayes, there are diverse opinions as to who should take credit for calling the meeting that actually launched NETWORK. After reading Mary's notes from interviews she conducted in the late 1970s for a proposed history of NETWORK, reflecting on my own experience of attending the founding meeting, and recalling subsequent conversations with major participants in NETWORK's founding and growth, there seems to be a consensus that the following persons and events were the main contributors.

Monsignor Geno Baroni grew up among coal miners in Altoona, Pennsylvania, and from observing their struggles moved to a lifelong commitment to social justice. Geno, as he was known by all those who learned from and were inspired by him, was also deeply involved in the civil rights movement. He marched at Selma, Alabama, and prodded the church at all levels to listen to African Americans and to respond to the injustices they experienced on a daily basis. Geno was also a strong advocate for members of white ethnic groups who felt neglected in urban neighborhoods. He set up the Center for Urban Ethnic Affairs to help organize them for political change and to form coalitions with African Americans to work on common agendas.

Another target in Geno's organizing for political involvement were the women religious. He recognized that United States sisters were already somewhat organized under the auspices of the Leadership Conference of Women Religious, whose members had recently changed the name of their organization from the Conference of Major Superiors of Women to reflect better their self-understanding following renewal chapters. Two other groups had been recently organized at the grass roots level: the National Coalition of American Nuns, NCAN, and the National Assembly of Women Religious, NAWR, who later changed their name to National Assembly of Religious Women, NARW, in order to be more inclusive. These organizations provided additional forums for sisters to come together across congregational lines and to join with other women in order to speak out on issues and to organize for social change. NCAN was the most aggressive group and could be counted on to have a press release ready on many issues of injustice, particularly those that affected women religious and the economically poor.

Geno had tried in vain to get priests politically involved, "I was frustrated that I hadn't been able to start a priests' group to lobby in Washington. I kept telling them that it's those damned public policy issues in the public arena that hurt you back home when you're talking about day care or housing or jobs or food stamps" (O'Rourke, 171–72). He then turned to the sisters and addressed LCWR members at their annual meeting in August, 1971, in Atlanta. He found some sisters who were interested, and apparently kept a list for future use, because Carol Jean McDonnell and Marcella Hess, both Adrian Dominicans, remember hearing Geno at LCWR, and later received and accepted his invitation to meet in Washington in December 1971, to discuss how sisters could become involved in political activities.

Marjorie Tuite, OP, met Geno through the Catholic Committee for Urban Ministry (CCUM). She remembered that he was always talking about legislation as a means of change, and how he believed in the strength of the American sisterhood and its potential for mobilization. As a founder and first chair of NAWR's Social Concerns Committee, Margie was already convinced about the strength of an organized base of sisters advocating social change and made sure that the regional contacts for the committee were invited to the first NETWORK meeting. Margie used the Women's Caucus at CCUM's 1971 fall meeting as a testing for the upcoming Washington meeting. Claire Dugan remembers Margie's disappointment, after asking how many sisters would be willing to go to Washington in December to initiate action for a "political thing," that of the thirty-seven women present, only seven raised their hands. Two of these were Claire Dugan and her friend and co-activist from Rhode Island, Mary Reilly, RSM.

Josephine Dunne, SHCJ, and Mary Hayes, SND, were the NAWR Social Concerns coordinators in Washington and helped with local arrangements before, during, and after the first meeting. I would not have

attended the founding meeting except that Jo Dunne had met Kathy
Gannon at a religious education conference in Miami that fall, and in
their brief conversation, Kathy told Jo about our work at the political
level for open housing and voting rights. Jo suggested to Kathy that she
might like to come to a meeting being planned in Washington. When
the invitation arrived, we both were intrigued by it, so Kathy asked if I
wanted to go with her.

Audrey Miller, CDP, from Pittsburgh, was also invited by Jo Dunne.
Audrey worked for the United Church of Christ then and was also involved in the Catholic Interracial Council that sponsored a rent-
withholding project in the Hill District of Pittsburgh.

Jerry Ernst worked for Geno at the Center for Urban and Ethnic
Affairs. He, too, was an organizer and drafted the invitation letter that
came out over Geno's signature. Jerry helped facilitate the December
meeting and probably helped put together the speakers. I suspect that
Rita Mudd, SP, who also worked for Geno, took care of the administrative details.

Forty-seven Sisters Launch a Network to Influence Legislation

The invitation letter to socially concerned members of religious congregations went out December 7, 1971. The purpose stated was "to plan
a network of sisters to deal with social policy questions." Geno hoped
that twenty-five would attend; instead forty-seven arrived on December
17, 1971, and settled in an art classroom at Trinity College, near The
Catholic University of America. Carol Jean McDonnell, OP, remembers
both the "starkness of the room and the energy of the sisters."

Both Geno and Margie gave talks—Geno drawing huge circles on the
blackboard to depict the various classes in United States society. His
diagrams showed where members of working-class ethnic groups were
located and he described their consternation at being bypassed as young
activists and sisters went to work with the more economically poor,
primarily African Americans and migrant farm workers. He illustrated
the connections among government, the private sector, and the voluntary
sector. He noted that we sisters were clearly in the voluntary sector and
were needed to promote the church's social teaching in the political
arena. Margie, who was a formidable presence from the onset, paced
back and forth across the classroom urging us to action. In her com-

manding voice she stated that it was time for sisters to move from service to change!—that we needed to be self-determining and involved at the base and in the centers of political power!—out of the convents and into the streets and the halls of Congress!

The next morning we went to Capitol Hill and heard, from an aide to Senator Edward Kennedy, how the political process works and about the black agenda for the 1970s from James Gibson, a close friend of Geno. That afternoon David Cohen from Common Cause, Anona Teska of the League of Women Voters, and John Esposito from Ralph Nader's Public Citizen organization explained different ways for citizens to become involved in the legislative arena.

Listening to these challenges and being on Capitol Hill was new for most participants, but my strongest remembrance is the high level of energy and the broadbased experiences of the sisters present. I had never been in a room with so many involved, strongly opinionated women in my life! And the most energizing moment occurred when Audrey Miller stood up and stated that if we were about creating a women's organization, why were men the main facilitators and most of the speakers? From that point on Jerry Ernst and Geno stayed in the back of the room and Audrey chaired the meeting. Her intervention became a galvanizing event and helped us find our collective voice. By Sunday morning, it seemed that we had come to a consensus and should take action, so when I offered a motion that the sisters "form a political action network of information and communication," it was approved by a 43-to-3 vote, with one abstention. Audrey then appointed a steering committee of nine to meet in January at Jo Dunne's house. As I recall, the main criterion for serving on the committee, besides interest, was having the finances to get back to Washington. We took up an immediate collection resulting in the modest sum of $147 to get the organization started. Those present agreed to try to find additional funding from their communities and other contacts.

The steering committee took on five tasks: (1) set up the network, (2) find permanent staff, (3) establish contacts with additional organizations, (4) explore various types of political action, and (5) plan for weekend and summer workshops to involve other sisters in political activity.

When the steering committee met in January, Geno joined us as an observer. After long discussions about our goals and objectives, we turned to the question of staff. The group felt that the first staff should include someone who had participated in the founding meeting. We thought about this and looked around the room. I distinctly remember

Margaret Smith, RSCJ, focusing on me and stating that I should be the one to do it. The committee agreed. It was a powerful moment for I realized that I was being called beyond myself and my current experiences; that it was going to pull me out of a compensated position I loved and away from my closest friends and family in Florida; that it would be a personal risk; and that I probably couldn't say "no" and live with myself! I felt lightheaded, off balance, and my heart was pounding with the decision being asked of me. I told the committee that I was willing to consider it, but needed to get permission from my provincial and prioress. I then left the room and, amazingly, was immediately able to locate our congregation's prioress, Rosemary Ferguson, OP, who was doing visitations in California. After a brief explanation of what we were proposing to do, Rosemary said it sounded like a good idea and something needed, and that I had her permission to proceed as long as it was all right with my provincial. I then talked to Mary Joseph Kennedy, OP, who also said "yes," as long as I could withdraw from my existing ministry in a responsible manner.

Afterward, a sister at the meeting commented on the rapidity of this decision: "If it had been my congregation, I would have been told to write up a proposal and submit it to the ministerial needs committee, which would meet in three months; and then send it on to the subsidy committee, which met two months later; and which would then send a recommendation to the general council, which met once a month!" I was grateful for the quick decision and the vote of confidence it represented. Later that year Rosemary asked me to come to Adrian and discuss my financial needs, because the council was willing to subsidize me until the organization was on its feet.

The Steering Committee members at this meeting included the following sisters: Monica Cahill, BVM; Carol Coston, OP; Claire Dugan, SSJ; Josephine Dunne, SHCJ; Ann Gillen, SHCJ; Mary Hayes, SND; Joan Linder, OSF; Audrey Miller, CDP; Margaret Smith, RSCJ; Marjorie Tuite, OP; and Jean Wood, BVM.

Alphonsa Puls, OSF, who attended the December meeting, had recommended that her sister, Joan Puls, OSF, be on the steering committee. Joan joined the group soon after and became the first elected president of the new board and served from 1973–75. (Margie Tuite had served as informal chair of the steering committee at the beginning.) Margie had recommended that Margaret Cafferty, PBVM, from San Francisco be added to the first board of directors and, as I recall, procured a small grant for Margaret to attend the first annual legislative seminar in 1972.

Margaret was board president from 1975–78, followed by Margaret Farley, RSM, 1978–79; Mary Luke Tobin, SL, 1979–82; Amata Miller, IHM, 1983–86; Barbara Bader Aldave, 1986–89; Dorothy Ettling, CCVI, 1992–1993; Dorothy Jackson, SCN, 1993–95; Mary Elizabeth Clark, SSJ, 1995–96; Beatriz Zapata, CSJ, 1996–97; and Elva Revilla, 1997–present.

Geno also helped financially. To get us started he offered me an immediate position at the Center for Urban and Ethnic Affairs that provided a small salary as well as office space and a phone number. When I returned to Washington full-time in April, 1972, I was joined by Margaret Hohman, SCN. By the time we held our first legislative seminar in August, the staff had expanded to five with the inclusion of Rosemarie Chase, SCN, Maureen Kelleher, RSHM, and Mary Rae Waller, OP. Mary Rae had just earned a master's degree in political science, and our provincial, Mary Jo Kennedy, had suggested to her that she come to help us as only she among us had a professional background even remotely connected with the legislative process! Margaret had a Ph.D. in organic chemistry, Maureen had a master's degree in English, mine was in speech and drama, and Rosemarie had a business degree.

In September, along with six other sisters, we set up the NETWORK house and office in northeast Washington, on Lawrence Street, in two wooden frame houses owned by Catholic University.

A Call to Action Follows the Call to Renewal

The sisters who founded NETWORK, both staff and board, had all been shaped by the renewal process engaged in by United States women religious beginning in the mid-1960s. This led us really to value a participative process of decision making and the assumption of personal responsibility for trying to shape congregational, ecclesial, and civil society's policies. We had been examining the contemporary "signs of the times," as well as our congregation's original charisms, and reflecting on how best to respond. Many of us had also been influenced by the experiences of our women who had served in Third World countries and by our own experiences working among the economically poor and discriminated against in this country.

One of the first assignments that the NETWORK staff and steering committee gave itself was to study Paul VI's Call to Action *(Octagesima adveniens),* which had been recently promulgated. We were particularly influenced by the calls to political action such as the following: "Politics are a demanding manner . . . of living the Christian commitment to the service of others" (46). "Political power . . . must have as its aim the achievement of the common good" (46). Christian organizations "have a responsibility for collective action" (51).

As the fledgling staff began to shape NETWORK as a Catholic lobby group, we undertook further study of the Synod of Bishops' Statement on Justice in the World and reflections on biblical passages such as Luke 4 and Matthew 25, Jesus' description of his ministry of justice and the passage on being judged by how one has fed the hungry, clothed the naked, and provided shelter for the poor, etc. We tried to apply these principles to legislative initiatives. We also studied liberation theologies from Latin America, and the staff set aside reflection days to share our own visions and religious motivations in order to formulate NET-WORK's mission and values.

In addition to these efforts, we also asked for and received professional advice on how to be a social justice lobby from Common Cause and the Friends Committee on National Legislation. Both groups were most generous with their time and resources and helped us shape our first legislative seminar in August 1972, as well as subsequent publications. As we became more organized, Common Cause let us use their long distance lines at night so that we could call our "congressional district" contacts or "state coordinators" to urge them to get in touch with their senators or representatives on a particular piece of legislation.

The Friends Committee urged us to register as a lobby organization because they felt that this action would be a good example for Congress on the importance of following the federal guidelines for disclosure of lobbying activities. This step required us to submit forms periodically, outlining the sources of our financial contributions as well as our expenses. These public documents were later used by *The Wanderer* newspaper in an attempt to discredit NETWORK. The front-page headline read "Priests Nuns Brothers Contribute to Leftist Lobby," and, after noting that the chief Catholic chaplain of the U.S. Air Force had contributed $2,000 to NETWORK, added, "Surprising also is the fact that the Franciscan Sisters of Perpetual Adoration of Wisconsin contributed $1,000 to NETWORK" (September 11, 1980). The author commented that many might presume that such a contemplative order would pay little direct attention to "such mundane affairs as national politics."

In 1972–73, as we began to learn our way around Capitol Hill and form alliances with other organizations that shared many of our values, we discovered that the majority of congresspersons and public-interest organizations perceived the Catholic Church as being predominantly interested in two issues: against abortions and for federal aid to parochial schools. When I later visited the United States Catholic Conference's (USCC) government liaison office to find out what legislative research they had that might help us craft our public positions, I browsed through their four-drawer lateral files and noted that three-and-a-half drawers were devoted to those two issues and half a drawer to the rest of the social justice agenda. The NETWORK staff and board felt strongly that, since these issues were being adequately addressed through the auspices of USCC, we needed to work on a much broader array of issues that would affect the common good, nationally and internationally.

Thus we began to educate ourselves, our members, and congresspersons on the connections between the biblical calls to justice and the tradition of Catholic social justice teachings, (Sylvester and Coston, 3–11) and the needs of the economically poor, as well as the need for a process of seeking peaceful solutions to global tensions. We also developed additional criteria to judge our public positions as well as our internal management and policies. These criteria—the NETWORK values of mutuality, participation, cooperation, stewardship and integration—evolved from extended staff sharing around our personal visions of a more just society and the values we thought should guide its creation. We identified these criteria as feminist values and felt they were the values to which we wanted to hold ourselves accountable. In the early years of NETWORK I had defined a feminist perspective as "a way of living, a way of critiquing present structures and systems, and a way of shaping a preferred future. It is based on respect for all persons regardless of sex. It deplores domination in any form—sexual, racial, economic, religious, militaristic, or political. A feminist perspective places high value on participation, mutuality, cooperation, and stewardship and uses these as a measure of evaluating present systems and structures."

Building from these roots we began to publish NETWORK'S first public voting records, giving all congresspersons a "+" or a "−", depending on whether or not they supported our positions on bills to halt funding for the Vietnam War, uphold migrants' rights in the proposed Sugar Act legislation, establish national health insurance, enact the Equal Rights Amendment, or pass the Cooperative Bank Bill. These voting-record issues were then distributed by hand to each of the five hundred thirty-five offices in the House and Senate. We also sent them to all our members and asked that they be used to issue local press releases and to schedule discussions with the congresspersons.

In 1975, in response to a suggestion made to me by Sister Kevin Ford, CSJ, NETWORK published the charts that I had used in my talk on Catholic social thought at the Leadership Conference of Women Religious Assembly. The chart outlined the social encyclicals from two perspectives: what injustices were being *denounced* and what alternative vision was being *announced*. It, and its many reprints up to the present time, has become the largest selling publication ever produced by NETWORK.

With these publications, our lobby visits, and our annual legislative seminars, we were able to broaden the public perception of Catholic concerns on national issues. We also contributed to educating our Catholic constituency on the social teachings of the church. In addition, we used the NETWORK values to articulate a feminist perspective on public policy and to illustrate their application to our internal participatory management polices and practices.

Sisters' Response to 1971 and 1976 Calls to Action

From the above account of NETWORK's beginnings, it is clear that women religious took seriously the calls to renewal emanating from the Vatican Council II documents and Paul VI's challenge to religious congregations. As a result, we had made many changes in prayer styles, religious garb, living arrangements, and types of ministries, including political ministry. Unfortunately, our enthusiasm for these changes was not always shared by the institutional church. It is one of the ironies of the last three decades that United States women religious have been so criticized and hampered by some of their ecclesial leaders for how we responded to their own directives. For many of us in NETWORK and our extended "networks," two of the more troubling situations were the responses of the National Conference of Catholic Bishops to the 1976 Call to Action Conference and Pope John Paul II's restrictions on religious in public office.

NETWORK had decided to participate fully in the Call to Action Conference, which was being held as a Catholic contribution to the 1976 Bicentennial Celebration of the United States, because we were assured by the planners that it would be a way to help shape the pastoral and social agenda of the United States church for the next several years. We were energized by the participatory nature of the process, by the chance to discuss the larger issues facing us as a church and a nation, by the regional hearings throughout the United States, and especially by the chance to gather in Cobo Hall in Detroit with representatives from every diocese and from most of the national Catholic organizations to debate the issues publicly and to vote our responses.

NETWORK staff obtained the lists of the diocesan delegates (all of whom were appointed by the local bishop) and began contacting those we knew or who were known by other NETWORK members. We worked in cooperation with other national and regional social justice organizations on issues of common concern, but had decided that we would focus most of our organizing efforts on garnering support for the Equal Rights Amendment (ERA). We also supported passage of strong statements on full employment and disarmament.

Maureen Kelleher, RSHM, was on the NETWORK staff at that time, but was also on the Peace and Justice Committee of the USCC, and thereby appointed to be a delegate. As such, she was later appointed to the Credentials Committee to help arbitrate disputes over which individuals or groups could be seated as delegates. I was the official NETWORK delegate, and many other NETWORK members were diocesan delegates. Maureen had prepared a survey on the Equal Rights Amendment that through concerted staff effort was filled out prior to the start of the proceedings. The survey showed overwhelming support for the ERA.

The small group discussions were lively and there was a strong sense of excitement around this new experience of being a participative church and of being together at such an historic gathering. The NETWORK members felt gratified at the final results. Resolutions in support of the ERA had passed in four different issue groups, and there were many other strong statements on other social justice issues that could help us in our political ministry efforts. We felt that the vast resources of the church would be channeled in new ways and that the calls for political involvement in the 1971 documents of Paul VI and the United States Bishops would be fleshed out by the directions set by this broad-based representative group of Catholics.

Our enthusiasm was short-lived. The official press releases following the conference did not mention the strong support for the ERA, and the USCC Call to Action office was closed soon after. We had hoped that this office would be the rallying point for education and implementation of the directives set at the conference. This did not happen, nor did the

USCC ever give support to the passage of the ERA at either the national or state level. And now, in 1999, the Chicago-based Call to Action group, which has tried since then to keep alive the spirit and direction of that original conference, has been under attack by conservative elements within the church, including some bishops.

Pope Prohibits Religious from Holding Public Office

The second area of disillusionment was John Paul II's prohibition against religious in public office. This forced people, such as Rev. Robert Drinan, SJ, and Sisters of Mercy Elizabeth Morancy, Arlene Violet, and Agnes Mary Mansour, to choose between ministries to which they personally felt called and membership in their religious communities. Clare Dunn, CSJ, the first woman religious elected to state office, was killed in a tragic auto accident in 1981 and thus was spared the difficult decision of whether to leave religious life or to resign from her ministry as an Arizona State Legislator.

Robert Drinan, SJ, was a highly respected United States Representative and a wonderful Catholic presence in Congress. He was always a strong supporter of NETWORK and our agenda and spoke at many of our seminars. Bob was an outspoken opponent of the Vietnam War, military dictatorships in Latin America, and discriminatory practices. He was a vocal supporter of human rights, health care for all, and everyone's right to food. His influence was enormous and the decision to leave Congress was quite painful to him and to his supporters. This prohibition was extremely hard to understand in the light of Catholic social teachings and in observation of Pope John Paul II's highly visible personal involvement in political matters in the many countries he so publicly visited.

Each of the three Sisters of Mercy who held state offices in Rhode Island and Michigan—Liz was a State Legislator; Arlene, an Attorney General; and Agnes Mary, a Director of Health and Human Services— made the painful choice to leave her community rather than to go against her conscience and what she felt called to do. Both Liz and Arlene served on the NETWORK board, and Liz was at the founding meeting in 1971. Their choice of elected office was a natural outgrowth of this type of ministry. When attempts at negotiation failed, these sisters chose to separate rather than put their congregations through any more anxiety or distress. Many of us resonated with the pain endured by these sisters and their congregations. A high level of distress and disaffection remains in recalling the lack of appropriate dialogue with those affected, the absence of due process, the disregard for the role of the congregational leadership, the discounting of personal conscience, and the forced separation of the sisters from their communities of many years.

Casting Our Lot with Those Who Reconstitute the World

Despite disappointments, such as those just described, as well as those that arise from often being on the losing side of legislative battles and seeing the needs of the poorest and most under-represented in our society being pushed aside in favor of the more privileged, there are many positive accomplishments to remember as NETWORK celebrates its twenty-fifth anniversary. The following stand out in my experience:

- NETWORK has always been an example of how women religious can collaborate on a common project—from the forty-seven sisters from many different congregations who founded the organization to the hundreds of others who were, and still are members of the staff or board, state coordinators, and congressional district contacts. In addition, as NETWORK has grown, members of the people of God from all walks of life have assumed positions of leadership within the organization.
- The leadership of women's congregations provided essential financial support throughout the twenty-five years, as well as encouragement for their members to participate. For example, LCWR's national assembly has passed three different resolutions in support of NETWORK. The first in 1972, when the group supported a resolution introduced by Mary Joseph Kennedy, OP, my provincial at the time, that stated: "The members . . . support the NETWORK in its efforts for social justice by letters of support, by financial contributions, and by encouraging other sisters to become active members." This was especially critical in the beginning when we were a new and untested type of ministry. In the 1992 publication for the twentieth anniversary, 312 religious congregations, predominantly women religious, were thanked for their "sustaining support."
- NETWORK was an active participant in various coalitions that won legislative victories in helping to stop the war in Vietnam,

supported the original Equal Rights Amendment as well as the extension of the ERA, pushed to pass the Family and Medical Leave Act, and successfully pressed for the Community Reinvestment Act that has helped many neighborhood groups get access to credit from local banks.

- NETWORK opposed the aggressive militaristic policies of the Reagan Administration, particularly toward Nicaragua and all of Central America.

- NETWORK is committed to and understands that *systemic change takes a long time* and that we must be persistent in our advocacy. For example, the first *NETWORK Quarterly* in 1972 featured an article by Mary Rae Waller, OP, on the need for national health insurance. The cover of the July/August 1997 issue of *NETWORK Connection* features seven news clips on the debate around health care reform and an article by Catherine Pinkerton, CSJ, entitled "Is Comprehensive Health Care Reform Dead?"

- In trying to use our feminist values as a lens for focusing public positions as well as internal policies, NETWORK has had to be willing to critique itself and make changes. For example, I was named "Executive Director" by the board in the early years, but when Nancy Sylvester, IHM, took over in 1982, it seemed more consistent with the values of mutuality and participation to change the title to "National Coordinator."

- The decision to change the salary policy is described in Nancy Sylvester's article for the twentieth anniversary publication: "Prior to 1981, there was a two-tier pay scale. Lay women received twice as much as sisters. At a time when there was a great awareness within the women's church community concerning the divisiveness of separating lay and religious and with increased emphasis on a just wage for all workers, NETWORK chose to reject this unequal model. After much discussion, especially around the way patriarchal society articulates how work is valued, often depreciating the value of women's work, the staff accepted a more countercultural model: equal pay for all staff. Rooted in the belief that the value of work emanates from the dignity of the worker . . . the value of each staff person as worker would be the base upon which the salary policy would be built . . . regardless of position, degrees, longevity, or experience."

- Within ecumenical settings, NETWORK has often been a consistent Catholic voice.
- Thousands of persons have been exposed to the legislative process, the social encyclicals, and ways in which to connect our faith and values to public policy.
- NETWORK provided a place for sisters to find support with each other as well as with other activists. It was encouraging for those who felt that they were lonely voices within their own congregations to be able to gather with others of similar beliefs. The NETWORK annual seminars were key to making these connections. Friendships formed through NETWORK have lasted for years and have helped sustain the organization.
- NETWORK staff and members have tried "to speak truth to power" in ways that are consistent with its values. The *Boston Globe* described it as follows: "Unlike lobbyists for business, who have been known to tempt lawmakers with campaign contributions, free lunches, and junkets, the NETWORK sisters inundate House and Senate Members with fact sheets and position papers designed to frame an issue in a moral context."

Can We Be like Drops of Water Falling on the Stone?

I want to close this remembrance by recalling the above image from the opening page: Are many drops of water able to wear away the rock?

Many times during its twenty-five year history, NETWORK's staff, board, and members have felt overwhelmed by the magnitude of the needs and the inadequacies of the legislative response. During most of this time, our political leaders in Washington were not sympathetic to the needs of the economically poor throughout the world, and many initiatives were put forth that would benefit the already rich. Often, our allies in Congress were insufficient in number to stem this tide and thus NETWORK staff members have spent countless hours in writing and lobbying from a "damage control" position, a discouraging process!

As we on the NETWORK staff plugged away at these efforts and at many Saturday workshops throughout the United States trying to garner more involvement in a particular issue or in the elective process, we were often asked: "How can you keep doing this year after year? How can you remain hopeful and enthusiastic when things appear to be so bad on Capitol Hill and U.S. policy is hurting millions of people globally?"

Faced with such questions, I found it helpful to recall the "Drops of Water" song by Holly Near and Meg Christian, and its origins as a Vietnamese poem. It evoked for me the image of a peasant population seemingly powerless against the overwhelming forces arrayed against them—beginning with colonial takeovers and evolving into the full force of U.S. military might during the Vietnam War. Somehow these under-armed and under-funded people managed to withstand a sustained military onslaught over many years, at a great cost to themselves and to the U.S. troops caught in an unpopular war but responding from a sense of duty to their country. Eventually, the resistance of the Vietnamese people, coupled with the growing U.S. and international coalitions of groups protesting the war, caused President Nixon to withdraw the U.S. troops.

In the light of such persistence on the part of the Vietnamese people, and of the thousands of resisters and revolutionaries in other countries fighting for human and economic rights for the poorest, could we do no less? And was it not possible that our "drops of water"—our seemingly fruitless efforts—could prove also to be transformative over time?

These musings took on new meaning for me recently when I witnessed a literal example of the power of millions of drops of water. Sisterfarm is situated just above a small creek, the Big Joshua Creek, that usually runs in a gentle fashion but which stopped running completely in 1996 during a ten-month drought. But beginning on Saturday morning, June 21, 1997, through Sunday, June 22, the normally blue skies turned dark gray and over the course of some twenty-four hours let loose more than twenty inches of rain. On Saturday afternoon, after only five inches of rain, the creek had risen about fifteen feet, flooding its banks and rushing downstream, converted into a muddy and turbulent river. On Sunday morning, while the rain was still pouring down, we could see that the creek water had risen even higher and that the dry-bed ravine, which cut through the property to the right of the house and ran down toward the creek, had turned into a roaring waterfall rushing toward the creek.

Later that afternoon the rain subsided enough for us to survey the damage. We were shocked! Sometime during the night the creek had become a powerful body of water that had crested twenty-two feet high and one-hundred-and-ten feet wide. Several giant cypresses were stripped completely of their bark, and one was now tilted at a forty-five-degree angle, its base concealed by a massive knot of logs, branches, and vines, with the trunks of two twenty-foot trees suspended, roots and all, in the tangle surrounding the cypress!

In many places, eighty to one hundred feet from the bank of the creek, more than two feet of sand had been borne by the surging waters and dumped. On the other side of the creek, across from us, the trees and shrubs whose greenery formerly concealed the country road some fifty feet beyond, were completely washed away, exposing not only the road but also a new landscape of whitewashed limestone rocks and rubble.

A few days later when we were able to navigate our way down the creek (the current was too strong in many places to wade in it), we were awestruck by the transformations to the landscape. The most incredible sight was of a massive concrete piling, which years ago had suspended a railroad trestle some twenty-feet above ground. The whole thing had been dislodged by the rush of water, and was now jutting out of the creek some fifteen yards downstream, having smashed and destroyed on its way the concrete slab that had served as a fording bridge for cars.

We have renamed the portion of the Big Joshua Creek that runs through Sisterfarm, the Kali Creek—a testament to the awesome power of drops of water which, over time, not only can wear the rock away but also, on occasion, raise it up in the air and toss it like a feather. Or as Hildegard of Bingen would express it: "A feather on the breath of God."

Works Cited

O'Rourke, Lawrence M. *Geno: The Life and Mission of Geno Baroni.* Mahwah, N.J.: Paulist Press, 1991.

Paul VI. A Call to Action. Apostolic Letter on the Eightieth Anniversary of *Rerum Novarum.* Washington, D.C.: United States Catholic Conference, 1971.

Rich, Adrienne. "Natural Resources." *The Dream of a Common Language.* New York: W. W. Norton & Company, Inc. 1978.

Sylvester, Nancy and Coston, Carol. "The Prophetic Tradition of Denouncing and Announcing." In *Shaping a New World. A Challenge for the 21st Century.* Washington, D.C.: Network, 1998.

12.

◆

Many religious congregations have stock portfolios in order to produce income to support health care, retirement, formation and education of their members, as well as to contribute to worthy efforts in ministry that otherwise would go unfunded. Holding stocks in profit making companies, however, involves tacit support of their policies and raises questions about possible complicity in unjust practices. Congregations of women engaged in collaborative efforts among themselves and with other like-minded groups to monitor investments, develop resolutions for presentation at stockholder meetings, and to assist in divestment of stocks when it was deemed advisable. Later they pooled resources for alternative investments to enable small businesses and loan fund organizations to get started.

◆

Women Religious Invest in Their Values

Sharing the Earth's Resources in a Spirit of World Communion

Carol Coston, OP

By holding in common all our resources, we place mutual trust in one another and challenge one another to coresponsibility in the use of those resources. (ADC)

The ferments of the late 1960s—student unrest, opposition to the Vietnam War, the civil rights struggle, new ideas from Vatican Council II, renewal in religious life, liberation theologies, feminism, critiques of United States foreign policy, antimilitarism—led to disturbing questions about the uses of power in all institutional settings. These ferments encouraged innovative approaches in seeking social justice that bubbled up into new expressions of social, academic, religious, and political activism. And just as an examination and subsequent rejection of the government's justification of the war in Vietnam led thousands to demonstrations, draft counseling, acts of resistance, political action, teach-ins, and prayer vigils; so, too, an examination of the role of multinational corporations led to new forms of shareholder activism in the 1970s.

As women religious, we lived in the midst of these societal ferments, as well as those we spawned ourselves in the renewal process. As Adrian Dominicans, imbued with a new sense of our responsibility for social justice, we found ourselves continually questioning how best to use our institutional resources—both human and financial—in furthering our mission, the mission of the gospel. The story that follows focuses on the way one congregation moved with the dynamic of creative leadership reciprocally engaging with the energies, questions, and suggestions of its members to establish a consistency between its stated values and the use of its financial resources. While it is one congregation's story, it reflects a broader movement among women religious that spread to form connections with other like minded organizations to become a significant force for societal change.

Ecumenical Cooperation in Exploring Corporate Responsibility

In 1971, when they filed the initial resolution against apartheid in South Africa, the Episcopalians became the first United States religious group to become publicly involved in corporate responsibility activities. They were assisted by the Corporate Information Center (CIC), a branch of the National Council of Churches in New York City. Organized Catholic involvement appears to have begun in 1973 with the formation of the National Catholic Coalition for Responsible Investment (NCCRI), sponsored by several Catholic religious orders in the Midwest. It was in that same year that Father Joseph O'Rourke joined the staff of the CIC as the Catholic Coordinator.

The Adrian Dominicans stepped into the corporate responsibility arena in January 1973, when Louise Borgacz, OP, was asked by Sister Rosemary Ferguson, prioress, and the general council at the time, to investigate the "role that the Church, as investor, has in proclaiming the Gospel" (RMRCI, May 1973). In an earlier report to the Council, Louise noted that taking our responsibility as "investors to help determine the course of action to be taken by corporations is a very new area for the Catholic Church to investigate" (RMRCI March 1973). She observed that "many other Christian denominations have done considerable work and have become quite sophisticated in their approach," whereas Catholics were "taking their first faltering steps in this endeavor." As a result, no clear-cut guidelines were readily available, and any "meaningful action" would have to be preceded by further investigation and reflection. This situation led Louise in the same report to observe: "I must admit to my impatience but I realize that precipitate action is rarely, if ever, effective."

In May of the same year Louise attended a symposium in Milwaukee entitled "Church Investment and Corporate Responsibility." The symposium was conducted by CIC, which soon after evolved into ICCR, the Interfaith Center on Corporate Responsibility. The topics covered included History of Corporate Responsibility and Religious Institutions, Theology of Corporate Challenge, Structure and Strategy of Multinational Corporations, Environment, Disclosure and Proxy Resolutions. The eighty participants were primarily sisters, the majority from the Wisconsin area. In her follow-up report to the general council, Louise noted that "It soon became very apparent that a great deal of education was needed by the participants before any group action could be taken."

During the evaluation session, NCCRI members decided to form a committee to plan subsequent meetings in the fall of 1973. Louise, Sister Assunta Stang, SC, and a NAWR (National Association of Women Religious) representative were on the committee, as well as Fathers Eugene Boyle, Joseph O'Rourke, Dale Olen, and Reid Mayo, who was president of the National Federation of Priests' Councils (NFPC). Interest was gathering momentum and two days later Louise and Kathryn Noonan, OP, attended a meeting of the Michigan and Indiana Treasurers of Religious Institutes where Louise addressed the group on the issue of corporate responsibility as it had been presented at the Milwaukee Symposium. The treasurers decided to sponsor a similar symposium at their LCWR (Leadership Conference of Women Religious) Region VII meeting in the fall at Adrian, Michigan. They would ask the major Superiors of that region to be co-sponsors.

Adrian Dominicans Encouraged to Develop Investment Guidelines

As concern for social responsibility in investments was mounting, Louise recommended to the Adrian Dominican General Council that a written policy statement and criteria on our investments, representing primarily funds set aside for the retirement needs of the Adrian Dominican Sisters, be prepared to be included in an annual report of the financial position of our congregation. She also urged a donation to the Corporate Information Center to support ongoing research into corporate activities. She recommended further that a portfolio review committee be established: to develop criteria for our investments; to review our portfolio on a continuing basis to assess our investments in accordance with our criteria; to initiate and/or cooperate in actions being undertaken with corporations whose policies were at odds with our criteria; to communicate with all the members of the congregation to educate on the moral aspects of corporate investments; and to appoint a member of the committee to act as liaison to other groups who share our agenda on corporate investments with us.

Evolving from her role of investigating the ways and means of corporate responsibility and suggesting the formation of a portfolio committee, Louise next took direct action. Representing the congregation through the Finance Office, she wrote in February 1974 to the corporations in which we owned stock and requested information on their policies in the following areas: fair employment practices, both domestic and foreign; attention to ecological balance and pollution controls; efforts to concentrate on peacetime as contrasted with military operations; improvement of the quality of life of employees by alleviating poverty and combating racism; and procedures to allow consumer groups a voice in corporation affairs.

The first education piece on corporate responsibility for the Adrian Dominicans appeared in the *Report to the Congregation 1968–1973* (ADA) in the section on finances in advance of the 1974 General Chapter. "General chapters" of the 1,200–member congregation are convened every six years to elect new leadership and set congregational priorities and directions articulated through chapter "goals" or "enactments." The pre-chapter report stated:

Now that we have liquidated some of our real estate and have purchased stock for the growth of our Education Fund, our Retirement Fund and our Dowry and Patrimony Fund, we are increasingly aware of our obligation as stockholders. The social impact large international corporations may have which injures our neighbor or destroys the environment concerns us deeply. In 1968, the Congregation owned a few shares of stock in various corporations and was relatively oblivious of the ethics of investments . . . Many sisters have expressed a concern regarding the Congregation's investments; the various portfolios are available for review in the Finance Office. *Presently being considered is a Portfolio Review Committee composed of members of the Congregation and others, that would develop criteria for investments and study the various issues involved.* (ADA 54. Emphasis added)

1974 General Chapter Endorses Evaluation of Congregation's Investments

As preparation for general chapter continued, members of the congregation, encouraged by the leadership's position, expressed interest in having the general chapter pass a strong mandate in the area of justice, that could encompass all the works and resources of the congregation, including our investments. A discussion about this issue took place in Washington, D.C., during the 1974 Annual Legislative Seminar sponsored by NETWORK, the Catholic social justice lobby, founded by forty-seven sisters in 1971 (see chapter 11). We had convened a gathering of the twenty or more Adrian Dominicans who were attending that seminar or were in Washington at that time. We discussed the general chapter and our hopes for it. As a participant in the discussion, I recall that four of the Adrian Sisters present were delegates to the general chapter and that they were urged to help pass a chapter enactment on using justice as a criteria in examining our investment portfolio. In August, 1974, the entire general chapter proposed as Goal IV that we:

> evaluate our congregational investments in relation to the Gospel social principles and identify means to effect change toward justice in the policies and operations of corporations in which we hold stock. (ADA)

That fall the General Council commissioned the Office of Financial Services to coordinate the establishment of a Portfolio Advisory Board (PAB), modeled on the proposal of Louise Borgacz. On October 10,

1974, Sisters Anne Guinan, OP, treasurer of the congregation, and Louise Borgacz, assistant to the treasurer, wrote to the congregation explaining the General Council's directive to them and the function of this new board, whose members would be appointed by the General Council "representing a cross section of the Congregation with knowledge in one or more of the following areas: theology, economics, social justice issues, business and finance." Anne and Louise noted that "while it is important that the board be composed of individuals with the knowledge outlined above, it is equally important that these members evidence self motivation and objectivity." They then asked for volunteers or for suggestions of sisters to be invited and attached a form indicating that it should be returned "on or before October 30, 1974."

First Portfolio Advisory Board Appointed

In December 1974, the following Adrian Dominican Sisters received an invitation from Sister Rosemary Ferguson, prioress of the congregation, to serve on the first Portfolio Advisory Board to help implement Goal IV: Margaret Andrezik, Louise Borgacz, Carol Coston, Anne Guinan, Marie Solanus Reilly, and Kathleen Woods. Although Marie had some banking experience prior to entering the congregation, and both Louise and Anne had some finance experience, all were relative novices in the area of shareholder responsibility. But in the time-honored tradition of many religious congregations of women we accepted the challenge and learned by doing.

The first meeting of the Portfolio Advisory Board was preceded by a workshop for the PAB members, the General Council, investment managers, and representatives of congregation-owned schools. Capuchin priest Michael Crosby from the Milwaukee Justice and Peace Center assisted with the workshop. The Board accepted the biblical model presented by Michael as its model for strategies for change. It included the elements of dialogue, coalition, litigation, and divestment. The Board determined that it would inform the congregation of its deliberations through the February issue of the *Bulletin of Coordinating Services*.

In the following months the board began to finalize its bylaws and to formulate criteria for socially responsible investing. The members drew up seven short-range goals including advocating for affirmative action in corporations, developing guides for voting proxies, identifying allies, informing the congregation, attending five stockholder meetings—all to be completed by May, 1975. They also drew up five medium-range goals around alternative investing, awareness of strip mining, investigation of our banks, identification of local areas of concern for social responsibility and organizing action projects for various congregation committees, such as the PAB, ADISS (Adrian Dominican Independent School System), the Justice and Finance Committees, as well as our individual sisters. There still remained the task of developing four long-range goals to initiate dialogue with banks, communicate guidelines to corporations, plan stockholders' actions for 1976, and establish formal and informal linkages with related groups. These were completed later in the year.

The first official act of the board was to send for information on equal employer opportunity to eight corporations. At the same time some of the sisters had their first experiences of attending shareholders meetings: Louise Borgacz, with IBM in Pittsburgh; Carol Coston, with General Electric in Boston; and Kathleen Woods, with 3M in St. Paul. Attendance at shareholders meetings was to become a continuing activity under the direction of the PAB and over time has involved many members of the congregation. One ongoing concern has been the presence or absence of women on corporate boards. As shareholders, congregation representatives chose not to vote at all for new board members when there were no women among the nominees.

Among other early activities of the PAB was the establishment of a study project on the infant formula policies of Abbott Laboratories as they were affecting women and children in poverty areas of the world. In this effort they were in concert with the other social responsibility groups with whom bonds were being forged, especially with ICCR with whom later they co-filed resolutions for the shareholder meetings of Abbott, as well as Bristol-Myers and American Home Products. Of particular interest to Adrian Dominicans were the policies of Gulf and Western in its treatment of employees in the Dominican Republic, a country in which the congregation had carried on ministry since the 1940s. Plans for congregation-wide education in the areas of agribusiness, consumerism and hunger were developed. And the possibilities of alternative investment began to be raised. Merely to review the activity of the PAB in its first years of existence is to gain a sense of the excitement and urgency that lay in this new arena of ministry for women religious as they reflected upon their responsibility to be communicators of Gospel values.

Initial reflection and activity led to the following position statement developed by the PAB and approved by the General Council of the Congregation:

The Portfolio Advisory Board of the Sisters of St. Dominic of Adrian, Michigan, will communicate the following guidelines to the corporations and financial institutions in which our congregational funds are invested. As responsible investors we hope to raise their consciousness regarding our investment priorities and to challenge them to make continued efforts to operationalize the promotion of justice in the following ways:

- by providing adequate benefits and equal opportunities for all employees in both domestic and foreign operations,
- by having representation of a broad range of society on their boards of directors,
- by affirming the dignity of the individual in their promotion and advertising policies,
- by utilizing their corporate profits in a just and responsible manner,
- by directing their products or services toward the health and welfare of the consumer,
- by making extensive efforts to convert from a military to a peacetime operation,
- by including in their planning the correction of exploitative practices in the Third World, and
- by displaying a sensitivity to the problems of ecological balance through their efforts to control pollution (ADA).

An immediate consequence of this position was to attend to the congregation's own corporate investments by researching the companies in which the congregation held stock, attending their stockholder meetings and investigating the social policies of the banks that held the congregation's funds. The criteria for socially responsible investment were sent to all of the corporations and they were informed that in the future the congregation's investment managers would be sending the proxies to the congregation's headquarters for voting. This latter step was important since most stockholders delegate this responsibility to their portfolio managers.

In 1976 the PAB's relationship with the Interfaith Center on Corporate Responsibility was firmly established. It was to be long term and mutually beneficial. A policy of co-filing resolutions with them in as many areas as possible was adopted. Tim Smith, executive director of ICCR met with the PAB to discuss strategies for stockholder meetings.

The congregation's particular interest in the condition of workers in the Dominican Republic has an interesting history of corporate responsibility activity with Gulf and Western. The firsthand experience of the congregation's members in that country, as they observed the deplorable conditions of the workers and the profligate use of the country's resources on the part of the company weighed heavily on the corporate conscience of the congregation. PAB members made investigative trips to the Dominican Republic. They contacted Gulf and Western corporate executives directly and met several times with their representatives in Adrian, New York and the Dominican Republic. The company insisted that they had a social policy governing their employee relationships, but it was several years before a written version of this policy was obtained.

The interaction continued for several years with a series of meetings held in the Dominican Republic with Gulf and Western's local management, government officials from the agriculture department, labor union leaders, community activists, workers in the sugar industry, the local bishop and Adrian Dominicans working in the country. PAB was careful to hear all sides of the issues. The process was a learning experience in many ways. It gave the PAB members a firsthand encounter with the enormous economic power of multinational corporations in stark contrast with the impoverished economy of a struggling nation. Labor union leaders took them to a worker camp where, since there were no lights, they had to make their way with flashlights. They walked through filthy sewage water and observed as many as eight people sleeping within a narrow room scarcely eight feet wide. There was one working shower for about two hundred people and all of the toilets were clogged. Many of these workers were Haitians, hired by Gulf and Western because the arduous work of cane cutting was rejected by the Dominicans. The Haitians were unorganized and easily susceptible to exploitation. From 1976 to 1979, the annual gross pay received by the cane cutters was $2.13 a day.

Such memories accompanied me as I attended the annual stockholder meeting of Gulf and Western in 1981. It was held that year at the elegant and exclusive Breakers Hotel in Palm Beach, Florida. We gathered in a high-ceilinged ballroom with huge windows opening out to the Atlantic Ocean under a clear Florida sky with swooping seagulls. The parquet floors were spotless, the expensive chairs neatly arranged and the speakers' platform adorned with lovely green plants and floral arrangements. The contrast between the two scenes was painful, as was the angry outburst of the Gulf and Western CEO, Charles Bludhorn, when I tried to convey what I had seen and heard during my recent trip. He clearly did not want to hear what I had to say, nor did he want any discordant note sounded during an otherwise upbeat meeting with well-heeled investors.

Sisters from other congregations involved in corporate responsibility activities had had similar experiences when they tried to convey the negative effects that highly funded multinational corporations can have on economically developing countries. It is an ongoing struggle to put the human faces of the workers and their rights in front of executives competing in the Wall Street world of profit margins and bottom lines.

Divestment Strategy with Defense Industries

Since the visit of Pope Paul VI to the United Nations in 1965 where he had passionately urged that there be "no more war," Catholic Christians generally had begun to recognize the horrible toll that war and the arms race exact in human lives and the world's resources. The experience of the Vietnam War had raised the issues in explosive ways that engaged the entire populace of the United States and the world community. The rising consciousness of the Adrian Dominicans and its PAB led to reflection upon the congregation's responsibility in supporting corporations that were heavily into the production of the weapons of war. An enactment of the General Chapter of 1982 made the following statement:

> Corporate America is geared toward profit and as multinationals move to the Sunbelt or other countries in order to secure cheaper and non-unionized labor they leave unemployment in their wake. Many corporations specialize in securing military contracts and become part of the "iron triangle"—the Pentagon, the Congressional Armed Services and Appropriations Committee, and defense contractors. This triangle is a major force in skewing the federal budget toward defense spending that is highly inflationary. (ADA)

Upon the further recommendation of the PAB, the General Chapter endorsed a specific action. "The Congregation will take a public stand for peace-making by divesting itself, within one year, of stock currently held in the top one hundred defense contractors." On February 16, 1983, Sister Carol Johannes, OP, prioress of the congregation, notified all the companies in our portfolio that were among the top one hundred in defense contracts that we would divest of currently-held stock, and that we would advise our investment managers not to invest in the others so long as they were on that list. There was immediate response from many of the companies whose basic message was that, while they did not agree with us, we had a right to our opinion. Some suggested that we were "naive."

Opposition to Apartheid in South Africa

The civil rights movement of the 1960s and 1970s in the United States was another strong influence in consciousness raising around issues of social justice for all Americans. Global awareness encompassed the issue of apartheid in South Africa and the role that multinational corporations played in sustaining that system. Beginning in 1977, banks and corporations in the Adrian Dominican investment portfolio were called to account for the effects that their holdings, practices, and policies had in sustaining the dehumanizing conditions in South Africa. By 1986 the situation had escalated to the point that the PAB was carrying on dialogue with thirty-two corporations represented in the congregation's portfolio. They were asked to explain how their business activities conformed to the Sullivan Principles, the guidelines elucidated by Reverend Leon Sullivan, one of the first African Americans to serve on corporate boards. In August of 1986 the PAB decided to co-file shareholder resolutions on South Africa with the New York State Common Retirement Fund, the New York City Employees Retirement Fund, and the National Council of Churches. Notifications were sent to twenty-two corporations advising them of our intention to file a shareholder resolution and asking them to withdraw from South Africa by May of 1987. Four of these corporations withdrew from South Africa during this period of dialogue, but in June 1987, Sister Nadine Foley, OP, prioress of the congregation, informed eighteen companies that the Adrian Dominican Congregation was divesting itself of their stock because of their intransigence on the issue of apartheid in South Africa.

    To dramatize another strategy showing our resistance to the evils of apartheid, PAB arranged a press conference on October 10, 1986, in the entrance lobby of the Congregation's Administration Building in Adrian,

Michigan. The point of the press conference was to announce our boycott of Shell products because its parent company, Royal Dutch/Shell, was doing business with the military and police of South Africa. Notices were sent out to sisters living on the campus and in the surrounding areas. Since many of them used Shell cards to purchase gasoline, the PAB gave everyone present the opportunity to participate in the symbolic cutting up of the charge cards. With characteristic cooperative response, dozens of Shell cards were produced by the sisters, and even by some of their relatives. A container full of scissors was provided; signs were made, including one featuring a large Shell logo crossed by a red line; a microphone was set up; the press was contacted; and people came from the campus and the surrounding area. The event took on the feel of a ritual of protest as each sister cut the card and dropped it in an envelope to be mailed to corporate headquarters. Sisters in other parts of the country joined in the action at their local areas. At one level, the action was a small symbolic gesture but, on another, it illustrated the strength of an institutional response to injustice and linked PAB's shareholder actions on behalf of the entire congregation with the power we have as individual consumers. The small symbolic action received a great deal of media attention, much to our surprise. It also generated some heated responses from Shell executives.

In the April 1995 issue of the congregation's publication *In Between*, celebrating PAB's twentieth anniversary, Sister Marie Michael, OP, who had coordinated much of PAB's South Africa resolutions, reflected on the cumulative effect this type of action had on the eventual dismantling of the system of apartheid:

> Little was known in the early years of the impact shareholder activism would make in the corporate and financial market world. For the first time in financial history, stock market prices had declined for companies who remained doing business in South Africa, and placing a company's name on the South African boycott list caused great concern among company leaders and policymakers. (10)

Alternative Investments Reap a Hundredfold

As work with responsible investments continued, the members of the Portfolio Advisory Board began to expand their vision to other areas for action on behalf of justice. The possibility for making some of the congregation's funds available for alternative investments, to assist those for whom high interest rates were prohibitive, became an exciting consideration. Upon appeal to the General Council of the Congregation a program for alternative investments was undertaken. In the same twentieth anniversary issue of *In Between*, Sister Corinne Florek, a member of the PAB for fifteen years, and who served as chair of the Alternative Investment Committee, wrote an article entitled "Alternative Investments Reap a Hundredfold." She described PAB's initial foray into this field:

> In 1978 the PAB made its first alternative investments in Chicago's South Shore Bank, a credit union in Texas, an ecumenical coalition in Ohio addressing unemployment, and St. Mary's Development Center in South Carolina directed by Ellen Robertson, OP. These projects put money directly back into poor communities in a very different way. They were loans, not giveaways or grants, which meant a change in expectations. First, the money would be returned. Second, there would be ongoing communication so that a relationship was begun. Third, there would be accountability for what happened as a result of the loan. Finally, interest would be paid on the loan. (8)

The 1978 General Chapter, in response to suggestions made by PAB, passed Enactment 39 that called for "the continued monitoring of our present investment portfolio and the increased utilization of alternative investments." Beginning with a $100,000 fund, which the General Councils gradually increased to $1.5 million in 1984, to $2 million in 1991, and to $3 million in 1998, the PAB made loans to a variety of worker-owned businesses, and to intermediary organizations that develop and support low-income businesses or housing projects. We also placed deposits in low-income credit unions and South Shore Bank, an innovative bank which became the prototype of "community economic development banks," and whose mission is to make credit available within low-wealth neighborhoods and to help reinvigorate distressed communities.

Learning by Doing

Just as we "learned by doing" shareholder resolutions and dialogue with corporate management, so too, we learned how to make credit available to underserved communities by beginning to make a few loans and deposits and then evaluating the results. For example, in 1978 we made two loans, two deposits, and purchased a few shares in the Ecumenical Development Cooperative Society (EDCS). By 1989 we had made eighty loans or investments totaling almost three million dollars. Thirty of these (29 percent) had paid back in full and we had lost three, representing 2.4 percent of the total loaned at that time. As of June 30, 1997, PAB had placed over $5.5 million in 155 loans and deposits. But these numbers alone do not really tell the story of why we began this work, how we saw lending as part of our mission, who was assisted by this credit, and how we evolved and matured as a committee.

When PAB first began, there was a small reference to the possibility of our making alternative investments, but a major factor in our moving in this direction was the Board's collective frustration in the early years of ever effecting real change in the corporations in which we then held stock. We dutifully filed shareholder resolutions, voted proxies, initiated dialogue with corporate management, and spoke up at annual meetings. The faith-based members of ICCR collaborated on resolutions and we often went together to the annual meetings, but our resolutions usually obtained very small percentages of the proxy votes cast—one percent to three percent. It was hard to feel any great sense of victory, even though we knew we were fulfilling a General Chapter and Gospel mandate. So the idea of doing something more proactive with our investments was quite appealing—to know specifically where our money was being used and who benefited from it.

The congregation's mission statement at that time spoke of our commitment to the mission of Jesus, to be bearers and recipients of love, and cocreators of justice and peace in a manner similar to his own life and teachings. We asked ourselves: With whom do we cast our lot and how should we create justice and peace with our investments? The experiences of divesting in corporations that produce nuclear weapons and contribute to an escalating arms race was a way of trying to create peace, and our opposing the racist policies of South Africa by urging the corporations to leave the country was a step for justice. And when we applied these questions to more proactive investing, it is easy to see the appeal of aligning ourselves with small credit unions, worker-owned cooperatives, and ecumenically supported housing projects.

Credit Unions Help Marginalized Communities

By 1989 we had made nine credit union deposits. Our connection with Quitman County Credit Union in Marks, Mississippi, illustrates the commonality of mission we felt with them. When Sister Maureen Fenlon and I visited Marks, it was easy to see the long history of segregation that the founders of the credit union faced as they began to think of developing a financial institution that would be accessible for their needs as African Americans. The small town was clearly divided by race, the blacks living, literally, on the other side of the tracks. The white power structure refused to give the credit union organizers a zoning permit to construct a building to house both the credit union, a small business, and the office of a community economic development corporation. The town's African American community united in an economic boycott of the white- and Chinese-owned businesses. The boycott was successful and the zoning permit obtained, but the local bankers were not interested in placing deposits in the credit union to help it increase its lending capital. The credit union belonged to the National Federation of Community Development Credit Unions that by definition have to have a field of membership that is over half low-income. The Adrian Dominicans, therefore, could make a $50,000 deposit and become partners with the courageous and determined activists willing to take a stand for their own empowerment. Their spirit had been demonstrated earlier, during the civil rights struggle in the 1960s, when the famous "mule train" caravan began in Marks. That caravan was a public demonstration of African Americans' demand to be treated equally under the law and to be able to register and vote in all elections. It was clear that their determination was still alive and well in Marks.

Worker-Ownership Creates Alternative Business Structures

Our investing in worker-owned cooperatives is another example of "throwing in our lot" with persons willing to take financial risks in order to achieve some self-determination and to create a work environment that is respectful, humane, and just. By 1989, we had invested in nineteen worker-owned cooperatives, and these experiences collectively provided our most colorful stories as well as learnings from our losses! Just the names and products illustrate the imagination and creative energies of the worker-owners: Eastern Casket Company (North Carolina);

Crazy Ladies Bookstore (Ohio); Rainbow Workers Cooperative (California), which tried to organize Asian, African American, and Latina women to produce upscale camping equipment such as tents and sleeping bags; Wild Oats (Vermont), which made maternity clothes; and Cooperative Cab Company (California), a former Yellow Cab Company taken over by the workers.

PAB members felt a great commonality with the structure of a worker-owned cooperative since it was similar in many ways to our own congregation's form of governance and our pooling of resources. But it was a very difficult structure for workers who were used to having a boss and being paid a regular salary and who now had to take on co-responsibility for all major business decisions and to rely completely on each other in order to make a profit. We North Americans are so imbued in a culture that values "rugged individualism" and "looking out for number one" that the concept of co-ownership became a major barrier. Three of the worker-owned cooperatives to whom we made loans, however—Cooperative Home Care Associates in the Bronx, Childspace Management Group in Philadelphia, and Equal Exchange in the Boston area—are among the most successful cooperatives still functioning today.

Equal Exchange and Adrian Dominicans: A Creative Partnership

When Michael Rozyne first called to tell me about a small worker-owned business that wanted to import coffee from small cooperatives in Latin America and sell to socially responsible consumers in the U.S., and whose three co-owner founders were white males with college degrees, I admit to having limited enthusiasm. But Michael is persistent and persuasive, and after PAB members, Corinne Florek, Maureen Fenlon, and I, met him personally, we recommended our first loan to Equal Exchange in 1987 and another in 1988. They have continued to be sound borrowing partners and we still have a loan with them in 1999.

Equal Exchange is an amazing enterprise. The worker-owners truly are committed to fair trade relationships with small coffee producing cooperatives. When Michael, Jonathan Rosenthal, and Rink Dickinson began the cooperative, they realized that the small producers were at the mercy of middlemen who bought low and sold high, thus creaming off the profits and leaving the coffee growers living at a subsistence level.

Equal Exchange determined to establish personal relationships with the growers, to offer portions of the payment in advance so that the small farmers could manage until the final sale, and to guarantee the purchase of specific amounts of beans each season. Another important policy decision was to pay the fair market price for the green beans, despite the fluctuations in the worldwide coffee market. This "fair price" was set by established fair trade organizations in Europe. As a result of the policy, Equal Exchange, in effect, has subsidized the growers during many years when the world coffee price was depressed. By 1998 they estimate this total subsidy to be over one million dollars.

Each year certain staff members visit the cooperative growers to keep up the relationships, to set up the contracts, to determine their technical assistance needs, and to share information on sustainable growing methods. Equal Exchange uses its newsletters and magazine to educate U.S. consumers to the economic reality of the small growers and often encourages college students and shareholders to make site visits to the producing cooperatives.

PAB members try to find ways to help sell Equal Exchange coffee within our own networks. For example, during a congregation-wide gathering, "Transformations '89," each coffeestand on campus used Equal Exchange coffee and included informational pieces on the cooperative that showed how our investment monies are used in solidarity with the economically poor. The sisters were encouraged to take home order blanks for their personal or institutional use. The coffee was in evidence again during the 1998 General Chapter for the same reason. In addition, I encouraged the financial officers of several Catholic health care systems to pass on Equal Exchange information to their purchase departments. The PAB sees socially aware purchasing as another aspect of corporate responsibility.

Learning from Our Losses

Part of PAB's lending philosophy is that we want to help those who have been left out or discriminated against by traditional lending institutions. These groups are often members of minority communities, women who have no business experience, or persons trying to establish different forms of business structures, such as cooperatives, that banks do not understand or choose to refuse loans, if they do. Another value is supporting alternative approaches to the production of goods or services. We also encourage local self-determination and community control, and ask if the project could lead to the breaking down of racial barriers.

Most of the groups to whom we have given loans embody several of these values and are able to establish successful businesses or housing projects. However, a few of our borrowers, especially the worker-owned cooperatives, have run into serious difficulties and had to close down their enterprises. These losses have been assumed by the Alternative Investment Fund. Working with a group that is confronting a failed venture is often painful and time consuming for PAB members or staff. When all bailout or regrouping strategies have failed, we try to help the workers or directors close down with a minimum of financial loss to us and the organization, and to do it in a way that respects the dignity of the participants.

As a part of our own sense of responsibility for overseeing the use of this part of our common fund, PAB members prepare a detailed analysis of each loan we have lost and then we have a discussion about the learnings and how to apply them to future lending. For example, Maureen Fenlon, OP, wrote the report when the Rainbow Workers' Cooperative in Oakland, California, failed. This cooperative began when public pressure on an upscale camping supply company that was trying to take the business out of Oakland forced the owners to offer the business to a group of predominantly women workers, who envisioned turning it into a worker-owned business. The workers included Asians, Latinas, and African Americans. The local community loved the concept of the "rainbow" and gave a lot of support to a sale of the products, which would be used to give each worker money to buy her individual "share" of the cooperative. A number of lenders also liked the idea and so the necessary capital for the transfer of ownership was raised. Despite everyone's enthusiasm, however, the business ultimately failed. Maureen's analysis pointed to four major reasons:

(1) Trying to convert to worker-ownership is difficult under the best of circumstances, but it is made all the more so by having to translate all worker instruction and meetings into three languages.
(2) The business of sewing tents, sleeping bags, backpacks, etc., is an extremely competitive one with many companies using sweatshop techniques or setting up off-shore and cheaper factories for production. So when the cooperative tried to pay a living wage to the workers, it became very difficult to remain competitive on price.

(3) The local technical assistance in financial management that the lenders had been assured was present was not, and this added to the floundering. By the time the problem surfaced in financial statements sent to the lenders, the cooperative was on a downward spiral.

(4) A new manager was hired who almost tripled the number of items to be produced. This completely out-paced the capabilities of the internal structure and systems.

Maureen made several visits to the cooperative during these troubled days and felt particularly sad that the women, who had such high hopes, were going to be let down and once again looking for decent paying employment.

In the past twenty years during which the number of religious congregations doing some kind of alternative investments, or "investments in alternatives" has increased, so has the spirit of collaboration. The size and complexity of the community economic development projects have also grown and therefore the need for more funding. Given this growth, congregations are reaching out to one another to create ways to be co-lenders in these projects, not only by agreeing to make loans to the same project, but also to develop "co-creditor agreements" so that the cooperation remains into the long term of these community investments.

Besides these joint efforts congregations are also challenging one another to increase the level of their alternative investment funds, not only as a demonstration of their commitment to this financial ministry, but also as a response to the growing need for this form of community investment. As an example, the Dominican Leadership Conference passed a nonbinding resolution at their October 1998 annual meeting that states:

To counteract the negative effects of globalization on people who are poor, we encourage each Dominican congregation or province to earmark five percent (5%) of their total investment portfolio for alternative/community investment by the year 2000, giving special attention to enterprises beyond U.S. borders.

What began as a small effort by a few is expanding to a sizable commitment on the part of many in concert with one another to address the economic pressures on the disadvantaged in the global markets.

Reflections on Adrian Dominican Leadership Style and the PAB

As I conclude this story of the Adrian Dominicans' establishment of our Portfolio Advisory Board, I want to reflect on the roles played by the General Councils, the General Chapters, the PAB members and staff, and the congregation at large.

I earlier explained how Louise Borgacz generously responded to the General Council's request to research ways to examine our investments in the light of social justice. When she came back to the council with suggestions about a forming committee, placing statements in the financial report, and holding a workshop in Adrian, the leadership acquiesced and encouraged her to keep pursuing the research. Soon thereafter, the general chapter responded to these and other suggestions, passing Goal IV "that we evaluate our congregational investments in relation to the gospel social principles and identify means to effect change toward justice in the policies and operations of corporations in which we hold stock."

Following the 1974 General Chapter, the General Council wrote a memo on October 5, 1974, to the whole congregation regarding the implementation of chapter goals. The council members noted that they recognized their responsibility "to direct the congregation's planning and development," and to make the initial decisions as to the types of programs needed and the way to mobilize the congregation's resources to carry them out. I believe, however, that the next paragraph aptly illustrates a leadership style that I have observed in our congregation:

We also know and believe that the initiative and creativity of all our sisters is our most valuable resource and that program designs must allow for their free expression. As we have spent days in dialogue, study and consultation, we have tried to make provision for that expression. *We have tried to take only such steps as will set things in motion and allow for further development as all of us become involved.* (ADA. Emphasis added)

Once the PAB had been "set in motion," we were encouraged to develop our goals and objectives on our own, in concert with the General Chapter mandates. We were trusted to make decisions and recommendations on the basis of our own research, study, and consultations with others in the field, and with the common good of the congregation in mind. It has been my experience that each subsequent General Council has treated the PAB in the same way.

It is clear that we are appointed by the council and ultimately responsible to them, particularly through the general council liaison to the committee. Our authority is limited to recommending the alternative investments but over the years our judgment has been accepted with rare exception. The PAB has the authority to take on shareholder activities as we see fit and to recommend the purchase of given stock if we want to be involved with that corporation because of a particular issue. We can also request that certain stocks be sold if our shareholder dialogues or resolutions do not bring about the changes desired. When we wanted to take a major action, such as divesting, or never purchasing stock in the top 100 defense contractors, we felt that this could have some financial ramifications, so we presented a proposal to the general chapter, who endorsed the idea. In this way, the action became a congregational response to the arms race in accord with general chapter directives. In short the PAB, while it has been given a wide range of freedom for its work, always acts in the name of, and with the authorization of, the congregation through its elected leadership.

Another way in which we engaged our sisters was to set up bus trips in Detroit and Chicago, where we have a large concentration of our members, to show them the alternative investments we had made in their name. We met the various borrowers and saw houses rehabbed, rentals turned into home ownership, and small businesses employing neighborhood residents. Then we had time for a debriefing and prayer service. These trips were well received.

Each year when shareholder resolutions are filed we notify the membership through the congregation's monthly bulletin of the place and date of the annual meetings and invite sisters to join PAB members in attending. This involvement of interested sisters also increases a sense of ownership of PAB's work. Since this essay is about using finances in ways that support the mission, I feel it is fitting to close with one final reflection on how Prioress Rosemary Ferguson and the Councilors "set in motion" the first PAB in the area of budgeting. From the beginning they made it clear that they were willing to approve a budget sufficient to cover the transportation costs for five team members from any geographical location to attend meetings in Adrian and also to cover the cost of transportation to five workshops or stockholder meetings. As a result, the PAB members could be chosen from anywhere within the congregation. Since 1975, the PAB has been funded sufficiently to carry out its mandate. As our work increased with the addition of alternative investments and increased shareholder research and activity, the one staff person also increased to two, three, and now four in 1999. The first budget in 1975 totaled $4,550; the 1998–99 budget was $105,214.

The number of staff and the location of the office continues to evolve—from sharing space with the finance office in Adrian, to an office in Detroit, then back to Adrian, another move to Silver Spring, Maryland, and then back to Adrian. The staff expanded to three in 1989 and is now moving toward a four person staff. Another innovation in 1998 is that two laywomen have been hired to be the alternative investments/community development coordinator and the corporate responsibility coordinator.

The View from the Outside

The financial and personnel support for PAB, as well as the demonstrated trust of the membership and leadership, freed us to work with confidence in the larger arena of socially responsible investing. In addition to influencing the ways in which the congregation's financial assets were directed, PAB members also helped shape other organizations' investment activities. For example, Maureen Fenlon now works for the Ecumenical Development Cooperative Society (EDCS), a $100-million international fund that lends to large worker-owned cooperatives. She helps shape the outreach to, and increase the investments from, other religious communities. Corinne Florek used her PAB experience and contacts in her earlier work with Campaign for Human Development's economic development fund. She now works for Women's Initiative, a California-based fund that offers technical assistance and loans to women micro-entrepreneurs. Judy Rimbey now directs a multi-million dollar grant and alternative investment fund for Catholic Healthcare West (CHW), a system in California, Nevada, and Arizona, cosponsored by eight religious communities. CHW's investment philosophy, as well as its sizable alternative investment fund, was partially influenced by the Adrian Dominicans who were in leadership or on the PAB at the time when the congregation became a corporate member in the late 1980s.

In 1988, I also brought my PAB experience to the Christian Brothers Investment Services (CBIS), when they asked me to be a consultant to help design an alternative investment for them to offer to their participants. CBIS is a for-profit business cosponsored by nine provinces of Christian Brothers to help other religious congregations manage their investment portfolios more profitably. The funds I designed, Partners for the Common Good Loan Fund and Partners for the Common Good 2000 (PCG 2000), evolved directly from the alternative investment activities of PAB. PCG 2000 is capitalized at almost $8 million. The ninety-nine investors are all religious institutions, including the Adrian Dominicans and Catholic Healthcare West.

How do we assess the results of our work with alternative investments? The words of those who have been assisted have been expansive in their appreciation and motivate us to continue. "We thought we'd have to close our doors, and then your check arrived. More than money, it gave us hope that this could work. We are a profitable business today because you took a risk with us" (Jonathan Rosenthal, founder and current president of Equal Exchange). "You were the first to give us a loan, help us to develop a business and give us a track record to leverage other monies for our recycling business" (Penny Penrose of Gulf Coast Recycling). "You do it all. You are not afraid of a long term battle with companies on very hard issues, whose time has not yet come and you are willing to put money in places of higher risk and lower return while others seek lower risk and higher return. You have not only taken on your own work but have taken on leadership roles in the national movement" (Tim Smith, Executive Director of ICCR).

While such accolades have given us affirmation and encouragement for work that has always seemed to us only what is to be expected of women committed to the Gospel, there have been other assessments that have called our very identity into question. These have not only been made of Adrian Dominicans but of other congregations of women religious who have been similarly involved in issues of social justice. The self-perception that we have discovered in the processes of renewal since Vatican Council II is at times at odds with long held preconceptions of who we are or ought to be.

A retired board member of a congregation-owned institution read of the congregation's shareholder filing against a company for its policies that were endangering the environment. He wrote an indignant letter to the president of the institution calling her to task and declaring that the sisters should "stay in the classrooms where they belong." The incident points out how far some of our lay sisters and brothers are from understanding the most basic responsibility of Christian discipleship, one incumbent not only on religious, but on all Christians. The women and men religious who have reflected deeply on their responsibilities and commitment to social justice have realized that they are in the world and that the world has claims upon them for the values that the Gospel preaches. There are many ways in which to preach the Gospel through ministry and religious have engaged in them through the centuries. But especially today in our global economic environment the pursuit of social justice in the places where it is violated, especially among those who are poor because they remain excluded from the economic systems of their communities and nations, is one of them. For, "action on behalf of justice is a constituent dimension of the preaching of the Gospel" (CU 6). Our commitment to that pursuit will continue.

13

The rising consciousness of women worldwide is evident within
congregations of women religious as they reflect upon their experience in
a patriarchal Church. Gospel mission impels women religious, and other
women as well, to an urgency to see their gifts and talents recognized and
employed in the ministries of the Church. Women's concerns are not
particularized and limited to certain spheres of human life. They are as
wide and comprehensive as those of all people in pursuit of human rights
in global context. Movements among Catholic Christian women in recent
years bring their insights and concerns into the mainstream of the
Church's agendas as they experience themselves fully alive with the
freedom with which Christ makes all people free.

◆

Religious Life and Women's Issues
Maria Riley, OP

*Let us note and celebrate the fact that "women-spirit rising" is a
global phenomenon in our time. Everywhere women are on the
move. What is coming into view now, for the first time, on a
worldwide scale, is the incredible collective power of women so
that anyone who has eyes to see can glimpse the power and
strength of women's full maturity. (Harrison, 44)*

"Sure 'n what happened to the good sisters since I left the church?" This
question was posed to me by a companion on an ecumenical journey of
reconciliation to Ireland in 1976. He was a former IRA (Irish Republic
Army) activist who had left Ireland and the church and moved to the
United States in the 1950s. This ecumenical journey of reconciliation,
sponsored by the National Council of Churches of the United States,
marked his first return to the land of his birth and a renewed encounter
with sisters and the Catholic Church that he had left behind.

The question was not easily answered since so much had occurred during his twenty-year hiatus: the Second Vatican Council with its turn to the world; the renewal process in religious communities; the series of social encyclicals, and particularly the 1971 Synod statement on Justice in the World,[39] the beginnings of liberation theologies; and the rise of people's movements, including the civil rights and women's movements in the United States and elsewhere. There had been a dramatic convergence of events in the church and in the wider society that had radically altered the perspective and self-perception of many women religious and communities. They had metamorphosed from the "good sisters" to ecclesial women, women who not only served the church but understood themselves as the church in mission to the world.

Opening the Way—1960s

The year 1963 is emblematic of the many forces and events that shaped the emerging consciousness of women religious. In that year, the Second Vatican Council was in its first session and Pope John XXIII issued his human rights encyclical, *Pacem in terris,* in which he identified women's new consciousness as one of the three characteristics of the modern age:

> Secondly, the part that women are now playing in political life is everywhere evident. This is a development that is perhaps of swifter growth among Christian nations, but it is also happening extensively, if more slowly among nations that are heirs to different traditions and imbued with a different culture. Women are gaining an increasing awareness of their natural dignity. Far from being content with a purely passive role or allowing themselves to be regarded as a kind of instrument, they are demanding both in domestic and in public life the rights and duties which belong to them as human person (PT 41).[40]

---

[39] All Vatican and Synodal Documents are taken from Walsh and Davies.

[40] The other two characteristics of the modern age John XXIII identifies are the growing power of working men throughout the world in claiming their rights as workers and the decline of colonialism as more and more nations achieve independence. John XXIII's use of "working man," but not "working women," is probably due to two pervasive characteristics of Catholic social teaching: the generic use of "man" to include men and women, and more importantly, its consistent position that women's primary role is motherhood. If women do work outside the home, Catholic teaching has consistently viewed that reality either as an unfortunate necessity or as an aberration.

It was also the year that *The Feminine Mystique* by Betty Friedan was published, the book that is generally credited with launching the second wave of the women's movement in the United States.[41]

The impact of the Second Vatican Council on the church and on women religious has been profound. Three documents of the Council became particularly important for women religious: *Lumen gentium,* the Dogmatic Constitution on the Church; *Gaudium et spes,* the Pastoral Constitution on the Church in the Modern World; and *Perfectae caritatis,* the Decree on the Up-to-Date Renewal of Religious Life.

Lumen gentium, with its declaration of the church as the people of God, profoundly changed many women's sense of their relationship to the church. They no longer perceived themselves as "daughters of the church" or even members, as if the church were extraneous to themselves. For the first time in history, women, both religious and lay, understood themselves as church, the people of God. This shift has been profound. It has transformed not only the sense of church and of who one is as church; it has also brought with it a strong sense of responsibility for the integrity of the Church and for its mission and ministries.

This sense of being church equally with clergy and hierarchy has led many women to insist that their gifts, experiences and voices be fully employed in all dimensions of church life, from the pastoral and liturgical to the sacramental and dogmatic. Unfortunately, most clergy and hierarchy did not embrace the symbol of the church as the people of God with the same breadth or passion. Hence, there is the famous story of the perplexed bishop who, in genuine confusion, asked "Who are these women?" as he tried to understand who, why, and by what authority a group of women were planning the first conference on women's ordination, Women in Future Priesthood Now—A Call for Action, held in 1975 (Foley 1976, 3).

Gaudium et spes opened another dimension of Catholic life with its strong affirmation of the Church's responsibility to be engaged in the modern world. It was a major shift from the defensive, antisecular, antimodernist positions that had characterized the church's then-recent past. Its ringing first paragraph has shaped the social, pastoral, and theological agenda since then:

---

[41]The nineteenth-century women's rights movement which culminated in the 20th Amendment to the Constitution giving women the right to vote in 1920 is generally defined as the first wave of the women's movement. The women's movement that began in the mid-1960s is defined as the second wave.

The joys and the hopes, the grief and anguish of people of our time, especially of those who are poor or afflicted, are the joys and hopes, the grief and anguish of the followers of Christ as well. Nothing that is genuinely human fails to find an echo in their hearts. For theirs is a community of people united in Christ and guided by the Holy Spirit in their pilgrimage towards the Father's kingdom, bearers of a message of salvation for all of humanity. That is why they cherish a feeling of deep solidarity with the human race and its history. (GS 1)

The Pastoral Constitution on the Church in the Modern World (*Gaudium et spes*, 1965), and the papal and episcopal documents that flowed from it, including On the Development of Peoples (*Populorum progressio* 1967), and Call to Action (*Octagesimo adveniens* 1971) by Paul VI, the Medellín Documents (1968) and the Synod Statement Justice in the World (1971) were challenging calls for women religious to become fully engaged in the struggle for justice and peace in the modern world, not only through the traditional ministries of education, medical services and social work, but also in such new ministries as community organizing, political advocacy and living and working with people in poverty as they sought to improve their lives. The enclosed character of religious life gave way to a new openness to the world and all its needs. Many sisters and communities were transformed in the process.

This call to be engaged in new ways with the people accompanied the council's call for renewal of religious life, *Perfectae caritatis* (Decree on the Up-to-Date Renewal of Religious Life). The Decree's mandate was extraordinary, not only in its vision, but also in its appreciation of the unique contributions that religious communities bring to the life of the Church. The renewal process was to be twofold: "(1) a constant return to the sources of Christian life in general and to the primitive inspiration of the institutes, and (2) their adaptation to the changed conditions of our times" (PC 2). For many communities of women religious this mandate not only engaged them in a return to an understanding of the original genius of their founders and foundresses as they sought to address the needs of their historical moment, but it also engaged the women in a renewed study of Scripture, theology, and the new and challenging task of "reading the signs of the times" as mandated by the Second Vatican Council.

It was truly a heady time, when the outpouring of the energy of the Holy Spirit on the study and deliberations of women's communities seemed palpable. Scriptural study brought them in touch with the new insights of the historical Jesus and his message of liberation and inclusiveness. Theological studies were validating their own experience as sources of truth. (See related chapters of this book for more comprehensive reviews of these issues.) Recent Catholic social teachings and liberation theologies were moving them to see the world through the eyes of those in poverty and on the margins of middle-class society. Contemporary psychological and sociological insights were informing their reading of the signs of the times.

By the late 1960s most communities were in the process of chapters of renewal. A fundamental question shaped many deliberations: What is the most effective way for a group of committed adult women to live together in communities of mission? For example, in the Adrian Dominican Congregation that question was answered with a series of basic principles that would govern our life together. Key to these principles was the recognition that the individual sister is at the center of community life and mission. From this first principle flowed all others, including a commitment to diversity, to participatory modes of decision making in all dimensions of our communal life, to assessment of corporate commitments and institutionalized apostolic works to ensure they did not inhibit our freedom to respond to the call of God's people, particularly those in critical areas of need who are least able to help themselves (Enactments of the General Chapter, 1968–71, ADA).

Implicit in these principles are the new learnings that had evolved from the study of Scripture, theology, Catholic social teaching, modern psychology, and sociology among many members of the community. These informing influences laid the foundation for the subsequent development of many local religious communities of women in mission. Future general chapters continued to elaborate these fundamental principles, particularly in the area of women's experience, and to call the women to work for justice in the world.

As many women religious moved through the initial experiences of renewal and began to participate in the critical questions of the wider world, they found themselves engaged in the civil rights movement, in people's movements against poverty and in the women's movement. This combination of the renewal process and the encounter with the people's liberation movements provided the final step for many women to raise the question of the role of women in the church as well as of how the church deals with women and their position and roles in the wider society. For many, particularly the bishops and clergy, this was an unanticipated and ambiguous outcome of the processes set in motion by the Second Vatican Council.

The question of women and their changing roles in society and church were not issues of any great concern during the Second Vatican Council. The documents reflect the traditional ambiguity that surrounds the Church's definition of women. In *Gaudium et spes,* the first time women are specifically mentioned is in relation to a perceived problem. In the section entitled "Imbalances in the World of Today" the bishops write: "On the family level there are tensions arising out of demographic, economic and social pressures, out of conflicts between generations, or *from new social relationships between men and women*" (GS 8) [emphasis added]. Setting the "new social relationships" under "Imbalances in the World of Today" reflects a clearly patriarchal interpretation of the changes related to women's rising consciousness. The imbalances of traditional relationships between men and women are not questioned.

In the section on culture in the document, the church's traditional ambiguity toward women is also evident. Recognizing that humans are the authors of culture, *Gaudium et spes* states: "In every group or nation, there is an ever-increasing number of men and women who are conscious that they themselves are the artisans and authors of the culture of their community" (GS 55). However, several sections beyond this statement of mutual responsibility and participation, in section 60, the document qualifies itself: "Women are now employed in almost every area of life. It is appropriate that they should be able to assume their full *proper role in accordance with their nature.* Everyone should acknowledge and favor the *proper and necessary* participation of women in cultural life" (Riley 1994, 988) [emphasis added].

The ambiguity arising from the Church's dual anthropology remains an unresolved question. Do women and men share a common human nature? Or is there a human nature, that is man's nature, and then woman's "proper nature?" (See McLaughlin, 213–66; Foley 1977 82–108.) The answer to that question either supports the church's continuing limiting and/or romantic interpretation of womankind or it insists that the church and society admit to the radical equality of women and men, as well as to their biological differences. For most women, the answer is clear: women and men share the same human nature and should enjoy the same human rights in all spheres of life, including church life.

From the point of view of women's empowerment, the synodal statement, Justice in the World (1971), is a critical and frustrating document.

It declares that anyone who ventures to preach justice must first be perceived as being just. It states:

Within the Church rights must be preserved. No one should be deprived of his [sic] ordinary rights because he [sic] is associated with the church in one way or another. Those who serve the Church by their labor, including priests and religious, should receive a sufficient livelihood and enjoy that social security which is customary in their region. Lay people should be given fair wages and a system for promotion. We reiterate the recommendations that lay people should exercise more important functions with regard to Church property and should share in its administration. (CU 41)

Because the document purports to speak of all people working in the church, the reader is initially lulled into believing that women are included under the generic *he* or *lay people* only to read in the following paragraph, "We also urge that women should have their own share of responsibility and participation in the community life of society and likewise of the Church" (CU 42). The words, "their own share" raise the questions: Is women's share different from men's? If so, why?

Justice in the World also speaks of the social movements among peoples as "a new awareness which shakes them out of any fatalistic resignation and which spurs them on to liberate themselves and to be responsible for their own destiny" (CU 4). Furthermore, it introduces the need to change social structures if justice is to become a reality in people's lives: "This desire [for human rights], however, will not satisfy the expectations of our time if it ignores the objective obstacles which social structures place in the way of conversion of hearts, or even of the realization of ideal charity" (CU 16).

This document brings together several powerful themes that support women's struggle for justice in the church and in the world. In calling for justice in the Church and in affirming social movements whereby people assume responsibility for their own lives to change oppressive structures, Justice in the World affirms women's struggle for liberation from all oppressive and inhibiting structures not only in society, but also in the church (Riley 1994, 989).

Discovering the Glass Walls—1970s

Ten years after the close of the Second Vatican Council, three years after the first ordination of seven Episcopal women, during the United

Nations International Women's Year, the first Roman Catholic conference on the ordination of women was held in Detroit in 1975. To anyone reading the signs of the times as well as the signs of the Church, the words of Nadine Foley, OP, in greeting the Assembly and those of Elizabeth Carroll, RSM, in her keynote address came as no surprise. In introducing Mary Lynch, the laywoman whose simple direct question, "Is it time in the International Women's Year, to raise the issue of the ordination of women in the Roman Catholic Church?" had precipitated the Conference, Nadine stated:

> I thought you should have the opportunity to recognize the power of one questioning woman. And that Mary should have a first-hand view of this thing which has come to pass. In a unique way I believe that our assembling today is a special instance of the urgency of faith that catches fire on the earth and forms a people. We come together as a legitimate and authentic expression of the Church in its self-understanding as a people of God. Our leaders have called us repeatedly in our time to assume responsibility for the mission of the Church (1976, 161–162).

Elizabeth Carroll invoked the same ecclesiology and symbol in her keynote address:

> We meet in many moods—angry or expectant, skeptical or impatient, fearful or exultant. But we meet as people of faith. We have confidence in that God who promised, "I will pour out my spirit on all humankind, your sons and daughters shall prophesy" (Joel 3:1). Under the influence of this Spirit who is the Spirit of Jesus, we proclaim that it is Jesus who is Lord, continually taking form in woman and man to build the Church, an ever new Church. We believe in this Church and in ministry and in the value of sacramental orders. We respond to the Spirit who calls us to be a speaking, listening, reflecting, responding Church. We are not the whole Church nor do we claim to speak for the whole Church. Some may even dispute our right to meet as a Church at all, for we have not been called together by any official of our hierarchy. We would have welcomed such an invitation, but none has been forthcoming. Therefore, we speak our part of the dialogue, publicly, unofficially, but nonetheless as Church" (1976, 13–14).

As subsequent events reveal, the revolution in women's self-understanding both in the church and in the world so clearly articulated at the first Conference on Women's Ordination in Detroit and at the

First World Conference for Women in Mexico City, both held in 1975, would begin to reshape the political, economic, social, cultural, and ecclesial terrain during the final quarter of the twentieth century. Many individual women religious and many religious communities have been part of that reshaping.

Significant events help to chronicle this changing terrain. In the church world, the Ordination Conference was followed by the National Conference of Catholic Bishops' U.S. Bicentennial Celebration, Call to Action in 1976; the Vatican's response to the question of ordination of women in 1977; and the second conference on women's ordination in 1978.

Call to Action was also held in Detroit a year following the 1975 conference on women's ordination. Through a highly participatory design, developed and fostered by Maria Riley, OP, with the help of Jeanne O'Laughlin, OP, the Call to Action meeting brought together hierarchy, clergy, laity, and women and men religious as equal partners in dialogue in framing the recommendations and resolutions of the meeting. The design reflected the consensus processes that the Adrian Dominican Community and many other women's communities had adopted in the process of their renewal chapters. It allowed for the emergence of voices heretofore not heard in official church gatherings. The voices of women naming their realities and agendas were clear. In the section on Justice in the Church the role of women was central. The final recommendations included issues that were already simmering in local churches and in communities, such as inclusive language, a continued call for ordination of women, participation of women in all levels of leadership and decision-making, equal status of women in church structures and women in ministry (A Call to Action 1977, 24–25).

The Vatican's response to the emerging-women's voice was swift and clear. In 1976, in response to the ordination of the Episcopal women, the Catholic Women's Ordination Conference and Call to Action, the Vatican issued its Declaration on the Question of the Admission of Women to the Ministerial Priesthood *(Inter insignores)*. According to this document the ordination of women is not possible due to the unchanging tradition of ordaining men and to the fact that women do not image Christ in their bodies. In 1978, the Second Women's Ordination Conference was held. Clearly, the lines were being drawn.

In the wider society, the women's movement was gaining momentum and political voice. In 1977, the first (and only) National Women's Conference sponsored by the federal government was held in Houston and a wide-ranging agenda, that included economic justice, social justice and antiracism, communication and culture, international issues, and reproductive choice, was developed. At Houston the lesbian community also articulated its agenda within the women's movement. These last two items, reproductive choice and lesbianism, became flashpoints for the Catholic Church. The lines were also being clearly drawn between the feminist community and the institutional Catholic Church.

Today, the United States Catholic Church and women's religious communities live with these lines of tension that symbolize the fundamental issues between women and the hierarchical church, namely the questions of ministry, authority, and sexuality as defined and dictated by an all-male hierarchical structure. The tensions pull in several directions: between the United States church and the Vatican, within the United States church itself, between some women's religious congregations and the Vatican, between some congregations and the local hierarchy and clergy, and within religious congregations themselves.

Signs of changing self-awareness among women religious and the tensions emerging are reflected in general chapter statements and in the struggle many communities have had in getting their new constitutions approved by the Vatican. For example, during the 1970s and early 1980s, a growing awareness of ourselves as women is evident in Adrian Dominican Chapter Statements. Policy II of the 1974 Chapter Document states: "The Adrian Dominican Congregation has its identity in the sisters who comprise it and in its mission in the church. The sister who by her profession assumes the identity of the Congregation at the same time accepts co-responsibility for its life and mission." That chapter also endorsed collegiality and diversity among its members and supported the allocation of resources directed toward persons in critical need. It further began using language that reflected the 1971 Synod statement Justice in the World. It specifically called for the promotion and respect for the dignity and worth of the human person, identified sexism and racism as justice issues, embraced cultural diversity and challenged the members to live the Gospel imperative of justice, and to be effective signs of justice (*Beginnings*—General Chapter Enactments 1974, ADA).

By the 1980s the Adrian Mission Statement strongly asserted our identity as women:

In the mission of Jesus we Adrian Dominican Sisters discover and identify ourselves as women called together to share faith and life with one another and sent into our world to be with others, bearers and recipients of his love, co-creators of his justice and peace. (ADC 6)

The rights and the realization of the full personhood of women, our-selves included, were part of the work for justice. The chapter delegates clearly intended justice for women in the church as part of our mandate. Enactment 6 states:

> As ecclesial women, we Adrian Dominicans will accept responsi-bility for the development of the role of women in Church and society by using personal and communal resources to understand the issues; to foster dialogue among all segments of Church and society; to confront specific injustices toward women; to take ac-tions that will lead toward women's full participation in both Church and society (General Chapter 1982, 3).

As with all chapter pronouncements, however, not all members fully understood or agreed with the work of justice for women in church and society. Internally, the community struggled with the use of inclusive language and female images of God in liturgies and communal prayer. Others were increasingly discomforted with criticism of the church and the call to challenge the church on issues of women's ordination, deci-sion-making and the predominate maleness of the institution members. The feminist spirituality movement with alternative rituals was deeply disturbing in the midst of the Christocentric faith of the community. Nor were there adequate forums in which seriously to explore the com-plexity of the ecclesiological and theological issues raised by a feminist critique of the institutional church, its hierarchical/patriarchal structure and how that had so deeply shaped its liturgical, sacramental, magiste-rial, canonical, ministerial, and community life.

Seeking Ways through—1980s

Two events in the early 1980s increased the tension between some women's religious congregations and the Vatican. The first was the oc-casion of Pope John Paul II's visit to the United States in late 1979; the second was the *New York Times* ad calling for dialogue on abortion that appeared on October 7, 1984.

Theresa Kane, RSM, as president of the Leadership Conference of Women Religious (LCWR), greeted the Pope in the name of all women religious at the Basilica of the Immaculate Conception in Washington, D.C. In respectful but firm words she spoke, not only of the enduring fidelity of women religious to the work of evangelization, but also of the need to open all ministries of the church to women. The event became a cause célèbre for all. The traditional voices of the church were outraged that she would speak to the pope in that way. The official handlers of the pope's visit could not understand why she had not submitted her text for approval (she had not been asked to); and the progressive women of the church were delighted that she had spoken out in their behalf. The event was highly covered by the media and the lines of tension between LCWR's religious communities and the official church were tightened.

The *New York Times* ad was a point of confrontation between the Vatican and many women's communities. It illustrated two critical points of tension, authority, and sexuality, and clearly affected all communities. Some fifty-eight women religious, along with hundreds of lay women and some men, signed a *New York Times* ad calling for dialogue on abortion. The Vatican contacted all the superiors of the signers and told them to demand from their members who had signed the ad a public retraction or, if they refused, to dismiss them from their congregations. Under the leadership of LCWR the superiors of all the signers worked with their members and with the Vatican authorities to reach a just resolution of the problem. A key principle governing the superiors' position was the primacy of intracommunity structures of relationship and authority that governed how they dealt with their members. No outside force could interfere with those structures. Individual solutions were reached between the signers and their communities with the quiet agreement of the Vatican and a crisis was averted. The event simultaneously heightened the fears of some members of communities and deepened the anger of others. It also clearly established, however, a new dynamic of relationship between women religious superiors and the Vatican.

Meanwhile, the National Conference of Catholic Bishops made the decision to write a pastoral letter on women in 1983. It was an effort to find some middle ground for women and for the United States church. The bishops' rationale for this decision was clear: "The women's movement is a sign of the times: the Church is compelled by its mission to address the new consciousness regarding the equality of women and their challenging roles current in American culture; the growing alienation of women from the institutional Church is a pastoral concern; the Church needs the bishops to take leadership in promoting the equality of women; and finally the preliminary groundwork of the ad hoc committee on Women in Society and the Church has created an atmosphere of increasing mutual confidence and hope between bishops and women" (qtd. in Riley 1984, 338). The bishops promised a wide consultation process and a four-year time frame. Ten years and four drafts later, the bishops voted against issuing the pastoral. The process had been long and painful. From a very wide consultation with women on the first draft to virtually no consultation on the last, the pastoral had lost credibility even to the majority of bishops.

The reasons were numerous, including the fact that many women voiced their serious questions on current church teaching and discipline, particularly in the areas of ministry, authority, and sexuality during the consultations. The bishops found it difficult to mediate between the new insights developed through feminist scholarship, particularly in theology, Scripture, and anthropology and the current Vatican positions. Two issues in particular were stumbling blocks: ordination of women and the church's dual anthropology, which continues to make the distinction between human nature, that is man's nature, and woman's "proper nature." Furthermore, because there was a lack of consensus, the *sensus fidelium*, among the Catholic community on many of the issues raised, a teaching document was premature. Finally, the pervasive problem of a select group of men again defining and limiting the personhood and role of women had become problematic not only to women but also to some bishops.

Many women religious had entered into the initial dialogues on the pastoral with great enthusiasm and anticipation, but when it became clear that the Vatican, not the voices and insights of women, would control the final document they became disillusioned. The hoped-for middle ground was not possible.

The 1980s also saw the growth of new structures specifically relating to women. Within the institutional church, many dioceses instituted commissions on women to address the particular concerns of women within the diocese and local churches. Typically these commissions included lay women, women religious, lay men, and clergy. LCWR and many women's religious communities also developed commissions on women with a variety of agendas, including the continuing education of their members in the emerging body of literature relative to women, particularly in theology and Scripture. Typically, these commissions also tried to open their resources to lay women. For example, the Adrian Dominican Commission for Women sponsored an annual Voices of

Women conference and set aside scholarship funds for lay women, particularly women from diverse cultures and backgrounds. The conference topics covered issues of current importance to women, including spirituality, psychology, ecology, poverty, and empowerment. The Adrian Commission also developed a women's resource center as an integral part of Weber Center, their retreat and conference facility, to ensure that retreatants and other groups that came to the motherhouse campus had access to current books, periodicals, videos, and tapes on women's issues and concerns.

Outside the institutional structures, the women-church movement developed. From its beginnings of small groups of women, both lay and religious, who gathered to share faith, ritual, and friendship in their struggle with the patriarchal structures of the church, the women-church movement has grown into "a global, ecumenical movement made up of local feminist base communities of justice-seeking friends who engage in sacrament and solidarity" (Hunt 1993, 2).

Women-church participants believe that a discipleship of equals is the foundational vision of the Christian community and they work to be agents of transformation within their churches. In the United States, Women-Church Convergence acts as the gathering point for many local women-church groups. Because the Convergence is a coalition of some twenty-eight autonomous Catholic-rooted organizations and groups, the United States women-church has a significant presence of Catholic women, both lay and religious.

Its first conference in 1983, "From Generation to Generation Woman-Church Speaks," was a public proclamation of women's claim to be equally church. The women gathered to speak and to identify their particular mission as church, a mission shaped by their experience of being women. The over two thousand women present represented a wide spectrum of the church, representing women in diocesan and parish ministries as well as women who no longer maintained clear links with the institutional church. They were Hispanic, African American, Euro-American, single, married, divorced, and lesbian. For the first time at such meetings laywomen outnumbered the women religious (Riley 1984, 336).

More than three thousand women gathered in Cincinnati in 1997 for the second conference, "Women-Church: Claiming our Power." The third meeting in Albuquerque in 1993 gathered over thirty-five hundred women and reflected the attempt to build a multicultural, multiracial movement. Because women-church is primarily locally based, it is difficult to estimate its exact number and strength. But it is the locus for women, lay and religious, to meet and pray together as they continue to struggle with the wider church to recognize the full personhood of women (Hunt 1993, 7).

Moving toward the 21st Century—1990s

The United Nations Fourth World Conference on Women, Beijing, 1995, proved to be a watershed event for the Global Women's Movement. It signaled the maturing of the movement after some thirty years of local and global effort. The more than thirty-five thousand women from all parts of the world who participated at the conference exhibited the confidence and sense of authority that been growing through the long years of building the movement. No longer were women seeking the legitimacy of their demands and rights, they were acting on them. Beverly Harrison's prophetic words of 1981 were no longer a glimpse, but an historical reality:

> Let us note and celebrate the fact that "woman-spirit rising" is a *global* phenomenon in our times. Everywhere women are on the move. What is coming into view now, for the first time, on a worldwide scale, is the incredible *collective* power of women so that anyone who has eyes to see can glimpse the power and strength of women's full humanity (44).

It should come as no surprise that a consistent flow of disinformation, particularly from traditional and conservative religious voices from all faith traditions, preceded and followed the Beijing event. Until Beijing, it was still possible to try to isolate the feminist voices to a narrow range of women. How often have we heard the Roman Curia and some of the United States hierarchy try to dismiss the women's movement by saying it was only the product of a few, white, middle-class, unhappy women from North America and Europe who were raising their voices. After Beijing, such an assertion is no longer possible unless it is driven by ideological and/or political interests.

The Global Women's Movement has developed during the early stages of globalization, an emerging period of human history that is fraught with difficulties and filled with promise. The Beijing Conference was the final conference in a series of United Nations Conferences addressing the issues of this new age of globalization: U.N. Conference on the Environment and Development (Rio, 1992); World Conference on Human Rights (Vienna, 1993); International Conference on Population and Development (Cairo, 1994); and the World Summit for Social Development (Copenhagen, 1995). Whereas women had been active in ensuring that their voices and agendas shaped each of these conferences, in Beijing a global consensus on the women's agenda emerged. It focuses on economic justice, human rights, including reproductive and sexual rights, ecological sustainability, political participation, and antiviolence.[42] The women of the world understand themselves to be a transformative movement toward greater justice and peace for all. The movement is not focused on self-aggrandizement as is so often asserted, but it is focused on the empowerment of women as essential to ensure the well-being of all, the building of community, and the preservation of creation—women's traditional roles now understood in a global political setting.

Beijing, however, was just the highly public and highly visible symbol of the work women have been doing and continue to do in all the local settings where they seek to empower women. The results are evident everywhere. There are a growing number of women in significant positions of leadership not only in the wider society, but also in the church. Although the effort to write a pastoral on women's issue failed, the process proved very enlightening to the bishops. They did learn of the exclusion and injustice women experience in the church. As a result some bishops have sought to bring women into positions of decision making and leadership in their dioceses. The church is reaping the benefits of women's leadership.

More and more women, furthermore, are acting upon their own authority, both within the society and within the church. Women are creating their own space and structures to exercise pastoral leadership and authority, such as retreat centers, women's centers, women's theological projects. Women-owned businesses are the fastest growing segment of

---

[42]The issue of reproductive and sexual rights needs to be understood in its widest application. In the U.S. and in the Catholic Church the tendency is to equate these rights with two highly controversial issues—abortion and lesbianism. In the global context these rights apply to the denial of women's rights in a multiple of ways, including sexual slavery and sex tourism, mail-order brides, sexual political torture, systematic rape during war, sexual domestic violence such as incest and marital rape, forced pregnancy or forced abortion, female circumcision (also called female-genital mutilation), forced sterilization, discrimination due to pregnancy, sexual harassment, and all the other ways women are degraded and discriminated against due to their sex.

the business world. More and more women are professionally qualified to do work that formerly was the exclusive domain of men. They are also forming strong networks and caucuses to empower themselves within worlds that are still predominately male.

But while celebrating the progress women have made, it is essential that we also recognize the multiple problems too many women continue to face, including poverty, discrimination, violence, and exclusion. Much has changed, and much has stayed the same. The work of empowering women and transforming social and ecclesial structures to ensure equity and equality of women is well begun, but it is not done.

As we move toward the twenty-first century several challenges confront us. First is the need to mentor and support the next generations of women, both within the church and within society. For women religious, this support means to understand the young women who are the products of our efforts to liberate women. They no longer have our hesitations. They expect to be able to voice their ideas, to sit at the tables of decision making—even ours—and to act on their own authority. Secondly, we need to continue to challenge all social and ecclesial structures to greater equality, equity, and inclusiveness. Thirdly, we need to build structures of solidarity with women across race, ethnicity, class, national boundaries, sexual orientation, and disabilities to ensure that we exhibit the inclusiveness we demand. Fourthly, we need to continue to do the hard work of respecting cultural and religious traditions, while challenging them for their failure to recognize the full personhood of women. Finally, we need to celebrate and find our strength and hope in "womanspirit" rising. Women religious have given significant leadership to this rising. In fidelity to this "sign of our times" we must continue to do so.

Works Cited

Adrian Dominican Sisters. *General Chapter of Renewal*. Adrian, Mich.: 1969.

Adrian Dominican Sisters. *Beginnings—General Chapter Enactments*. Adrian, Mich.: 1974.

Adrian Dominican Sisters. *General Chapter*. Adrian, Mich.: 1982.

Carroll, Elizabeth. "The Proper Place for Women in the Church." In *Women and Catholic Priesthood: An Expanded Vision*, Ed. Anne Marie Gardiner. New York: Paulist Press, 1976

Foley, Nadine. "Greeting to the Assembly." In *Women and Catholic Priesthood: An Expanded Vision*, Ed. Anne Marie Gardiner. New York: Paulist Press, 1976.

———. "Women in Vatican Texts. 1960 to the Present." In *Sexism and Church Law*, Ed. James Coriden, 82–108. New York: Paulist Press, 1977.

Harrison, Beverly Wildung. "The Power of Anger in the Work of Love: Christian Ethics for Women and Other Strangers." *Union Seminary Quarterly Review* 36, supp. (1981): 41–58.

Hunt, Mary E. "Women-Church: An Introductory Overview." In *Women-Church Sourcebook*, Ed. Diann L. Neu and Mary E. Hunt. Silver Spring, Md.: WATERworks, 1993.

———. "An Historical Word about Women-Church in the United States." In *Women-Church Sourcebook*, Ed. Diann L. Neu and Mary E. Hunt. Silver Spring, Md.: WATERworks, 1993.

McLaughlin, Eleanor. "Equality of Souls, Inequality of Sexes. Women in Medieval Theology," *Religion and Sexism*. Ed. Rosemary Radford Ruether. New York: Simon and Schuster, 1974.

National Conference of Catholic Bishops/U.S. Catholic Conference. *A Call to Action: An Agenda for the Catholic Community*. Washington, DC: U.S. Catholic Conference, 1976.

Riley, Maria. "Women, Church, and Patriarchy." *America* (May 1984): 333–38.

———. "Women." In *The New Dictionary of Catholic Social Thought*, Ed. Judith A. Dwyer. Collegeville, Minn.: The Liturgical Press, 1994.

Walsh, Michael and Brian Davies. *Proclaiming Justice and Peace: Papal Documents from Rerum Novarum through Centesimus Annus*. Mystic, Conn.: Twenty-Third Publications, 1991.

14.

◆

Religious congregations of women, like United States society in general, has had to address the issue of cultural inclusiveness. They have done so more or less well, although today most include the eradication of racism as a critical item in their agendas for the future. The experience of being a woman of color in a congregation of predominantly Euro-American members can best be related by one who has had that experience. The reflection goes beyond policies of individual congregations to the public teaching of the church and the degree to which it has been sensitive to its racially diverse membership both in theory and in practice.

◆

Religious Life and Cultural Inclusiveness

Jamie T. Phelps, OP

If the Church is to be in a position to offer all women and men the mystery of salvation and the life brought by God, then it must implant itself among all these groups in the same way that Christ by his incarnation committed himself to the particular social and cultural circumstances of the women and men among whom he lived. (AGD 10)

I. Introduction

Consultation with religious congregations on the issue of racism and cultural diversity and teaching at a graduate school of ministry whose student body is comprised of diverse religious groups of men and women have provided empirical documentation of historic and continued patterns of ethnic and racial exclusion of men and women from some religious congregations or provinces in the United States. Many congregations and orders of women and men religious were established along ethnic lines while others established multiple provinces based on similar patterns of ethnic homogeneity. Still others that accepted diverse European ethnic populations within a single congregation often splintered internally around issues of inclusion. Power and authority issues manifested a pattern of the cyclic domination of one ethnic-cultural group over another. These in-group/out-group dynamics sometimes ended in the separation and establishment of separate religious congregations.

African American, Hispanic American, Asian American, and Native American women have often been rejected or "discerned" unsuited for membership in religious congregations of women and men religious because of unspoken racial or cultural considerations. They were perceived as potential sources of heightened fragmentation in the already tense ethnic-cultural experience of the institutes.

Today, U.S. religious congregations gather regularly for their chapters of affairs and election to "read the signs of the times" and revise their mission statements and set new goals consistent with their congregations' particular rules and charisms for a set period of years. In the process many have come to the realization that some aspects of United States society, e.g., its endemic racism and patterns of cultural ethnocentrism, have historically infected the very moral structures and processes of American communities of religious life and thus have proved a stumbling block to the congregations' implementation of their missions. With a renewed moral consciousness some have set goals to address the issues of racism, sexism, classism, and cultural imperialism as these impact the life and structures of their religious families. As a result, the historical pattern of ethnic-cultural homogeneity and racial exclusion are being challenged from within. Some U.S. religious provinces of men and congregations of women have admitted Hispanic and Asian Catholic candidates in increasing numbers and African Americans and Native American Catholic candidates at a slower pace.[43] In the past those African, Hispanic, Asian, and Native Americans who were admitted to

---

[43]The 1996 and 1997 annual meetings of the Dominican Leadership Council, an assembly of the elected leaders of U.S. Dominican men and women's provinces and congregations, have been focused precisely on this issue and represent a conscious effort of this leadership to lead their institutes toward being more racially and culturally inclusive. At the same time the unevenness of admission is conditioned, not only by admission policies, but also

predominately European-ethnic congregations were, with few exceptions, relegated to domestic roles, restricted to nonvowed (or for men nonordained) membership and/or subjected to other patterns of marginalization in subtle, informal but consistent practices. Only intellectual and moral conversion over time will alter such informal customs.

Despite these historical difficulties, this essay will argue that contemporary religious congregations in the United States are called to stand on the theological and moral high ground by participating in the prophetic mission of Jesus, the eschatological and liberating prophet. This essay will proceed in three steps. First, it will document select examples of the historical pattern of cultural and racial patterns of exclusive ethnocentrism as the predominant pattern of religious congregations founded during the nineteenth century that continued with few exceptions during the twentieth century. Second, it will outline briefly the multiple legal, social, and cultural factors that undergirded the pattern of cultural exclusiveness. Third, after providing a very brief sketch of the social cultural shifts occurring in our globalized urban centers within the United States and throughout the world, it will point to some basic ecclesial and theological doctrines that could encourage religious congregations to embrace new prophetic patterns of cultural inclusiveness.

II. Cultural Diversity: Historical Considerations

Within the Eastern United States, the worldview and culture of White Anglo-Saxon Protestants, the descendants of the English colonizers, was dominant and immigrant Catholics, with few exceptions, occupied the lower rungs of the American social-political hierarchy. Catholic labor movements, parochial school systems, and separate national Catholic parishes arose from the human need to provide immigrant Catholics with a sense of belonging to contradict the sense of isolation, marginalization, and alienation they felt within the religiously or culturally diverse milieus and churches that surrounded them.

Though anti–Catholic feelings and interethnic conflicts among Catholics fluctuated during various periods from the seventeenth to the early

---

by the number of candidates presenting themselves for candidacy. The times are such that other social and cultural factors, such as increased secularization and alternative opportunities for religiously motivated Christian service, exist and militate against large numbers of women and men from any U.S. cultural group considering religious life. The issue of culturally diverse religious vocations is a complex one.

twentieth centuries, immigrant Catholics felt most comfortable and confirmed in their religious and cultural identity by maintaining national parishes of homogenous members from the same nation of origin. The differing cultural expressions of Catholicism that characterized various nations in Europe did not merge into a common "American Catholicism" but was strengthened by national parishes.[44]

A. European American Religious Congregations

Nineteenth- and twentieth-century ethnocentrism and racism in the United States formed the seedbed for the practice of establishing culturally exclusive congregations of women (and men) who admitted members exclusively from one ethnic, cultural, and racial group. It was common practice in these religious congregations to maintain a pattern of singular cultural identification, that is, to identify itself as a Polish congregation founded to serve the Polish Catholic community; or as a German congregation founded to serve a German Catholic community, etc. Some congregations did embrace more than one cultural group. The foundation of the Dominican congregation, from which my own religious congregation of Adrian Dominican Sisters took its origin, is illustrative of the latter.

Our Dominican history contains several instances that illustrate the impact of cultural considerations in the beginnings of this one group of Dominican women religious in the United States. In 1853, having departed from the Dominican Convent in Ratisbon, Bavaria, four German-speaking Bavarian women, dressed in peasant-looking black dresses and bonnets, emigrated to New York to begin ministry among the German immigrant community. The letter of Dom Boniface Wimmer, OSB, to Mother Benedicta Bauer, prioress in Bavaria, proudly announced that the suburb in which the sisters were living had "30,000 inhabitants, 15,000 of whom are German Catholics" (Ryan, 36).[45] Later, in the same

---

[44]The history of American Catholic immigrants is a much more complex and nuanced reality than this brief summary suggests but nevertheless national parishes continued into existence officially until the early twentieth century and unofficially to the present time, though many contemporary parishes serve ethnically diverse populations. (See Dolan, *The American Catholic Experience* for an overview of the immigrant Catholic experience.)

[45]Mary Philip Ryan, *Amid the Alien Corn*, 36. Dom Boniface Wimmer was a Benedictine missionary priest who was stationed in the United States and who had suggested to Sister Benedicta, the elected prioress, that the Dominican Sisters from Holy Cross Priory in Ratisbon, Germany, consider entering the missionary fields in the United States. He promised that if they came to the U.S. he would take care of their initial needs and placements.

letter, Dom Wimmer indicated his awareness of the need for cultural sensitivity to forge an effective missionary endeavor.

> But there is something which needs immediate attention: you must admit one or two postulants who are well versed in English. You may not object to this because the nature of the case demands such. One who endeavors to attain the object must of necessity use the means. One who has not from youth been brought up in the use of the English language will never be able to master the English language sufficiently well to teach it. You are at liberty to send us German teachers or postulants but we ourselves must admit and train English postulants here. (Ryan, 37)

Although Dom Wimmer expresses concern only about language, implicitly he is expressing concern about cross-cultural communication. Acknowledging that it takes time to learn a language and thereby begin to enter into the worldview of another culture, he suggests that the presence of English speaking postulants will assist the German sisters' ministry of teaching in an English speaking context.

As the sisters established and expanded their educational ministry, culture was an acknowledged issue. Although German and Irish Catholics worshiped in culturally homogeneous parishes, the Dominican sisters adopted a pattern of intentional multicultural living. School policies introduced by the Ratisbon nuns were reasonable and practical. Irish candidates had been accepted into the novitiate when it was initiated in New York. Such inclusion made it possible to honor requests from schools in Irish as well as German parishes. In an era when the German people, like others of foreign descent, felt the need for parish schools with classes taught in their own languages, our Dominican schools were staffed in proportion to the prevailing nationality. If German, there were three German nuns and one Irish nun; if Irish, the reverse. As American-born candidates entered the novitiate, the proportion changed according to the demography of the areas from which they came (Ryan, 59). Unfortunately, the pattern of cultural inclusiveness established at the roots of our Dominican history in its transition from Germany to the United States did not continue.

As women from other European American ethnic communities emerged from the diverse cultural milieus among whom the Adrian Dominicans labored during the remainder of the nineteenth and twentieth century, not all ethnic cultural groups were treated equally in the Adrian Dominican processes of community building. Although our missions have embraced service to urban, suburban, and rural communities populated by a wide diversity of European American ethnic groups (e.g., Germans, Irish, Polish, Italian, and Central European Americans, etc.) and communities populated by African Americans, Hispanic Americans, Asian Americans, and Native Americans, our congregation has maintained a predominantly European ethos and pattern of membership that reflects the major streams of immigration of the late nineteenth and early twentieth centuries.

Cultural and racial considerations were a conscious aspect of the foundation of parishes and religious congregations in the past. Cultural exclusivity, born of cultural ethnocentrism, was a voluntary custom reflecting the ethnic separatism that characterized the social and ecclesial patterns of the day. Racial exclusivity, on the other hand, was not only in accord with the social and ecclesial patterns of the day but was reinforced by legislation that forbade the cohabitation of persons of different races. The emergence of separate congregations of black women religious occurred within this context of both legal and social racial segregation.

B. African American Religious Congregations of Women

Religious life among black Catholics began in Kentucky in 1824 when Charles Nerinckx, a Belgian priest, who founded the Sisters of Loretto, encouraged three young black girls to become the first members of a separate religious congregation slightly different from the Sisters of Loretto but under his guidance and direction. When Nerinckx was transferred this latter foundation was abandoned (Davis, 98–99). Five years later, the Oblate Sisters of Providence, founded by Jacques Hector Nicolas Joubert de la Muraille, was initiated by four women of color of Cuban and Haitian ancestry—Elizabeth Lange, Marie Madeleine Balas, Rosine Boegue, and Almeide Duchemin Maxis. These four women made their first profession of temporary vows on July 2, 1829, in Baltimore, Maryland, with the support and blessing of Archbishop Whitfield, the ordinary of Baltimore (Davis, 99–100).

The second congregation of black religious, the Sisters of the Holy Family, has a more complex foundational history. The congregation, supported by Abbé Rousselon, vicar general for Bishop Antoine Blanc and pastor of St. Augustine's parish in New Orleans, was established on the Feast of the Presentation, November 21, 1842, by Henrietta Delille, a free woman of color born in New Orleans, and Juliette Gaudin, a Cuban

Haitian, whose family had emigrated to New Orleans. A year later, they were joined by Josephine Charles, a member of a prominent New Orleans Creole family. These three women engaged in ministry of education and service to destitute and enslaved black men and women for whom they provided food, clothing, and shelter. In 1852 the three women professed their first canonical vows, although they were not fully recognized as women religious because of civil laws. Despite the legal ambiguity these women religious served the poor of New Orleans. Their heroic services as nurses during a yellow fever epidemic eventually gained them official public recognition as women religious (Davis, 105–7).

While several attempts to found other congregations of black women religious failed, a third successful foundation was inaugurated by the collaborative efforts of Ignatius Lissner, a member of the Society of African Missions, who had been appointed superior of the mission for black Catholics in Savannah, Georgia, and Elizabeth Barbara Williams, a black woman who became the foundress and first member of the Handmaids of Mary (Davis, 240). This congregation was founded in 1916 in Savannah, Georgia, to provide black teachers for black children. Anti-Catholic laws were under consideration that would have outlawed white teachers in schools for black children. When these laws were not passed, the Handmaids, lacking financial resources and moral support, were left without a mission and had to endure many hardships. It was the personal fortitude and faith of Mother Theodore Williams, the former Elizabeth Barbara Williams, who kept the congregation together by refusing to succumb to discouragement. At the invitation of Cardinal Hayes, the Handmaids relocated to New York to begin a day nursery in Harlem in 1922. With very few resources their mission expanded to include a soup kitchen, a kindergarten, and a home for homeless children. In 1929, Mother Theodore affiliated the Handmaids with the Franciscan Order and they became known as the Franciscan Handmaids of the Most Pure Heart of Mary (Davis, 241).

III. Cultural Diversity: Legal, Philosophical, and Psychological Considerations

The foundation of separate congregations of women religious in accord with their racial and ethnic ancestry conformed to the social customs and racial laws of the nineteenth and early twentieth centuries. Class and cultural homogeneity characterized the life and institutional structures until the middle of the twentieth century. The prevailing legal, philosophical, cultural, and psychological theories of the period supported an ideal of uniformity at the expense of diversity. Within the confines of this essay I will note only three: (1) the institutionalization of white-supremacy ideology; (2) the philosophical, scientific, and cultural ideal that undergirded modern racism; and (3) the fear-hate-fear pattern that characterizes the underlying psychology of black-white relations within the United States.

During most of the nineteenth century and early twentieth century, racial segregation was legal in the United States. The laws prohibited intermarriage between blacks and whites and living together in the same domicile. Segregation was rooted in a white supremacist ideology that considered African peoples to be less human, less intelligent, and less moral than whites (Webster, 59).[46] The establishment of the economic institution of slave trade and the social institution of slavery had predated the institution of legal segregation. Under both rubrics, African peoples and their descendants were thought to have been created to serve the needs of white Europeans. Their descendants, whose "manifest destiny" entailed caring for the enslaved, were to provide them with proper behavioral and moral rules, work, housing, clothes, and food to ensure their survival in the new world and salvation in the heavenly kingdom (See Goldberg and Eze).[47]

According to Cornel West, modern racism emerged as the result of the confluence of three post-Enlightenment developments, namely, Baconian and Cartesian philosophies, false scientific theory, and the retrieval of the Greek classical cultural ideal that made it impossible for Europeans and Euro-Americans to recognize the full humanity of black people and others of color (West, 47–68).[48] The philosophies of Francis Bacon and René Descartes are generally acknowledged as providing the philosophical ground of the scientific method. Bacon promoted the importance of the inductive method to arrive at "general laws to facilitate

---

[46] Webster traces the construction of the "myth of race" in the fields of natural and social science and finds it to be the root of the social political reality of racial categorization and racism.

[47] These authors provide a critical discussion of the philosophical origins of the "myth of race" and racism during modernity. Goldberg concludes his text with an extended argument for a pragmatic antiracist practice.

[48] West notes that François Bernier, a French physician, first employed race categories in 1684. The publication of the preeminent naturalist Carolus Linnaeus's *Natural Systems* in 1735, however, served as the foundation for subsequent race theories.

human mastery." Descartes "associated the scientific aim of predicting and explaining the world with the philosophical aim of picturing and representing the world." The scientific field of natural history led to the categorization of animals and human bodies based on " visible, especially physical characteristics." The category of race, based primarily on skin color, led to initial identification of the "four races" and the association of positive characterizations of the "white race" and negative characterizations of the "black race." The subsequent development of the anatomical sciences of phrenology and physiogamy that interpreted human potential and character on the basis of skull structure and face structure, respectively, further contributed to white supremacist ideology. The adoption of the Greek aesthetical ideal "of beauty, proportion, and moderation" as the norm for the classification and ranking of human bodies, coupled with the other indicators, led to the hierarchial arrangement of the races that resulted in the "black race" being deemed the most inferior (West, 51–58).

Years of the slave-master dynamics of white domination and social segregation led to social and psychological interracial patterns of fear-hate-fear. These emotions undergird the contemporary patterns of institutionalized racism and the periodic rise and decline of white supremacist groups. Institutionalized racism is maintained by members of the dominant culture who hold an irrational fear and hatred of blacks and other institutionally oppressed groups who are considered to be intellectually, morally, and culturally inferior and predisposed to violence and criminality.

While the inaccuracy and limitation of these "enlightenment" views gradually became apparent to many, they were not refuted before the falsity of these scientific, philosophical, and cultural notions had become an unconscious constituent part of the "normative gaze" of most European peoples. African peoples were outside the pale of the European concept of humanity and thus were never considered capable of participation as equals within the social and political dynamics of the society. The influence of this "normative gaze" produced a "black/white schism" within the human family. White racism, and with it white supremacist ideology, constructed a psychological barrier to the possibility of religious congregations and other social institutions admitting African Americans and other non-European peoples as fully vowed and participative members within predominately European American congregations of women and men religious.

IV. The Contemporary Challenge

A. Social Cultural Shifts

The changing patterns of our society and the theological principles of church mission seem to demand that religious congregations of men and women examine their often undeclared admission policies and customs that restrict the admission and maintenance of African, Hispanic, Asian, and Native Americans and other persons of diverse cultural, ethnic and class backgrounds. Diverse European American ethnically homogenous communities are still evident in urban, suburban, and rural towns in the United States. While an increasing number of these geographic areas are experiencing an influx of a select few African Americans, Hispanic/Latino Americans, Asian Americans, and Native Americans, the majority of these latter cultural populations inhabit our large cities. The culturally pluralistic character of our country challenges the assumptions of the American melting pot prevalent in previous eras of our nation.

The shift from the classicist normative gaze identified by Cornel West to a more historically conscious view of the world within the postmodern consciousness is one response of this challenge. The radical plurality of reality has had an impact on the social and cultural consciousness and worldview of many human cultural groups. Some Americans in the United States, whose work and social contacts have expanded their experience of culturally diverse peoples within the United States and other nations of the world, have developed a more expansive understanding of humanity and its diverse cultural expressions. The continuous flow of immigrants and refugees from Asia, Africa, Latin America, and Europe makes it increasingly difficult for persons to live their entire lives in culturally homogenous contexts. As a consequence an unspecified number of U.S. citizens have abandoned the ethnocentric practice of restricting their primary social and professional associations to persons of their own ethnic, racial, and religious heritages. Many have made considerable progress in embracing social and professional relationships across previously well-established ethnic, cultural, and national barriers.

Despite the civil rights movements' transformation of the legal patterns of racial segregation and theoretical debunking of fallacious race theory, the institutionalized patterns of racial and class isolation have proven to be more difficult to overcome (Wittberg 1994, 58–70). Persistent racist, class, and cultural supremacist perspectives often influence the understanding and prioritizing of social and moral issues of institutional decision makers. Uncritically adopted European American middle class values and concerns constitute the a priori assumptions of many of the declared mission statements and goals of religious congregations. Contemporary research suggests that people generally join orders that share their cultural, ethnic, and class perspectives and assumptions about religions life (Wittberg 1996, 114; 1994, 16–17). If, then, contemporary U.S. congregations of religious men and women wish to admit and maintain a culturally diverse membership, the worldviews of these culturally diverse groups must be reflected in the construction and interpretation of the mission statements and goals of their institutes. African American, Hispanic/Latino American, Asian American, and Native American members of religious congregations find that issues surfaced from their distinct social cultural contexts and worldviews are often overlooked or not incorporated because they are viewed as less significant than those issues and concerns shared by the dominant cultural group(s). Culturally diverse membership becomes impossible within those congregations that hold uncritically to an ideology of cultural homogeneity. Attempts to assimilate members from diverse cultural groups is in reality a process of cultural imperialism. While members from culturally diverse groups must adapt to the religious charism of a particular congregation, e.g., a Dominican congregation, they must be encouraged to interpret the congregational charism in a manner that enriches, and is enriched by, their own cultural heritage and that of their missionary contexts (Wittberg 1996, 113–18).[49]

---

[49] Wittberg, contrary to this essay and argument, advocates the continuance of the homogeneous patterns of separate religious congregations. She suggests that Black and Latino Catholics establish separate congregations in order to "cherish and safeguard their distinctive cultures and separate institutions . . . [and] enflesh their own spiritual focus and to [overcome the ethnic dynamics of oppression] which bar them from opportunities for leadership and professional growth." While she honestly identifies the sociological patterns and dynamics that militate against patterns of full inclusion in predominantly European American congregations, she labels efforts to draw minorities as "noble . . . but . . . naive." While some attempts deserve such labeling, Wittberg seems oblivious to genuine multicultural and trans-cultural shifts in the social and cultural patterns in the United States and throughout the world and disparages the possibility of effective multicultural membership coming together for a common mission. As a sociologist, she does not critique the origin of culturally inclusive patterns and has no recourse to the ecclesial and theological teachings of the church that would argue for religious congregations to assume the role of prophetic leadership in furthering these movements toward the establishment of communities that are sacraments of God's own image.

B. Ecclesial and Theological Foundations

The emerging of a "world church" with the convening of the Second Vatican Council provided the impetus for the church's initial shift from a classicist worldview to a historically conscious and pluralistic worldview. This shift has led to the deepening and widening of historical critical and social cultural methods in biblical and theological interpretation that have spawned a host of new biblical and theological methodologies and a concomitant plurality of interpretation of church traditions. (Küng and Tracy)[50]

1. Missiological Considerations

Despite this plurality of interpretation, the fathers of the Second Vatican Council affirmed the assertions of *Lumen gentium*, The Dogmatic Constitution on the Church, that stated that the Church "is a sacrament, a sign and instrument, that is, of communion with God and the unity of the entire human race" (1). Its Decree on the Church's Missionary Activity (*Ad gentes*) further specifies that the church's essential universality demands that it preach the Gospel to all (1). This latter document suggests that

> [The] work of implanting the church in a particular human community reaches a definite point when the assembly of the faithful, already rooted in the social life of the people and to some extent conformed to its culture, enjoys a certain stability and permanence; when it has its own priests, although insufficient, its own religious and laity and possesses those ministries and institutions which are required for leading and spreading the life of the people of God under the leadership of their own bishop. (19)

While this vision from the Council of Vatican II clearly had in mind the so-called mission countries of Asia, Africa, and Latin America, by analogy one could speak of the necessity of nurturing and sustaining the ministries of priests, sisters, and laity from the diverse ethnic-racial and

---

[50] This work details a conference of North American, Latin American, and European theologians documenting and legitimizing the emerging pluralism of theological methods while cautioning against the virus of ideology that seems to infect old and new theological methods.

cultural groups that comprise the church in the United States. If the church's contemporary mission within the United States is to be a manifestation of the church as a "universal sacrament of salvation," it cannot continue to perceive itself as a church primarily committed to serve diverse groups of white European Americans and recent Hispanic/Latino immigrants and refugees, exclusively. The Catholic Church in the United States and its religious congregations must open its doors to embrace all the culturally diverse groups who constitute the national and cultural mosaic of the United States, including African Americans, recent continental Africans and members of the African diaspora emigrating or seeking political asylum from Africa and from other nations worldwide.

2. Trinitarian and Ecclesiological Considerations

The church teaches that God is by nature one God, i.e., the supreme reality, divine substance and essence, in three persons. Each of these persons is distinct from the other but at the same time they are persons-in-relation who constitute one being, God (CCC 1994, 253–55, 260).

The human race in the original order of creation was created in the image of God and as such was designed to reflect the unity in diversity of God's creation. We constitute one human race in extraordinary cultural diversity. Our fundamental unity as the human community, however, was broken by original sin. This original fragmentation of creation is manifested in the social institutions of the United States constructed by individuals who consciously or unconsciously embrace as part of their *a priori* assumptions the myths of cultural and racial superiority of European peoples that undergird the social sins of racism, sexism, classism, and so forth. Human distinctions have become the term of human divisions and systems of oppression.

Current church teachings promulgated by the twentieth-century popes, papal offices, and the United States bishops argue that practices of racial, cultural, and gender oppression in any form are sinful. These teachings are based on the notion of communion as a key aspect of the church and society. In a 1992 document entitled *Some Aspects of the Church Understood as Communion*, the Congregation for the Doctrine of the Faith states:

> The concept of a *communion* ecclesiology lies "at the heart of the Church's self understanding" insofar as it is the mystery of the personal union of each human being with the divine Trinity and

with the rest of [hu]mankind, initiated with faith, having begun as a reality in the Church on earth, is directed toward its eschatological fulfillment in the heavenly Church (3).

The document goes on to suggest that the reality of ecclesial communion has both an invisible and a visible manifestation. Its invisible aspect is constituted by the "communion of each human being with the Father through Christ in the Holy Spirit, *and with others who are . . . sharers in the divine nature, in the passion of Christ, in the same faith, in the same spirit"(4)*. Furthermore, invisible communion and visible communion possess an intimate relationship based on the church's hierarchical ecclesial order, its apostolic teaching, sacramental ministry of announcing and witnessing "to make present and spread the mystery of communion which is essential to her, *and to gather together all people all things in Christ" (4)*.

The mission of the church, understood as communion, has the mandate to embody spiritually, sacramentally, and historically, the church as the realization of that communion to which all humanity and creation are called. The ecclesial community comprised of distinct and individual human persons and cultures is made in the image and likeness of God and has the divine vocation to express sacramentally the unity-in-person, the unity-in-community, and the unity-in-diversity characteristic of the Triune God. The church, as the historical embodiment of the image of God, is commissioned to continue the mission of God inaugurated by Jesus of proclaiming the coming of the Reign of God in its word and deeds. It must continue the process directed toward the full realization of the reign inaugurated by Jesus. Religious congregations are ecclesial institutions called to participate in some aspect of the general mission of the church through their particular charisms. Those religious congregations that refuse, because of their cultural heritages, to welcome African American women and men, and other men and women from non-European cultures, who have discerned a call to the consecrated life, contradict the current teachings of the church on its universal mission. These institutes are concrete historical examples of what *Lumen gentium* identifies as the church that is always in need of renewal and purification, the church that does not yet perfectly manifest itself as the Church of Christ (8).[51]

---

[51]*Lumen gentium* 8 states that "[The] church, constituted and organized as a society in the present world, subsists in the Catholic Church," and later, "The church, however,

3. Moral Considerations

The documents of the U.S. Catholic Bishops that focus on the social sins of racism, sexism, and economic justice are all attempts to call the U.S. Catholic community to conversion from its complicity with patterns of sinful human interactions that constitute the negative aspects of American culture (*Brothers and Sisters*). These documents echo similar calls for the world wide conversion of the church and society manifest in Roman episcopal and papal documents (See GS, PP, CU, AGD, etc.).

Combined, the ecclesial documents on church and society represent the social teachings of the church on its role in its own social transformation and that of the world. For the purposes of this essay, I will highlight the two documents that focus exclusively upon the social sin of racism as a fundamental dynamic that mars the church's communion and mission, since racism seems to be a primary deterrent to the establishment of culturally inclusive religious congregations.

The 1979 pastoral entitled, *Brothers and Sisters to Us,* the U.S. Bishops' Pastoral on Racism in our Day, clearly identified racism as a radical evil and social sin that divides the human family and called for an "equally radical transformation, in our own minds and hearts as well as in the structures of our society" (10). Later in the text it called for the "fostering of vocations among minority groups" and the establishment of culturally sensitive programs for the formation of priests, deacons, and men and women religious that did not "entail an abandonment of culture and traditions or the loss of racial identity" (11). In the minds of the bishops this agenda would entail programmatic changes and the development of racial-cultural education for seminary faculty and students. Such programmatic changes and racial-cultural education are similarly necessary in formation programs for women and men religious.

The 1988 Vatican's Pontifical Commission on Justice and Peace issued a later document entitled *The Church and Racism* and offered a wider analysis of racism as it impacted world history through colonial imperialism accompanying the discovery of the New World and the black slave trade (10). After an historical overview it identifies the many types of racism evident in the world today, among them systems of apartheid, ethnocentrism, social racism, anti-Semitism, etc. After portraying racism's various manifestations as contrary to a biblically based

---

clasping sinners to its bosom, at once holy and always in need of purification, follows constantly the path of penance and renewal."

theological anthropology that asserts the basic dignity of the person (man and woman) created in God's own image and likeness, it affirms the essential unity of all human persons based on their common origin and destiny "to form one sole family according to God's plan established 'In the beginning' " (*Church and Racism*, 20).

The document turns to the Scriptures as a source of its theological position that through the Incarnation "the work of salvation carried out by God in Christ is universal." The universalizing of the covenant fulfilled and sealed through the suffering and death of Christ obtained the redemption of sinful humanity through whose cross, "religious division, which had hardened into ethnic division between the people of the promise that was already fulfilled and the rest of humanity," was abolished (21).

Although *The Church and Racism* focuses primarily on the struggle of the church in her mission of social transformation it concludes by asserting that "the Church's doctrine affirms that all racist theories are contrary to Christian faith and love" and states further that " the Church wants first and foremost to change racist attitudes, including those *within her own communities*. Her mission is to give soul to the immense undertaking of human fraternity [sic]" (22). Earlier in the document, the Commission acknowledges that equality in dignity does not mean equal physical, cultural, intellectual, and moral strengths, i.e., not uniformity but rather equality in treatment that recognizes the "diversity and complementarity of one another's cultural riches and moral qualities" so that no human group can claim "a natural superiority over others" (23). The document affirms that the recognition of all people as equal in dignity requires the establishment of mutual respect, community, and effective solidarity among all but, in particular, between the rich and the poor.

The church's magisterium has called for the end of racism, the admission of men and women from minority groups to seminaries and, by extension, to religious congregations of women and men, and has called the members to change the racist attitudes manifested within their own communities. These calls seem to mandate the development of culturally inclusive religious communities as one manifestation of the Church's mission to be an instrument of universal salvation. The development of culturally inclusive communities of women and men, who are the sacramental signs of mutual respect, fraternal and sororal community, and human solidarity, is made possible by the presence and power of the Spirit. African Americans, Asian Americans, European Americans, Hispanic/Latino Americans, and Native Americans can give witness to the

transforming power of God present within all human beings who acknowledge themselves as creatures of the living God by gathering in
communion with one another as they engage in the mission of the
church.

4. Biblical Considerations

The life and ministry of Jesus and that of some of the early Christian
communities provide additional rationale for the development of culturally inclusive communities.

(a) Jesus' Embodiment and Preaching of the "Reign of God" Jesus'
own lifestyle embodied a pattern of inclusivity. The Bible is replete with
examples of Jesus transcending the laws and customs of his day when
these laws and customs seem to violate the spirit and principle of God's
universal love, and to set up boundaries to social interaction between
the rich and the poor, men and women, and persons of diverse cultures.
Although his primary ministry was among his own cultural community
of Jews, Jesus' preaching and inauguration of the "reign or rule of God,"
as indicated through his parables and sayings about the reign of God,
interpreted through a social historical theological lens, suggest that Jesus'
redemptive life, death, and resurrection had universal intent and social,
historical, cultural, and political consequences. As such, no person or
cultural group was beyond the scope of God's redemptive act nor the
call to community and discipleship (Gal. 3:28).

While it is true that Roman Catholic Christian customs eventually
excluded women from ordained ministries and public ministry, most
would agree that women were never totally excluded from membership
within the early Christian community or from the exercise of some aspects of Christian ministry. Similarly, no person or cultural group should
be excluded from church membership, religious life, and ecclesial ministry for reasons of ethnic-racial or cultural identity. Such exclusion is
contrary to the implications of Jesus' preaching of the coming reign of
God as a reality that will unite all human persons and "nations in the
universe" into a community of peace, love, and justice empowered by
the mystery of the communion in the Triune God.[52]

---

[52]Contemporary theologians, regardless of their cultural and social location generally agree
that Jesus' central message was the inauguration and proclamation of the future reign of
God. (Cf, Kasper, 73, and entire section 72–87). "Love includes the commitment to justice
for everyone. . . . Love is the power and the light which enables us to recognize the de-

(b) The Witness of Early Christian Communities The issue of cultural inclusiveness in the Christian Church has been rooted in the pouring out of the Spirit in which all those assembled in community heard the proclamation of the Good News of the Resurrection in their own "native tongues" on the occasion that tradition has called Pentecost, i.e., the outpouring of the Holy Spirit (Acts 2). It was further addressed at the Council of Jerusalem in Acts 15. This Council was called to resolve the conflict surrounding the baptizing of uncircumcised Gentile Christians within the Jewish Christian community. Arguing that the prophet Amos had foretold the restoration of Israel and the conversion of the rest of the human race, James convinced those assembled that Paul's insistence that "all are saved through the grace of the Lord Jesus" suggested that distinct cultural practices (e.g., circumcision) of one Christian community should not be imposed upon another cultural community. Jewish Christians should not put obstacles to Gentile conversions. For the sake of the table fellowship, however, Gentile Christians must make certain compromises, such as refraining from eating meats sacrificed to idols, a practice that would prohibit the communion of Jewish Christians and Gentile Christians at a common table (See Karris, 1039–42, 1055–56).

This inclusion of Gentile and Jewish Christians at one table could be interpreted as a normative principle of inclusion of diverse cultural Christians within one eucharistic celebration, and church congregation and by analogy the inclusion of diverse cultural Christian groups within one religious congregation.

V. Conclusion

Generally speaking, insofar as a religious congregation constitutes a type of "particular or local church," made distinct by its particular charism and mission, such a congregational church is like the other local churches that constitute and manifest the universal Church in their celebration of the Eucharist. Religious congregations, as types of a particular or local church, are called to embody the message and mission of

---

mands of justice in changing situations and to meet them appropriately" (Boff, 87 and 72–87). "This insistence on the absolute indiscriminate nature of love within the kingdom is the dominant perspective of almost all of Jesus' teaching" (Boff, 90, and full text, 74–99).

Jesus the Christ who proclaimed and embodied the inauguration of the future universal reign of God. Religious congregations must be sacraments of universal salvation that image the unity-in-diversity of those who individually and collectively image and embody the communion of the Church and world with the Triune God.

Shifts in the social cultural reality of U.S. society and world, as well as social historical interpretations of major ecclesial, sacramental, Trinitarian, and Christological doctrines, validate moral arguments for the inclusion of men and women of African American, Hispanic American, Asian American, Native American, or any other cultural group as members of religious congregations. Exclusion of such members solely on the basis of their ethnic-racial or cultural identity constitutes social sin. To my knowledge no theologically sound ground for such exclusion has been developed. The practice lies entirely within the realm of social custom at odds with the mission and witness of Jesus Christ and the early Christian communities.

The patterns of ethnic-racial exclusion that continues in religious congregations have primarily been motivated by social and cultural ethnocentrism which has been identified as a type of racism. Within the last decade Adrian Dominicans, like so many other congregations, have begun to reexamine its patterns of racism and cultural domination and exclusivity. Responding to the call for moral conversion and social transformation they have explored ways to move toward more cultural inclusiveness. A formation program has been set up within the Dominican Republic and its admission process is open to candidates from the diverse class, ethnic-racial, and cultural groups that comprise the Dominican Republic. As these candidates complete their candidacy and become novices they are participating in a collaborative international novitiate in the Dominican Republic, rather than in the St. Louis-based common novitiate to which they were formerly sent.

On the mainland, we have developed an increasingly culturally diverse group of associate members and established a "house of hospitality" in California to attract women as associates and full members from the Asian, Pacific Rim community. I trust that our congregation will continue in its creative response to the Spirit's urging us to become a sacrament of cultural diversity and communion. We will find creative ways to invite and nurture associate and vowed membership from the African American, Hispanic American, and Native American communities that are within the current mission context of our members. One aspect of the process is the continued participation of current associates and vowed members in mission situations and experiences that will help us recover from our personal racism and ethnocentricism. A second aspect involves a continual examination of our institutional policies and structures to eliminate the residues of institutional racism and cultural imperialism that persist in the our own institutions and in the institutions and contexts in which our sisters minister.

The Adrian Dominican commitment to the search for truth, authentic preaching and holiness impels our ongoing conversion. We recognize that continued refusal to enter into the process and struggle of social, intellectual, moral, and social conversion necessary for religious congregations and individuals to be prophetic agents of God's call to communion is a serious moral failure.

Congregations who say "yes" to the Spirit's call to communion mediated by their prophetic members and/or individuals who respond positively to the call within the inner recesses of their hearts are recovering from the institutionalized social sins of racism and ethnocentrism. Through their moral and spiritual conversion they are living up to a constitutive aspect of their identity as ecclesial women and men called to live prophetic lives. Their congregations are sacraments of God's universal will that each person and community have life and live it to the fullest in a manner that is consistent with their cultural family of origin and the Gospel. They are healing and reconciling agents of God's unconditional love and mercy. They are embodiments of the evangelizing and justice mission of Jesus Christ with its liberating hope that generates a vision of full communion under the reign of God. Congregations that embrace the creation of culturally inclusive religious congregations are transcending spiritual, sacramental, and historical death and embracing new life in the risen Christ.

Works Cited

Boff, Leonardo. *Jesus Christ Liberator*. Maryknoll, NY: Orbis Press, 1982.

Brothers and Sisters to Us. U.S. Bishops' Pastoral Letter on Racism in Our Day. Washington, D.C.: United States Catholic Conference, 1979.

The Catechism of the Catholic Church. Liguori, Mo.: Liguori Publications, 1994.

Clarkson, John F. et al., ed. *The Church Teaches: Documents of the Church in English Translation*. Rockford, Ill.: Tan Book Publishers, 1976.

Davis, Cyprian. *The History of Black Catholics in the United States*. New York: Crossroad, 1990.

Dolan, Jay P. *The American Catholic Experience: A History from Colonial Times to the Present*. Garden City, NY: Doubleday, 1985.

Eze, Emmanuel Chudwudi. *Race and the Enlightenment.* Cambridge: Blackwell Publishers, 1977.

Goldberg, David Theo. *Racist Culture: Philosophy and the Politics of Meaning.* Cambridge: Blackwell Publishers, 1993.

Karris, Robert J. *The Collegeville Bible Commentary.* Collegeville, Minn.: Liturgical Press, 1992.

Kasper, Walter. *Jesus the Christ.* Frank V. Green. New York: Paulist Press, 1985.

Küng, Hans and David Tracy. *The Paradigm Change in Theology.* New York: Crossroad, 1990.

Pontifical Commission on Justice and Peace. *The Church and Racism.* 1982.

Ryan, Mary Philip. *Amid the Alien Corn.* St. Charles, Ill.: Jones Wood Press, 1967.

Senior, Donald. *Jesus: A Gospel Portrait.* New York: Paulist Press, 1992.

"Some Aspects of the Church Understood as Communion." *Origins* 22, no. 7 (1992):108–112.

Webster, Yehudi O. *The Racialization of America.* New York: St. Martin's Press, 1992.

West, Cornel. *Prophecy Deliverance: An Afro-American Revolutionary Christianity.* Philadelphia: Westminster Press, 1982.

Wittberg, Patricia. *The Rise and Fall of Catholic Religious Orders.* New York: State of New York University Press, 1994.

———. *Pathways to Re-Creating Religious Communities.* New York: Paulist Press, 1996.

15.

◆

Most United States religious congregations of women have some measure of cultural diversity in their membership. Those sisters who are from Latin America bring a unique viewpoint on religious life as a result of the movements toward liberation that have taken place there. For women religious these movements have had both positive and negative influences upon them. Their experience in evaluating the progress in religious life since Vatican Council II is important to the larger movements in religious life globally, as well as to women's agendas worldwide.

◆

Theology of Religious Life: A Latin American Perspective

Margarita Ruiz, OP

If theology is not primarily a prefabricated "system," if its most basic task is to interpret and illuminate religious life, one could speak of a specific theology of religious life in Latin America insofar as an original experience of religious life is taking place. (Palacio, 39)

Introduction

The changes in Latin American religious life after Vatican Council II began in 1968 with the Conference of Latin American Bishops in Medellín, Colombia. This conference was the beginning of a process of change in the centuries-old structure of the church that, wherever it spread, showed similar characteristics all over the world. The adoption of *aggiornamento* dictated by the documents of Vatican II within the understanding of our common history of salvation made it necessary for religious in Latin America to initiate adaptations more consonant with the diverse contextual reality in which religious life was immersed. Given a spectrum of cultural difference, it became impossible to understand religious life in relation to the parameters set in Europe centuries earlier.

In order, therefore, to present the theology of religious life from the Latin American perspective it is necessary to situate its responses and experiences, as well as to identify the spirituality that has accompanied these thirty-two years of commitment in a reality plagued with injustice and oppression.

For a better understanding of the changes that have occurred in religious life, they can be approached by dividing the period into decades to describe the real-life conditions, the biblical and theological challenges, and the spirituality that have been interwoven progressively with these changes. In order to acknowledge the individual importance of each phase, the approach in this reflection is one of respect for each school of thought that developed and the new comprehension that surfaced out of each of them. An important question that emerged centers around the understanding of spirituality. In what follows here this question is central: Is spirituality a personal experience, a school of thought, or an ongoing communal search?

The experiences to be examined for each decade are not the only expressions of religious life, nor are they necessarily the experience of the majority. In fact, the experiences may represent only a minority of the different currents of thought in this moment. In any case, the journey of a small but significant group of women religious who are committed to the liberating changes prompted by the poor is the focus of what follows. This group of religious uniquely represents the evolution of the changes inspired by the Spirit of God actively present in the reality of Latin America.

The 1970s

This was a period of expansion and freeing thought. It was the time of the church awakening to the situation of oppression suffered by the majority of the population since colonial times. It was the period of vitality experienced among leftist political parties and popular movements. Rural and urban guerrilla groups, supported by a significant number of the largely Christian population, broke out in almost all Latin

American countries. Governments allied themselves with the powerful and exerted strong repression, resulting in more frequent and generalized roundups, massacres, jailing, and torture inflicted on women and men (See Ress, 2–11; Codina, 39–41; Condor, 1–25).

The bishops who convened in Medellin in 1968, having used social analysis to find the causes of the contrasting conditions of their people, declared the situation on the continent and in the Caribbean as one of "institutionalized violence." Notwithstanding these findings, growing groups of Christians who were faced with their exploding reality found the pastoral activity promoted by the church to be insufficient. A situation of tension in the church resulted and caused conflictive clashes among its members. Within its ranks three ideologies could be easily identified: the traditional conservative, the modernizing liberal, and the radical liberationist. The division experienced at the social level was also evident among the faithful and the hierarchy. This was the moment in which liberation theology took root. It assumed the categories of Marxist theories since it analyzed reality from the perspective of the impoverished classes. It was not possible to continue within the parameters of the prevailing system because its perspective served to justify the injustice and the oppression in which the great majority of people were living. The theology of liberation based its methodology on a three-step scheme: to see (analyze the reality), to judge (discern by the enlightenment of the Word of God), and to act (in favor of social transformation). The task consisted of a critical reflection based upon praxis within a specific context of oppression. The poor were seen as the theological *locus* or starting point.

Through its methodology the theology of liberation adopted the biblical tradition of acting from experiential truth. The theologians departed from abstract reflection on which to base correct knowledge, thought, and speech. They sought to maintain an intimate relationship between life and faith in order to discover where divine revelation was actually occurring. The criterion of moving from reality to reflection and back to reality guided the praxis. It in turn could not be directed against the impoverished majorities, but had to serve to heighten the consciousness of Christians toward a "correct way of acting." Fundamentally, this theology tried to provide a criterion for human action, namely, that salvation required its human intervention, since it did not occur independently of history (Ruiz 1977, 113–219).

One of the biblical texts that greatly inspired Christians in their new journey was the Exodus story. In its message one found, not so much a justification for any given program of social actions, but rather a strong motivation and inspiration informing courses of action in the face of conflicting reality. Similarly, many references were made to the classical period of Hebrew prophesy, of the eighth to the sixth century B.C.E. This was a time of enormous political, moral, and religious crisis. Due to the close resemblance between the reality of that period and the one lived at the present time in Latin America and the Caribbean, texts from Amos, Isaiah, Hosea, etc., were chosen for reflection (Berryman, 46–60).

The historical challenge found a response in many Christians, including some women religious, who separated themselves from the dominant society with which they had been connected since colonial times. This response necessitated their separating themselves from the type of work they had known so well and the familiar places where they had ministered. That exodus was not only seen as an exit; it was also seen as a promising entrance. It was not only to take a stand against a long-held system, but it was considered an opportunity for a new future. It did not signify only a protest, therefore, but also a promise. The sisters made an option for the poor under strong criticism from their previous allies. They left their schools, their pastoral works in upper-class parishes, and they went to live in the slums and in rural areas among the very poor.

When the sisters started their new endeavor they decided to take a contemplative stance by getting to know the reality, becoming friends with the people, identifying their common needs, adapting themselves to their new surroundings. Gradually the sisters took a more active position, motivating the formation of basic Christian communities and establishing other working groups. They offered Bible courses and taught reading and writing; they did social analysis, cared for the sick, promoted healthcare, etc. They wanted to help set up community organization within the framework of an integral liberation. Soon they began experiencing small successes. The popular sectors were no longer anonymous but began to show themselves capable of organizing to demand their rights, present their basic needs, and claim their just rights for employment. These accomplishments permitted them to glimpse the possibility of establishing a different society, where the oppressed could lay claim to their own space and opportunities (Gebara 1992, 7–31).

The theology and the spirituality that the sisters brought to these new places, however, did not correspond to the surroundings of poverty and the scarcity of opportunities experienced by the people. Neither were the sisters prepared to embrace the customs, the popular religiosity, nor the spontaneous and informal expressions used by the people in referring to

God. They had been trained to transmit or impose learned truth. The doctrine of the church and monastic traditions had led them to seek union with God in silence and solitude within the walls of their convents. Likewise, the transcendent concept they had of God demanded that they live on two levels, and when they prayed they had to empty themselves of all activities, images or distractions in order to live the contemplative dimension of their consecration. The dualism that excessively valued the eschatological/spiritual and disregarded the worldly/material dimensions had taught them to flee and separate themselves from the profane reality of this world. Therefore not all the sisters were able to insert themselves and recognize the presence of God in the people's realities and religious expressions.

It was difficult to reconcile religious life traditions with a new commitment and way of life. Nevertheless, a significant number of sisters immersed in poor surroundings were becoming convinced that the struggle for the survival and the dignity of the impoverished could not be set aside until "the wicked would leave their ways and the evildoers their evil thoughts" (Isa. 55:7). As the sisters became more involved in their work among the poor, they began to value the mysterious presence of God within them. They came to realize that all deeds done in favor of justice and oriented toward standing in solidarity with the poor were salvific actions.

Gradually a new theology and spirituality were set in motion, centered in the new understandings of Vatican II and *Evangelii nuntiandi*, both of which take into account the historical reality of the people. A new reading and understanding of the sense of mission within the church was established as an outcome of the option for the poor. One began to understand that the "sending of Jesus" constitutes only one reality within the mystery surrounding God's revelation in him. Jesus assumed the will of God in a particular time and space. His ministry took place in Palestine, in the midst of the poor and among the multitudes. It was also carried out in confrontation with the Pharisees, Sadducees, and Herodians. Jesus did not avoid the challenges of that socio-cultural and political moment but rather, from his response to those challenges, he translates, by his gestures, words, and actions, the message of the reign of God.

The new challenges presented by the reality, feelings, and intuition are digested and integrated by each Christian disciple in a very slow process. The experience of God, considered divine truth that cannot be questioned nor changed, has been lived and transmitted for centuries and has become dogmatized for traditional ecclesial communities. Thus the two positions (conservatives and radical liberationists) become polarized, making dialogue, comprehension, and community living difficult tasks. Desertions from both groups took place and a considerable number of members left their religious congregations. Despite the exodus, however, immersion within the popular sectors, that allowed direct contact with the poor and vulnerable, did not happen in vain. Through the option for the poor, the continent opened itself up to the possibility of a theological reflection that could face the challenges of inculturation in the world of the poor, of the Afro-Latin American, of the indigenous people, and so forth.

The 1980s

The rise in the price of petroleum and the devastating effects of the external debt upon struggling countries left the already poor of Latin America in a deepening economic crisis. The Latin American bishops, who met in Puebla, recognizing the negative impact of these events, declared with urgency the preferential option for the poor. At this time the Latin American church tried to identify the face and cosmology of the poor with resulting implications that brought about a new focus in theological discourse.

Central America became the focus of attention and the boiling point of the continent and the Caribbean. Armed clashes between guerrilla fighters and dictatorships took place in this area, creating great motivation and strong expectations toward changes within the popular masses throughout all of Latin America. The Sandinistas triumphed in Nicaragua and this victory strengthened the revolutionary ideals in the area. On the southern continent dictatorships fell in disgrace, yielding their place to the so-called restricted democracies.

The United States, led by Ronald Reagan, supported a struggle on various fronts to recover what they believed to be their area of influence, leaving behind the human rights policy that characterized Jimmy Carter's administration. A rise in violence, whose victims included priests, religious, and lay people, became evident in the area. Because of his declarations in defense of the impoverished masses, a rightist group in El Salvador deprived Archbishop Romero of his life in 1984. Likewise, in 1989, six priests were assassinated, together with two innocent women who were in charge of the upkeep of the house.

At this time the Catholic Church began to prepare a celebration of the five hundredth anniversary of Christian presence in Latin America, and in 1983 Pope John Paul II pronounced in Haiti the challenging task of a new evangelization. During the same period the Vatican published the document by the Congregation of the Doctrine of the Faith, led by Cardinal Joseph Ratzinger, that condemned the theology of liberation. Well-known theologian Leonardo Boff was silenced by the Church for his harsh criticism, a result of his decisive stance in favor of the poor. Thus the confrontation continued to gain the religious dominance that would give support to the challenges presented by the new paradigm. But each of the groups went on to entrench themselves in their own worldview, a standoff that impeded a positive advancement that could help overcome the immense problems caused by massive poverty, injustice, and domination.

Meanwhile, the open dialogue held between women and men theologians on women turned out to be quite significant. Women theologians stressed that women's issues do not include only women, but are issues that need to be understood in terms of a situation of subordination that affects all of society. All should be urged to commit themselves to change the existing reality, even though the leading role belongs to women who need to claim their own full personhood.

The women theologians who proposed the use of new forms in theological discourse claimed that the traditional form was too classic and analytic. It was centered in economics and was too rigid and rational. Furthermore, they promoted the recovery of feminist elements, both in the interpretation of the Bible and in the attributes assigned to God. At this time dialogues and contacts were made with feminist theologians of the First World. The exchange was very fruitful, providing for some the needed socio-economic and cultural dimensions, while for others it provided the insight of a long struggle based on the theories of gender.

The decade ended in 1989 with the surprising and spectacular fall of the Berlin Wall. The consequences of this event, which continue to be felt, led to the reevaluation and regrounding of many theories regarding the concepts of social structures and revolution. Christians committed to the cause of liberation had begun this period with great enthusiasm and with the hope of seeing their dreams come true. The meeting in Puebla had advanced the cause by making the preferential option for the poor. But the consciousness acquired and the evaluation of the events had helped many to perceive that the first stage of this option had been done, not by the grass roots or lower classes, but from the top, by the upper classes, in favor of, or for, the poor.

This experience led to the understanding that inculturation is the fullest and most positive response to the option for the poor. The option evolved from a theoretical and vertical posture to a true inculturation based on mutual enrichment and participation in the people's reality.

The ecclesial debate held by means of a theological discourse went a step forward. Openly it was accepted that in Latin America there had been no true evangelization. Furthermore, there had been a deculturation that required indigenous people and the Africans to rid themselves of their cultures in order to become Christians. They were not permitted to maintain their customs, their family structure, and their economic, social, and political organizations. Once the coherence of their daily life had been removed, new beliefs and religious expressions were imposed upon them because their own were considered magic, witchcraft, or, in other words, the works of the devil.

The contradiction between those who held the official position of the church and those adhering to the theology of liberation arose from what each understood about inculturation and about how the task of evangelization was to be addressed. The official church's position was to recognize the elements of truth, "seeds of the Word," in non–Christian religions. At the same time it perceived Christianity as a unifying, normative, and inspirational principle capable of transforming and recreating the different cultures. This perspective did not seek to include the internal expressions of life, the historical processes, or the interpretations demanded of the mystery of God according to the logic of other cultures (Ruiz 1993, 255–67). On the contrary, the official Church sought to remain distant in order to be "objective" so that it could "purify" the beliefs and practices of other people.

For the second group the liberating ecclesial expression "inculturation" meant open dialogue based on a respect for the experience of God as it was held and expressed by other cultures. Inculturation, therefore, did not imply a transmission of doctrine but an exchange of shared faith that permitted mutual enrichment. This exchange was understood to be possible by God's ongoing revelation. The second group also demanded that a clear distinction be made between faith and Christian religion. It was their position that what had been brought to the different peoples was a Christianity of domination, tied in with a strong centralization of power, maintained until the present moment.

The liberating groups, on the other hand, recognized another strong Christian tradition that had been represented throughout history, especially by the religious orders. These new groups did not seek to assume power; on the contrary, they wanted to give witness to the gospel by reaffirming life, service, and the option for the poor. They believed that the Christian religion could not be transmitted, for essentially the only thing achieved in traditional evangelization was the annihilation of the socio-cultural and religious richness of peoples. They believed further that the one universal reality was the original Christian faith experience. Since faith implied radical encounter with the mystery that is present in the world, it could then be expressed through other cultural codes, in other ways, and from distinct historical processes. The liberating groups believed that the faith-encounter is a possibility offered to all human beings, gathered in the midst of their people, with the intention of providing them a means for their salvation, that is, a covenant established between God and the people. Therefore, the Judeo-Christian faith expressed as a "utopia" could motivate the people to live the "now but not yet" in the lived experience of their historical processes. At the same time this utopia would help them question their concrete actions by keeping, as the ultimate horizon, the absoluteness of God (Boff, 58–69).

In fact, the two ecclesial positions recognized that to bring about inculturation one did not need to go to another country. One only needed to cross the bridge, to shorten the distance, to be immersed in the different worlds which today are present in our society. For inculturation is as valuable in approaching ancestral cultures that still exist in Latin America, as it is in those cultures which have sprung out of our modern and postmodern world.

It is difficult to determine the general response of religious groups to the two positions. But sisters working in slum areas knew very well that some of the doctrinal/theological details held in debate escaped their understanding, especially since they were so accustomed to fixed traditions and their subsequent conditioning. Nevertheless, even though the sisters would admit their doubts, they could perceive that hegemony, based on only one belief imposed on peoples and dominating their conscience through the mechanisms of religious forces, could not continue. Above all, they were able to recognize the difficulty presented to religious life, since for so long it had remained fostered out of the necessity to expand the white, Western Christian culture as if it were the salvation of the peoples.

Regardless of the challenges, the confrontation generated astounding creativity. Many methods and materials, such as theological reflection, the study of real life cases, the *Lectio Divina*, etc., were developed to be used by the base Christian communities. Meanwhile, the official church, mistrustful of the doctrinal teaching conveyed in these materials, suppressed the use of them in most of the Latin American countries. A case in point: the workbooks *Your Word Is Life* were forbidden because supposedly they made a one-sided reductionist view of the Bible.

In the local religious houses, community living continued to experience tension around the different perspectives maintained over the concept of salvation/mission. One of the best spokespersons on the spirituality of religious life, Ivone Gebara, stated: "We talk about unity, but we are not able to incorporate it into our lives. We talk about integrating the dichotomies that divide our lives but instead we insist on maintaining dualistic positions." And referring to inculturation she indicated: "The present moment demands that we take a new stand regarding evangelization or we shall continue risking the destruction of groups of people. It is necessary to welcome dialogue, equality, solidarity, and the exchange of experiences as an integral part of humanity's makeup, which is always full of variety. The spreading of the good news also demands that we renounce our own schemes, based on a traditional comprehension of what it means to evangelize, as if evangelization were something to be taught, learned and lived as though it were merely a lesson" (1992, 171).

Living among the poor and employing the praxis of liberation helped confirm the necessity of an incarnated spirituality. On the one hand, criticism was made of a spirituality that was based on principles that ignored history as the place where fidelity to God finds its concrete expression. On the other hand, it was discovered that there were no more autonomous or automatic channels for the spiritual life. What one could find were primary channels integrated with life and history. More and more committed Christians experienced a vivid desire to express their lives in spiritual practices that were different from what they had customarily practiced. They were convinced that these new practices did not come from any prior consideration, but came from real life demands.

There was a perceived need in Latin America for a spiritual expression that would serve to enlighten history as much as to motivate life. Slowly, a theological reflection evolved from a disincarnated spirituality that was oppressive and universal, to an incultured and historically effective spirituality. For it was being understood that there is no history without a spiritual sense and no spiritual life without history, since spirituality is the force of life.

Theologians such as Jon Sobrino and Gustavo Gutierrez were able to mold into their theologies the expectations and experiences of those groups committed to the emergence of a new Church and a new society. Jon Sobrino described this spirituality from the signs he perceived in the emerging groups. "It is by no means difficult to point to concrete persons or religious groups who live and manifest that life, that spirit. These are communities of religious women living among peasants, members of base communities, women and men toiling unselfishly for the good of others, with great commitment and generosity, with humility and eagerness to be of service to others. Their actions tell us better than words ever will what it means to live history with spirit" (10).

Likewise, Sobrino indicated the steps that were taken in a Christian journey by people becoming, in history, persons "akin to God." Sobrino explained, "The God of creation, life, justice and liberation is approached through a kinship with God in the practice of the bestowal of life and the furthering of justice . . . God incarnate, incredibly close to the poor, and oppressed in the scandal of the cross, is approached through a kinship with God in incarnation among the crucified of history—in persecution, in the surrender of our very lives with and for them. The God of hope, of the nearness of the reign, of resurrection, of the new sky and the new earth, is approached by a kinship with God in the stubbornness of hope, in, through, and against history" (40).

Gustavo Gutierrez helped clarify how all spirituality was connected to the historical moments of its own time, whether it be Benedictine, mendicant, Ignatian, or the spirituality of John of the Cross and Theresa of Avila. From there Gutierrez indicated that in Latin America the historical movement which centered in the process of liberation of the poor was the place where a new reading of faith and a new eruption of God occurred among the poor and in those persons who made an option for them. In this liberating process spirituality came to be understood as a community venture, a revelation for a people who must make their own path in the following of Jesus (42–51).

Soon the new situation created by the liberating process that rose against the misery and exploitation existent in Latin America provoked serious questions, ruptures, and a new search for understanding the

Christian life. The inquiry occurred because those who were marginated and exploited, those who felt estranged in their own lands, suffering the lashes of those who oppressed them, began to recognize and identify with the experience of the Israelites. In the Hebrew Scriptures, the land was understood as an object of promise; it was the place where sons and daughters of God lived as inhabitants and not as foreigners. The spirituality that emerged in Latin America during this journey recovered the Israelites' conception and overcame the idea that existed in the church up until Vatican Council II. Prior to that time spirituality was regarded as the province of an elect few and belonged to a "state of perfection." But now spirituality could no longer be only an exercise in individuality whereby a person cultivated a personal interior relationship with God.

Gutierrez specified that to affirm the following of Jesus as a collective adventure did not imply discarding the personal dimension. On the contrary, it meant giving the personal its proper sense as an answer to the call of the Father/Mother. It was then understood that the journey begun in this new path faced the same challenges as those confronted by the Jewish people in the desert where one had to walk in the midst of shadow and light, doubt and certainty. The people of Latin America realized that they too were in an immense desert where no prior precise route was marked. There, as in the sea, the footsteps would not be recognized. The spiritual path was and continues to be a permanent creative action that demands always to discern the creative presence of the Spirit of God (18–124).

The 1990s

This decade could be considered as belonging to apocalyptic times, in the double perspective of having both crisis and revelation. We have become conscious that we no longer live in an "age of change" but that we are experiencing a "change of age." Our contact with reality, the new scientific discoveries, the worrisome social and economic changes have placed us in a crossroads introduced by the challenges of the new paradigms. Theological reflection finds its limits, as the theologians realize that within the parameters previously conceived it becomes insufficient to orient the many tasks demanded by the construction of the future.

The events responsible for shaking the consciousness of many Christians are varied. At the international level we have the breaking down of socialism in Eastern Europe, the Persian Gulf War, the invasion of Panama by the United States, the loss suffered by the Sandinista Front in the elections in Nicaragua, the adjustments demanded by the new neoliberal economic order based on the globalization of the market, the weakening of the leftist parties and the popular social movements, the environmental summit in Rio de Janeiro, the Fourth U.N. General Conference of Women in Beijing, and, more recently, the new crisis produced by Iraq's retention of biological and chemical arms of mass destruction, the collapse of the stock market in Asia caused by the crumbling of the economic model in the region, the meeting in Ottawa that started an important control of land mines, the climate summit in Kyoto with its innovative proposal to reduce the atmospheric gases responsible for the warming of the planet.

At the ecclesial level, we have the celebration of the Fourth Latin American Bishops Conference, in Santo Domingo, with the theme of new evangelization. Even though the bishops reaffirmed the option for the poor and proposed a decisive action in favor of inculturation, the document does not have the acuteness of earlier pronouncements. The Fourth Interamerican Religious Conference, that centered around themes related to the scandalous increase of poverty in this hemisphere, became important for religious life newly aware of the rising tide of neoliberalism and its global effects. Finally, the Synod of Bishops of the Americas that took place in Rome was a hopeful encounter inasmuch as the official church decided to assume the task of contributing to the dismantling of the perverse mechanisms of the macroeconomic system that obliges poor countries to become poorer.

At this point, the topic of historical subjects becomes one of the most important themes of discussion in the effort to identify the protagonists who can lead the transformations that seem urgent for the next millennium. There is a wide range of challenges from the defense of human dignity, including all generations—children, youth, the elderly; the new vindication relating to identity in marginal cultures; feminism; the impact of global communications; ecology; and the rights of all who exist, not only the poor, but humanity itself.

All these problems question the responses given thus far. The theology of liberation is also challenged in its methodology and projection by the new vision of the cosmos derived from the studies of astronomy and physics. Feminists also criticize the theology of liberation. They recognize that this theology remains within the parameters of a patriarchal discourse, even though it may try to use feminist themes when it talks of the feminine attributes of God. The women theologians propose to use new and emerging theories of gender in order seriously to analyze the subordination to which women have been subjected for centuries in Latin America and elsewhere. Above all, the theology of liberation demands the firm acceptance of a dynamic character and must always remain connected to reality. According to the women theologians, this makes theology of liberation provisional in its own essence. At the same time the women demand that the theology of liberation should assume, like all other sciences, its own limitations and arrive at truth by means of trials, approaches, errors, and failures.

Realistic analysis helps us to see the necessity of forming a new global social project. This agenda has its own implications for the church. It seems urgent that the church define its works or ministries as service in and for the world by all its members. Men and women theologians also point out that this moment asks that all of us be humble. Together we must learn and become educated to help construct justice and peace in the world. Together we must try to save the planet. Together we have to establish the possibility of a collective future.

This task is overwhelming. We are conscious that before us lies a radical challenge, for it implies reinventing the whole of Christian theology. In the face of this monumental task, Ivone Gebara suggests we go beyond what we have learned and deduced from the biblical texts. We must try to recognize that the Word of God is the broadest revelation of the divine and cannot be limited to the understanding of reality and the faith of one particular people, gathered in some books labeled "sacred." According to Gebara, "What is important for us is not saving the text, but the life of humans," the earth, all the species, "to which the text indirectly is referring and where it finds its true inspirations." Therefore, she continues, "the scriptures cannot be a kind of an archetype of history and of human beings, but the written expression of the history and cultural expressions of people in which we find our religious roots." At the same time Gebara indicates to us that, "to take the anthropological and the religious models present in scripture as realities in themselves, is to canonize certain cultural models, without taking into account the evolution of human history and the high cultural productions of other ethnic groups" (1995, 108).

Following the challenges imposed on us by a "change of age," Leonardo Boff proposes, "To overcome the crisis we have to construct a new dream and articulate a new sense in life. In a religious discourse we might say that we need a new spirituality, a new encounter with the central Sense of life and of history, understood as the Mystery present in the world, the Reason behind evolution and the Direction of time" (85).

But such a spirituality cannot be disconnected from today's questions and from where the "change of age" is leading us. The confrontation with the new paradigms, ecological, feminist, and social, demands a true revolution, a global change of structures, as much mental as social and global. We especially need to take into account the obstacles caused by the existing separation in the religious realm that impedes spirituality from becoming a humanizing and liberating factor for our time. The Christian representatives committed to the new outcome of history point out that all transformations, economic, social, and political, are interdependent. They perceive, therefore, that the Christian churches cannot renew their religious institutions without changing their vision of the cosmos, their anthropological views and the analytical perspective that presides at the readings of Scripture and its articulation with the dogmas and the magisterium; in other words, without modifying their vision of reality that serves as the basis for its understanding (Gebara 1995, 109).

Ecological awareness leads to the need for a new doctrinal approach that takes into account the fact that our planet and all its creatures—animate and inanimate—constitute one living system. Humans are not separate beings, but are the conscious expression of the earth, totally dependent on the living community, the extended body of our existence that is the planet, the universe. All people are marked by a unique consciousness of the environment in which they live and they form images to conform to their perceptions of it. This awareness and imagery influence their social behavior and their responses to the questions they are confronting today. For those reasons we need to educate ourselves and others to form our consciences in ecological awareness. We need a serious commitment to care for and love the environment in which humans live in interdependence and where future generations need to live as well.

Given a new ecological awareness in Latin America and the Caribbean, the question has surfaced as to whether or not we should continue in favor of an option for the poor. Leonardo Boff clarifies the difficulty, "The transformation can not only be human and social; it also ought to be cosmic. . . . Out of this new covenant, in favor of the common cosmic and human good we need to redefine the sense given to the social transformation . . . It is true we need revolutions in order to bring about the transformations that cannot be forgotten or postponed. The path we must take to bring about these transformations today must be a different one. Structural transformations are not sufficient; we also need to have a subjective transformation in persons" (90).

To think of a new social and world organization, therefore, brings us to recognize the need for an ecological social democracy. An ecological social democracy is aware that human history is inseparable from its environment and from the types of relationships that were woven in the dynamic mutual influence that took place over millions of years. At the same time the ecological social democracy presents a direct relationship between social and ecological injustices, for it understands that poverty is the outcome of a lack of infrastructure to provide subsistence and a dignified life. It seems clear, then, that without a minimum of social justice it would be impossible to have an ecological justice. We ought to have, as a religious and political mandate, an ecological education that would help human beings learn to live together with all that exists as citizens of the same world society.

For religious in Latin America and the Caribbean it is not easy to bring about a change of mentality, after almost three decades of an intense and direct struggle to pursue justice in favor of the poor. The temptation is to go back, to remain with what seems more familiar or not to continue the journey that is ahead. But life demands stretching and opening horizons, in fact, all of the tasks imply the need to call one another to bring about solutions.

We must be open to dialogue with the theologies that have preceded us. In this respect, Michael Dowd's words help us see that the drastic change we must make in how we perceive and organize ourselves should not disturb us. The new ecological consciousness is not totally new for us, for it is something that has been dormant in us. To reaffirm "the radically new perspective on life is why faith is utterly indispensable in our day. Not faith that the beliefs we have grown up with are true in spite of evidence to the contrary, but faith that God is God, and that all truth is God's truth. Moreover, if this cosmology is a revelation of God, if it is the truth about the nature of reality, then not only will it not contradict the truth of Christianity, it will further open up its deeper meanings and unleash its transforming, prophetic power" (20–21).

We know too well that to answer faithfully to the God of life we do not start from nothingness. We have already traveled part of the journey, but there are miles still to go. Simon Pedro Arnold, realizing how religious life is a frontier vocation, one that takes risks in the face of historical challenges, asks that it take new roads migrating into "multiple forms ready to move and change from our certainties." And he indicates that "What truly belongs, what is part of religious life, is its spiritual and moral ability to be nomads, always ready to be on the go since ours is the demand to rid ourselves even of those convictions which were purchased by the shedding of blood" (3).

Another theologian, Victor Codina, suggests that we "go from Exodus to Exile, that is, from a situation where the objective (the promised land) and the strategy (to leave Egypt and cross the Red Sea) seem quite clear, to a situation of generalized impotence in the midst of an all-powerful culture and empire, with no clear cut alternatives, and no leaders (exile); yet the exile is the time of purification, of hope, of prophecy, and of spiritual growth" (43).

Challenging and motivating all religious to initiate a new mission—for if we don't do it, who will?—Simon Pedro Arnold tells us that "religious life, by its own charism and vocation, plays a prototype role and offers a historical commitment. Truly, religious life has always been an alternative proposal, under the form of an ideal micro-society . . . And this is especially true of Latin American religious life after Medellin. No doubt religious sisters have been, and continue to be, in the vanguard of putting into practice the great options of the church in this continent and the Caribbean" (3).

Thus it is that different groups of women and men religious have started to journey, have begun a new pilgrimage, even though they might not have started a second migration. Among them we have to mention the efforts initiated by the Mercy Sisters, the Franciscans, the Dominicans, who have begun to have meetings and workshops in order to help their members become aware of the new situations. Much more, these groups have established structures in order to form federations that would help them become more effective in confronting the problems set before them. Likewise, the Latin American Religious Conference (CLAR) has begun an ambitious project that aims to recover the history of women religious. They have proposed it to all the countries in South America and the Caribbean, trying to initiate a reflection, a discernment and a commitment toward the challenges that religious life will be facing in this third millennium" (CLAR 1).

The decisive position taken by the Jesuit provincials in Latin America has been commendable. In their working paper they stated, "Before this reality, which is contrary to the work of our Creator, a demand of faith in order that God can be God among us, we are called to resist the dynamics which destroy our brothers and sisters and resolve to work with many others to bring about change, to help construct a society closer to the ideal of the Gospel Reign of fraternity and solidarity. We don't count the cost of taking this stand. We do not have another alternative . . ." (*Documento Jesuitas*, 8).

By all that has been said, it seems clear that to accomplish all the pending transformations, we need to develop an integrated/holistic spirituality that will motivate, sustain and guide our efforts. In past years, if it was not easy to describe our spirituality, we could at least refer to the great spiritual schools in church history. And more recently, we could direct our lives by participating in the spirituality of the poor as we were guided by Medellín, Puebla, and the theology of liberation. But things have changed and we are once again searching for a spirituality that will organize, articulate, and put the pieces together that arise from our questions and concerns. Today it is not easy to define the steps of a spiritual journey. We more or less know what we don't want, what does not help us. In spite of the crises, the criticisms, and rejections, we also have some essential certainties that are permanent and continue to be valid.

Nevertheless, to enter into dialogue with modern cosmology, with the demands of our epoch and life's ultimate sense, we need, beyond reaffirming those things learned throughout history and in our Christian tradition, to let our creative imagination come up with new understandings and new challenges resulting from the contacts made with new realities. We ought to take advantage of all reserves found in each culture and all peoples. Intuition together with collective wisdom will bring about the needed transformation. Our call is still to "choose life," the life that has spanned all of history. Such a choice does not imply that we should adopt an ethereal or abstract conception, but it means to perceive what goes beyond all those things that absorb our daily attention and work.

We have then opened a reflection, a discussion, a new practice in order to delineate a new concept of what we call "mission." This task will go beyond the norm of our present doctrinal contents, though it does not negate their implementation as they defend the vital values of human existence. We also open the possibility of starting a joint campaign to have a new understanding of the cosmos, to learn all that is human and develop a collective responsibility in favor of life. Such a perspective, instead of rejecting old traditions, proposes a new opening for dialogue and for slow and gradual growth, taking the concrete realities of peoples as a point of departure.

The challenge remains for us to rediscover the spiritual in all that surrounds us, in life's simplicity and complexity, in its enchantment and disenchantment, in its delight and frustrations, in its beauty and ugliness. Let us set ourselves to transform our minds and hearts so that we may live with a more profound sense of our existence and may experience a new integral and just social relationship with creation and with our brothers and sisters. Let us recover the true sense of the Spirit of God, who teaches, animates, and motivates, especially human beings, to marvel at, respect, and love all that exists.

Works Cited

Arnold, Simón Pedro. "Pensar la fe como religiosos/as: claves hermeneúticas." *Revista CLAR* 35, no. 2 (1997): 3–33.

Berryman, Phillip. *Teología de la Liberación.* Mexico: Siglo XXI, 1987.

Boff, Leonardo. *Nueva Era: La civilización planetaria.* Navarra: Verbo Divino, 1995.

CLAR. *Recuperación de la Memoria Histórica de la Mujer en la Vida Religiosa Femenina de América Latina y el Caribe.* Bogota. Sept. 1995–99.

Codina, Vistor. "La Misión de la Vida Religiosa ante los nuevos aerópagos," *Revista CLAR* 35, no. 2 (1997): 39–41, 43.

CONDOR. *Periodización Histórica para la Recuperación de la Memoria Histórica de la Vida Religiosa Femenina de America Latina y el Caribe.* Sto. Domingo: Policopiado, May, 1997: 1–25.

"Neoliberalismos en América Latina." *Documento de Trabajo de los Jesuitas.* Policopiado: Mexico, 1996.

Dowd, Michael. *Earthspirit.* Mystic, Conn.: Twenty-Third Publications 1991.

Gebara, Ivone. *Vida Religiosa: De la Teología Patriarcal a la Teología Feminista.* São Paulo: Paulinas, 1992.

———. *Teología a ritmo de mujer.* Mexico: Ediciones Dabar, 1995.

Gutierrez, Gustavo. *Beber en su propio pozo* Lima, Peru: CEP. 1983.

Palacio, Carlos. *Reinterpretar a Vida Religiosa.* São Paulo: Paulinas, 1991.

Ress, Mary Judith. "Elsa Tamez: Tres fases de la Teología Feminista en América Latina," *Conspirando* 18. Santiago, Chile: Mosquito Editores, 1996: 2–12.

Ruiz, Margarita. *La realidad Dominicana presenta un desafío a la Pastoral de la Iglesia*. Tesis de Licenciatura. Lumen Vitae. Encuadernación Sto. Domingo, 1977.

———. "La Iglesia que renace desde los pobres y a partir de las distintas culturas." *Human Rights and the Quincentenary*. River Forest, Illinois: Rosary College, 1993.

Sobrino, Jon. *Spirituality of Liberation: Toward Political Holiness*. Maryknoll, NY: Orbis Books, 1998.

The Contributors

Carol Coston, OP, is currently the director of Partners for the Common Good 2000, an eight million dollar alternative loan fund whose ninety-nine investors are religious congregations. She also directed its predecessor, the Christian Brothers Investment Services. She was a founding member and first director of NETWORK, a national Catholic social justice lobby in Washington, DC. Instrumental in establishing the Adrian Dominican Portfolio Advisory Board, she also directed its program for alternative investments. She holds a master of arts degree in speech and drama from The Catholic University of America.

Nadine Foley, OP, is historian for the Adrian Dominican Congregation and professor of Religious Studies at Siena Heights University, Adrian, Michigan. She has served as prioress, vicaress and general councilor of her congregation; as president of the Leadership Conference of Women Religious; and as United States delegate to the International Union of Superiors General. She holds a doctorate in philosophy from The Catholic University of America and a master's degree in theology from Union Theological Seminary, New York. She writes and speaks frequently on religious life and on women in the Church. She has previously edited two books: *Claiming Our Truth* (LCWR) and *Preaching and the Non-Ordained* (Liturgical Press).

Carol Johannes, OP, a former prioress of the Adrian Dominican Congregation, is currently ministering as a spiritual director and instructor in pastoral theology at the Dominican Center for Religious Development in Dearborn Heights, Michigan. She holds a master of divinity and master of theology in Spiritual Direction from Weston School of Theology, Cambridge, Massachusetts. She gives conferences and conducts retreats on religious life and spiritual development in a variety of settings.

Carol Jean McDonnell, OP, is director of Human Resources and Planning Coordinator for The Night Ministry, an organization in the Chicago area in direct service for and with the people of the nighttime streets. She is a former member of the General Council of the Adrian Dominican Congregation and former executive secretary and chair of the Department of Ministries for the diocese of Lansing, Michigan. She has had overseas experience teaching at St. Kizito Seminary in Malawi, Africa. She holds a master's degree in mathematics from the University of Detroit, Detroit, Michigan.

Donna J. Markham, OP, is president of the Southdown Institute, a residential treatment center near Toronto, Ontario. She is a former member of the General Council of the Adrian Dominican Sisters, a former president of the Leadership Conference of Women Religious, and founder and former director of the Dominican Consultation Center for low income people in Detroit, Michigan. She holds a doctorate in clinical psychology from the University of Detroit. She is a frequent writer and lecturer on psychological issues and leadership, in relation to contemporary religious life. She has recently published *Spiritlinking Leadership: Working through Resistance to Organizational Change.*

Miriam Mullins, OP, is the diocesan director of English Catechesis in the Diocese of Las Vegas, Nevada. Previously she served on the General Council of the Adrian Dominican Sisters and coordinated the work of writing the Constitutions and Statutes of the Congregation. She has a background in adult faith formation on a parish level. She holds a master's degree in the sciences from Siena Heights University, Adrian, Michigan, and a bachelor of theology degree from the University of St. Paul, Ottawa, Canada. She has done additional advanced study in ecclesiology and Scripture.

Virginia O'Reilly, OP, is an adjunct professor of Psychology at Siena Heights University in Adrian, Michigan, and assists in the University's archives. She has a master's degree in science from The Catholic University of America, a master's in education from Siena Heights University and a doctorate in clinical psychology from the California School of Professional Psychology, pursued through funding from the Danforth Foundation. She has worked as consultant in psychology for congregations of women religious in the Western United States and in South Africa.

Jamie T. Phelps, OP, is visiting professor of Systematic Theology at Loyola University, Chicago, Illinois, and the associate director and adjunct professor for the degree program of the Institute for Black Catholic Studies at Xavier University, New Orleans, Louisiana. She was formerly professor of Doctrinal Theology at the Catholic Theological Union, Chicago, Illinois. She has a master's in social work from The University of Illinois, a master's in theology from St. John's University, Collegeville, and a doctorate in theology from The Catholic University of America.

Maria Riley, OP, is on the research staff and coordinator of the Women's Project at the Center of Concern in Washington, D.C. A popular speaker and writer on women's issues, she is the author of *Transforming Feminism* and co-author with Nancy Sylvester, IHM, of *Trouble and Beauty: Women Encounter Catholic Social Thought*, as well as many periodical articles. Currently she is working on a book on the global women's movement. She holds a doctorate in literature from Florida State University, Tallahassee. In 1996 she received the NETWORK "Women of Justice" award.

Margarita Ruiz, OP, teaches pastoral theology at the Dominican Theological Institute in Santo Domingo and serves as Formation Director for the Adrian Dominican Sisters in the Dominican Republic. She holds a licentiate in Pastoral Theology from Lumen Vitae, Brussels, a master's degree in sociology from Universidad Iberoamericana, Mexico, and a diploma in spirituality from the Religious Conference Spirituality Center, Rio de Janeiro.

Anneliese Sinnott, OP, is vice president for Academic Affairs and dean at Ecumenical Theological Seminary, Detroit, Michigan, and is the assistant director of the Pastoral Ministry Program at Marygrove College, Detroit, Michigan. She has taught at Ss. Cyril and Methodius Seminary and St. Mary College in Orchard Lake, Michigan. She holds a master's degree in divinity from Ss. Cyril and Methodius Seminary, a master's in religious studies from The University of Detroit, Detroit, Michigan, and a doctorate in systematic theology from Katholieke Universiteit, Leuven, Belgium.

Patricia Walter, OP, is the immediate past prioress of the Adrian Dominican Congregation and former representative of the United States women religious to the International Union of Superiors General. She holds a doctorate in theology from the Graduate Theological Union in Berkeley, California, and has taught theology at Siena Heights University, St. Mary Seminary in Cleveland, Ohio, the Center for Pastoral Leadership, Wickliffe, Ohio, at the Angelicum in Rome, Italy, and currently at the Aquinas Institute of Theology in St. Louis, Missouri.